THE TV THEME SONG TRIVIA BOOK

THE TV THEME SONG TRIVIA BOOK

MIND-BOGGLING QUESTIONS
ABOUT THOSE SONGS AND THEMES YOU
CAN'T GET OUT OF YOUR HEAD

VINCENT TERRACE

A CITADEL PRESS BOOK
Published by Carol Publishing Group

Carol Publishing Group Edition, 1998

A Citadel Press Book
Published by Carol Publishing Group
Citadel Press is a registered trademark of Carol Communications, Inc.

Editorial, sales and distribution, rights and permissions inquiries should be addressed to Carol Publishing Group, 120 Enterprise Avenue, Secaucus, N.J. 07094

In Canada: Canadian Manda Group, One Atlantic Avenue, Suite 105, Toronto, Ontario M6K 3E7

Carol Publishing Group books may be purchased in bulk at special discounts for sales promotions, fund-raising, or educational purposes. Special editions can be created to specifications. For details, contact Special Sales Department, Carol Publishing Group, 120 Enterprise Avenue, Secaucus, N.J. 07094

Manufactured in the United States of America
10 9 8 7 6 5 4 3 2

Library of Congress Cataloging-in-Publication Data

Terrance, Vincent, 1948-
The TV theme song trivia book : mind-boggling questions about those songs and themes you can't get out of your head / Vincent Terrace.
p. cm.
"A Citadel Press book."
ISBN 0-8065-1786-7 (pbk.)
1. Television music—Miscellanea. 2. Television programs—United States—Miscellanea. I. Title.
ML68.T47 1996
781.5'46—dc20 95-48088
CIP
MN

Contents

INTRODUCTION

In those good old television days it seemed that every show had a theme song that related the plot with a catchy, singable theme. Test your knowledge of television themes—from *Howdy Doody* (1947) to *Friends* (1994)—nearly six decades of memories packed into nineteen question-filled sections that will not only make you think, but also provide you with a treasure trove of TV trivia.

The 501 questions that follow comprise mostly quotes to which you either supply a program title or the next line of a particular theme. All of the themes presented in this book were transcribed directly from the actual programs.

While compiling this book of questions, I came to appreciate the work of the hundreds of songwriters and lyricists—many anonymous—who have contributed greatly to our popular culture. I'd like to thank them all for the memories.

So sit back, put on that thinking cap, and join "Jed and all his kin," "seven stranded castaways," and "a man named Masterson" on a nostalgia-filled journey through the unforgettable world of TV theme songs.

How to Use This Book

This book is divided into nineteen sections. Each contains questions and answers pertaining to particular shows. For your convenience, the question page always precedes the answer page. Questions are grouped separately from their respective answers. (A *Q* represents a question, while an *A* indicates an answer.)

The questions and answers are current as of September 1995.

THE TV THEME SONG TRIVIA BOOK

1

Opening Themes

Identify the series by the excerpts of the TV themes listed below.

Q1. "This is it, this is life, the one you get...enjoy the view, keep on doing what you do, hold on tight, we'll muddle through [name of show]."

Q2. "She's mine alone but luckily for you, if you find a girl to love, only one girl to love, then she'll be [name of show] too."

Q3. "And there ain't no nothing we can't love each other through; what'll we do baby, without us."

Q4. "For the names have all changed since you hung around, but those dreams have remained and they've turned around. Who'd of thought they lead ya, back here where we need ya."

Q5. "Hello, world, here's a song that we're singing, come on get happy. A whole lot of lovin' is what we'll be bringing, we'll make you happy."

A1. *One Day at a Time* (1975)

A2. *That Girl* (1966)

A3. *Family Ties* (1982)

A4. *Welcome Back, Kotter* (1975)

A5. *The Partridge Family* (1972 theme)

Q6. "It's about two astronauts, it's about their fate, it's about a woman and her prehistoric mate. And now [name of show]."

Q7. "Loving one who loves you and I'm taking that vow; nice work if you can get it and if you get it, won't you tell me how."

Q8. "She's my very own guiding star, a 1928 Porter, that's my mother dear. She helps me through everything I do and I'm so glad she's here."

Q9. "Where Indian fights are colorful sights and nobody takes a lickin'; where paleface and redskin both turn chicken."

Q10. "...you're doomed to wander, on beyond this land so lonely. So roam in search of home, cross this land so lonely."

Q11. "From San Antone to the Rio Grande, on mountain peaks or desert sand, every outlaw feared the hand of danger, this Texas Ranger."

Q12. A foreign spy arrives by the name of U-31. On his first day in he's done in by a hit-and-run. Got to find a man with the same face as 31, but who?

Q13. "I've traveled here, I've traveled there, I guess I've been most everywhere, but I like it where I am today, and here is where I'll stay."

Q14. "He's a man of his word and the road he's chosen to follow brings him to this place and time; now he wears the badge—[name of show]."

Q15. "From the coonskin cap on the top of ol' Dan to the heel of his rawhide shoe, the rippinist, roarinist, fightinist man the frontier ever knew."

A6. *It's About Time* (1966)

A7. *Cybill* (1995)

A8. *My Mother the Car* (1965)

A9. *F Troop* (1965)

A10. *A Man Called Shenandoah* (1965)

A11. *Rango* (1967)

A12. *The Double Life of Henry Phyfe* (1966)

A13. *The Californians* (1957)

A14. *Nashville 99* (1977)

A15. *Daniel Boone* (1964)

Q16. "Just the good old boys, wouldn't change if they could, fightin' the system like two modern day Robin Hoods."

Q17. "He and she, you and me, the sweet blend of milk and honey, always together. We'll go through life discovering good things come in pairs."

Q18. "Still they're cousins, identical cousins, and you'll find they laugh alike, they walk alike, at times they even talk alike; you can lose your mind when cousins are two of a kind."

Q19. "No one you see is smarter than he. And we know [name of show] lives in a world full of wonder, lying there under, under the sea."

Q20. "You'll see him smile, right from the start, he'll play it smart. Beware of [name of show], he's such a lover, you'll discover when he steals your heart."

Q21. "We're tiny, we're tooney, we're all a little looney, and in this cartoonie we're invading your TV."

Q22. "We're just tryin' to be friendly, come and watch us sing and play; we're the young generation and we've got something to say."

Q23. "Yippie-I-Oh-Ki-A, galloping all the way; great big star on his chest, outdraws all the rest, fastest gun in the West."

Q24. "Come on now and meet everybody and hear us singing. There is nothing better than being together when we're singing."

Q25. "Lady Godiva was a freedom rider...Isadora was the first bra burner...and when the country was falling apart, Betsy Ross got it all sewed up. And then there's [name of show], that uncompromising...anything but tranquilizing, right on [name of show]."

A16. *The Dukes of Hazzard* (1979)

A17. *The Dumplings* (1976)

A18. *The Patty Duke Show* (1963)

A19. *Flipper* (1964 theme)

A20. *Flipper* (1967 theme)

A21. *Tiny Toon Adventures* (1990)

A22. *The Monkees* (1966)

A23. *Quick Draw McGraw* (1959)

A24. *The Partridge Family* (1970 theme)

A25. *Maude* (1972)

Q26. "And so I go my lonely way, every day filled with danger, even to myself a stranger, wondering who am I."

Q27. "He just keeps a-movin', ladies keep improving, every day is better than the last. Blue jeans and better scenes, and best of all I don't pay property tax."

Q28. "I'm a good guy; hey, you're another one too. Like a brother, each to the other one true blue."

Q29. "Dream away little man, dream as long as you can; don't grow up I beg of you. Dreams are made for children, and we're children as long as we can dream."

Q30. "People let me tell you about my best friend, he's a warmhearted person who'll love me till the end…he's a one boy cuddly toy, my up, my down, my pride and joy, he's my best friend."

Q31. "He was cursed with a quick and restless gun and he played the game that no man ever won; but his killing turned him cold, he grew bitter, he grew bold, and he fought the world with cold and hungry guns."

Q32. "She was a grandma to this lad, he was the son she never had, and together they hit the trail for Cal-i-forny."

Q33. "Girls, girls, girls, don't you wanna love 'em…some made of sugar, some made of spice, all made of everything that's nice, girls, girls, girls."

Q34. "I'm gonna make it forever, light up the sky like a flame…I want to live forever, baby remember my name, [name of show]."

Q35. "Take me home to the land of the Pecos, hear that stream, let me dream 'neath the sky…"

A26. *Coronet Blue* (1967)

A27. *B. J. and the Bear* (1979)

A28. *The Good Guys* (1968)

A29. *Shirley Temple's Storybook* (1958)

A30. *The Courtship of Eddie's Father* (1969)

A31. *The Legend of Jesse James* (1965)

A32. *Dirty Sally* (1974)

A33. *Sugar Time* (1977)

A34. *Fame* (1982)

A35. *Judge Roy Bean* (1955)

Q36. "Welcome to a land that's way under Down Under; the sky's always yellow in rain or shine…"

Q37. "I wanna a happy ending, I'm tired of pretending, won't let 'em get the best of me. [name of show], the game is survival…and plan my arrival [name of show]."

Q38. "She's fantastic, made of plastic, microchips here and there; she's a [name of show] and brings love and laughter everywhere."

Q39. "In the eyes of a ranger, the unsuspecting stranger had better know the truth of wrong from right. 'Cause the eyes of the ranger are upon you."

Q40. "Whenever I think of yesterday, I close my eyes and see that place just over the [name of show], that will always be home to me."

Q41. "We've got a gorilla for sale…see in the window…full of charm and appeal; handsome, elegant, intelligent, sweet; he's really ideal."

Q42. "He was a bold adventurin' man…his blade was tempered and so was he, indestructible steel was he…he was a fighter, a fearless, a mighty adventurin' man."

Q43. "On your mark, get set, and go now, got a dream and we just know now, we're gonna make that dream come true—and we'll do it our way, yes, our way…make all our dreams come true for me and you."

Q44. "He's my man, ah, he's my man; yeah, let me tell ya about him, can't do without him, just one of a kind; now he's the man, [name of show]."

Q45. "It's fun to look at yourself as other people do. How's your sense of humor, there's a rumor laughter's on its way. Smile, you're on [name of show]."

A36. *Tazmania* (1993)

A37. *Gimme a Break* (1981)

A38. *Small Wonder* (1985)

A39. *Walker, Texas Ranger* (1995 theme)

A40. *Brooklyn Bridge* (1992)

A41. *The Magilla Gorilla Show* (1964)

A42. *The Adventures of Jim Bowie* (1956)

A43. *Laverne and Shirley* (1976)

A44. *The Six Million Dollar Man* (1973 theme)

A45. *Candid Camera* (1963 theme)

Q46. "Like a streak of lightning flashing across the sky; like the switftest arrow whizzing from a bow; like a mighty cannonball he seems to fly."

Q47. "There's a little hotel called the Shady Rest at the junction...it is run by Kate, come and be her guest at the junction...[name of show]"

Q48. "With beauty and grace as swift as can be, watch it flying through the air. It travels in space or under the sea and it can journey anywhere."

Q49. "Whistle me up a memory, whistle me back to where I wanna be, whistle a tune that'll carry me back to [name of show]."

Q50. "Yes, he's only a man, and he walks like a man along a path full of hills to climb without pause, climb them because he's a man."

Q51. "Bigger than big, taller than tall, quicker than quick, stronger than strong, ready to fight for right against wrong."

Q52. "I'm standing on the edge of tomorrow and it's all up to me how far I go...standing on the edge of tomorrow today."

Q53. "He was innocent, not a charge was true, but the world would never know. [name of show], scorned as the one who ran; what do you do when you're [name of show] and you know you're a man?"

Q54. "Rollin', rollin', rollin', keep movin', movin', movin' though they're disapproving; keep them dogies movin' [name of show]."

Q55. "Overture, turn up the lights, this is it, the night of nights; no more rehearsing and nursing a part, we know every part by heart."

A46. *The Adventures of Champion* (1955)

A47. *Petticoat Junction* (1963)

A48. *Supercar* (1963)

A49. *Tombstone Territory* (1957)

A50. *Headmaster* (1970)

A51. *Gigantor* (1966)

A52. *Saved by the Bell: The College Years* (1993)

A53. *Branded* (1965)

A54. *Rawhide* (1958)

A55. *The Bugs Bunny Show* (1975)

Q56. "I'm not the kind to kiss and tell but I've been seen with Farrah...I've gotten burned over Cheryl Tiegs, blown up for Raquel Welch...I'm the unknown stuntman who makes Eastwood look so fine."

Q57. "It's a grand life, it's an I've-got-the-world-in-my-hand life. It's an almost-more-than-you-can-stand life; strike up the band, it's a grand life."

Q58. "Thank God there is someone to pick up the phone, be my cornerstone; I'm not alone, thank God for a friend like you."

Q59. "You're never too old for love; never say no to love. Until the twilight comes, we'll take what time allows."

Q60. "How do I fit in, in a room full of women when they don't even know I exist? Daily I rehearse 'Ladies first,' 'Up with women'; still I'm at the bottom of the list."

Q61. "If I'm crazy, then it's true, and it's all because of you...but it just may be a lunatic you're looking for..."

Q62. "You couldn't call him pretty, yet you'd have to say he's kind of witty. Joey, Joey, Joey."

Q63. "He protects and he saves his friends under the sea, that's where you'll find [name of show]."

Q64. "It's a rare condition in this day and age to read any good news on the newspaper page; and love and tradition of the grand desire, some people say is even harder to find..."

Q65. "She was working in a bridal shop in Flushing, Queens, till her boyfriend kicked her out in one of those crushing scenes; what was she to do, where was she to go, she was out on her fanny..."

A56. *The Fall Guy* (1981)

A57. *Marblehead Manor* (1987)

A58. *Hope and Gloria* (1995)

A59. *A Touch of Grace* (1973)

A60. *Ladies' Man* (1981)

A61. *Dave's World* (1993)

A62. *The Joey Bishop Show* (1962 theme)

A63. *Diver Dan* (1960)

A64. *Family Matters* (1989)

A65. *The Nanny* (1993)

Q66. "Hit the road, Jack, don't you come back no more, no more, no more! Hit the road, Jack, and don't you come back no more..."

Q67. "Thank you for being a friend, traveling down the road and back again. Your heart is true, you're a pal and a confidante."

Q68. "Everywhere you look there's a heart, a hand to hold on to...When you're lost...and all alone, a child is waitin' to carry you home, everywhere you look."

Q69. "The dream got broken, seemed like all was lost; what would be the future, could you pay the cost? You wonder will there ever be a second time around."

Q70. "He'll dry clean your clothes, be a butler or a porter, if it means another quarter in the bank. He'll get his degree, his Phi Beta key and get 'em both for free, that's [name of show]."

Q71. "Life goes on and so do we; just how we do it is no mystery. One by one we fill the days; we find a thousand different ways..."

Q72. "Standing tall on the wings of my dreams; rise and fall on the wings of my dreams...My life, my dreams, nothing's gonna stop me now."

Q73. "According to our new arrival, life is more than mere survival and we just might live the good life yet."

Q74. "Life is a riddle and you're in the middle and the puzzle is how to survive. Well you keep a-hopin' and you keep a-copin' and the answer will come to you [name of show]."

Q75. "There is a path you take and a path not taken, the choice is up to you my friend. Nights are long but you might awaken to a brand new life around the bend."

A66. *Unhappily Ever After* (1995)

A67. *The Golden Girls* (1985)

A68. *Full House* (1983)

A69. *Step by Step* (1991)

A70. *Hank* (1965)

A71. *Empty Nest* (1988)

A72. *Perfect Strangers* (1986)

A73. *Mr. Belvedere* (1985)

A74. *Out of the Blue* (1979)

A75. *Who's the Boss?* (1984)

Q76. "If the teacher pops a test I know I'm in a mess and my dog ate all my homework last night...if I can hand it in tomorrow it'll be all right...'cause I'm [name of show]."

Q77. "Life goes on, right or wrong; now it's all been said and done...seems we've sung love's last song, poor John, seems we've sung love's last song."

Q78. "We've got laughs from coast to coast to make you smile, a real bright look at each of you...it's the honest things you do, America laughs at you."

Q79. "There's no place like home, with your family around, you're never alone. When you know you're loved, you don't need to roam because there's no place like home."

Q80. "Your friends will be there when your back is to the wall; you'll find you need us 'cause there's no one else to call...You better be ready to, be ready to jump [name of show]."

Q81. "...an angel on a visit to his brother here below can cause a lot of trouble; there's miracles from the start, but they always come apart on ...."

Q82. "I don't know, I don't care, I just got to be there. California, here I am and I love you; I've got the fever for you, fever, fever, fever."

Q83. "There's a new girl in town with a brand new style; she was just passing through but if things work out, she's gonna stay for a while."

Q84. "There's a hurricane a blowin' in over the water, waitin' in anticipation for the action to begin."

A76. *Saved by the Bell* (1989)

A77. *Dear John* (1988)

A78. *America's Funniest Home Videos* (1993 theme)

A79. *227* (1985)

A80. *21 Jump Street* (1987)

A81. *The Smothers Brothers Show* (1965)

A82. *California Fever* (1979)

A83. *Alice* (1976)

A84. *Thunder in Paradise* (1994)

Q85. "Look right down any crowded hall you'll see there is a beauty standing; is she really everywhere or a reflection...could there be two different girls who look the same at [name of show]."

Q86. "Show me that smile again...don't waste another minute on your crying, we're nowhere near the end, the best is ready to begin."

Q87. "Where is the best defense against the rising tide of crime? Where is the man who gives the law his heartiest support? I'll tell you where, it's [name of show]."

Q88. "You'll never guess [name of show] who's on the inside hanging out...sometimes this double life gets out of hand, but it's all in a day's work for Ultra Man."

Q89. "It's hard to lick the U.S. government; they're taxin' us and takin' every cent. The money comes and goes and we're paying through the nose..."

Q90. "It was you...you made me leap without taking a look; I never thought forever was the best I could do. Then came you, it was you and me and you, and then came you."

Q91. "Little bones and little hearts can sometimes end up broken; medicine works twice as well with understanding...Just give them love, a little love because tomorrow depends on [name of show]."

Q92. "When you're at the top, you've got it made...don't be afraid; when a chance comes along you must take it. You'll go far; the world's gonna know who you are..."

Q93. "So come along, my barefoot love, you can be that child of three as we laugh and play all the way knee deep in daisies with you."

A85. *Sweet Valley High* (1994)

A86. *Growing Pains* (1985)

A87. *Sirota's Court* (1976)

A88. *My Secret Identity* (1988)

A89. *The Kallikaks* (1977)

A90. *Webster* (1983)

A91. *The Little People* (1972)

A92. *A Year at the Top* (1977)

A93. *Barefoot in the Park* (1970)

Q94. "Don't go to bed with no price on your head...don't do the crime if you can't do the time..."

Q95. "Hey there, there's a world where we don't have to run...living free in harmony and majesty. Take me home, take me home."

Q96. "He stands for justice, he has no fears; he's the agent they call when trouble is near."

Q97. "Fame and fortune waiting to be won...a smile in the limelight and a place in the sun. I want it all, I want it all."

Q98. "Here comes Sabrina, and all your friends are here again with you; and with Sabrina, there's fun and magic to keep you laughing too."

Q99. "Virginia, Virginia, Virginia, there's always something new in everything you do. Virginia, Virginia, Virginia, you've got a winning point of view."

Q100. "Love is crazy, it's unwise, it can take you by surprise."

Q101. "Archie's here, Betty's here, Veronica too. Reggie's here, and here comes Jughead and Hot Dog too, so everything's Archie; come on let's go with [name of show]."

Q102. "It's in the air, it's everywhere, people really startin' to care; they're gettin' [name of show]."

Q103. "Goin' down that long lonesome highway, gonna live life my way."

Q104. "Once before we took a chance and even though it didn't last [name of show]. Even though we share one life with your ex-husband and my ex-wife [name of show]."

A94. *Baretta* (1975)

A95. *The Life and Times of Grizzly Adams* (1977)

A96. *Lancelot Link, Secret Chimp* (1970)

A97. *Blansky's Beauties* (1977)

A98. *Sabrina, the Teenage Witch* (1971)

A99. *The Virginia Graham Show* (1970 theme)

A100. *Bridget Loves Bernie* (1972)

A101. *The Archie Show* (1969)

A102. *Getting Together* (1971)

A103. *Then Came Bronson* (1969)

A104. *Here We Go Again* (1973)

Q105. "You're my inspiration, days are never blue. After all is said and done, there is really only one [name of show], it's you."

Q106. "She's laughter, she's magic, she's mine. She's an angel and angels are few. So everything I've ever dared to dream has come true."

Q107. "There's a new boy in the neighborhood; lives downstairs and it's understood he's just here to take good care of me like he's part of the family."

Q108. "He's smart as a fox, he's strong as an ox, but he's soft as a teddy bear. If you're backed up against the wall, all you gotta do is call [name of show], that's the man."

Q109. "...'cause each day is what you make it, our hopes are riding high and it's better when you share it, but we'll never know until we try."

Q110. "Love is harmony, love is family, love is you and me...and here is where the love is...right here for us all."

Q111. "There is a man the legends tell who stands for what is right. Like Wyatt Earp, he never shrieks or cowers from a fight."

Q112. "If we're ever puzzled by the changing times, there's a plate of homemade wishes on the kitchen windowsill and [name of show] to fill our lives with love."

Q113. "We're in the air and everywhere, flying high, flying loose, flying free as a summer breeze...we're in the air and everywhere."

Q114. "When the world never seems to be living up to your dreams, it's time you started finding out what everything is all about. When the boys you use to hate you date, I guess you best investigate [name of show]."

A105. *Margie* (1962)

A106. *Nancy* (1970)

A107. *Charles in Charge* (1984)

A108. *Big Eddie* (1975)

A109. *A New Kind of Family* (1979)

A110. *Shirley* (1979)

A111. *The Misadventures of Sheriff Lobo* (1979)

A112. *Eight Is Enough* (1977)

A113. *The Bugaloos* (1970)

A114. *The Facts of Life* (1979)

Q115. "You talk to people all day for a living, but all those easy answers you are giving—are you really living your life that way? Portland is a long way from L.A."

Q116. "Here he comes, here comes [name of show], he's a demon and he's gonna be chasing after someone."

Q117. "If you're in doubt about angels being real, I can arrange to change any doubts you may feel. Wait until you see my [name of show], you'll want her for your valentine..."

Q118. "We all had an uncle and his name was Sam; we had to go in and get him out of a jam; the job wasn't easy, but the burden was shared, back in the forties when everyone cared."

Q119. "There's a man who leads a life of danger and everyone he meets he stays a stranger. With every move he makes, another chance he takes; odds are he won't live to see tomorrow."

Q120. "Stop, look, listen, 'cause you're gonna hear a brand new story 'bout a great engineer. He's the greatest of them all we claim; Number One's his engine, [name of show] his name."

Q121. "You don't have to be a Mia or Sophia, this is the year of the Tom; be the shapiest, ickiest [name of show]."

Q122. "Katie, all the fellas fall for Katie, 'cause Katie is the gal they adore."

Q123. "At a party she's a stomper, a rock 'n' rollin' romper; everybody's glad she came, hey that's [name of show]."

Q124. "Who lives down in deepest, darkest Africa? Who's the one who brought the jungle fame? Who's the king of animals in Africa? [name of show] is his name."

A115. *Hello, Larry* (1979)

A116. *Speed Racer* (1967)

A117. *Gidget* (1965)

A118. *The Goodtime Girls* (1980)

A119. *Secret Agent* (1965)

A120. *Casey Jones* (1957)

A121. *The Ugliest Girl in Town* (1967)

A122. *The Ann Sothern Show* (1958 theme)

A123. *Karen* (1964)

A124. *Kimba, the White Lion* (1966)

Q125. "All the world is waiting for you and the powers you possess; in your satin tights, fighting for your rights, and the old red, white, and blue."

Q126. "Take me back so I can see the way it was my legacy; I need to find what once was good in traces of my childhood."

Q127. "I'll tell you a story, a real true life story, a tale of the Western frontier; the West it was lawless, but one man was flawless and his is the story you'll hear."

Q128. "Who likes it hot, who's getting steamy, who snores a lot, who's feeling dreamy; who cuddles and coos, who's loaded with animal drives [name of show]."

Q129. "I'm solid gold, I've got the goods; they stand when I walk through the neighborhood...I've got the chance, I'm takin' it, this time in life I'm [name of show]."

Q130. "Mission impossible is what they called our plan...we could have used a miracle or two; never thought we'd see it through [name of show]."

Q131. "Hey look at me, I'm ready to fly; I'm ten feet off the ground, bound for the clear blue sky."

Q132. "Life is a game we're playing, let the game begin; love is the word we're saying, better let it in."

Q133. "Here comes the daydream drifting down on you...follow the dream until you see where it's going; like a kid, you're gonna feel yourself growing."

Q134. "School's out, summer's comin'...just can't imagine what the world would be without a West Coast woman gettin' next to me. School's out, summer's comin'..."

Q135. "Come to Bongo Congo, meet the ruling king, good King Leonardo, how that king can swing."

A125. *Wonder Woman* (1976)

A126. *The Family Holvak* (1975)

A127. *The Life and Legend of Wyatt Earp* (1955)

A128. *Husbands, Wives, and Lovers* (1978)

A129. *Making It* (1979)

A130. *In the Beginning* (1978)

A131. *The Waverly Wonders* (1978)

A132. *The Harvey Korman Show* (1978)

A133. *Who's Watching the Kids?* (1978)

A134. *Richie Brockelman, Private Eye* (1978)

A135. *The King and Odie Show* (1960)

Q136. "It's just another day, it's up to you to make it special. So enjoy it friend, today could be the day to find that rainbow again."

Q137. "Leavin' the city, taking a chance to do what we wanna do. [name of show] for something really new."

Q138. "If you have you and me, here in this shining world, there will be dreams to dance and summer's to sing…if you have you and me there will be love."

Q139. Like magic he appears, a hero to save the day. And just when you think he's here for good, that's when he goes away. 'Cause it's [name of show], he's never gonna settle down…"

Q140. "Let the times roll, let your love grow; let the rain shower, let the rose flower. Love it seeks, love it finds, love it conquers; love it finds, love it seeks, and love it finds."

Q141. "Pick out a star and wish, crazy as it may seem. Don't be afraid to hope, don't be afraid to dream…"

Q142. "They're crazy wild, and they're rough and rude; the dean don't like their attitude; they're animals…Baby, baby, let's go down to the [name of show]."

Q143. "Not gettin' hassled, not gettin' hussled, keepin' your head above water, makin' a wave when you can…"

Q144. "Rollin', rollin' round and round, pick yourself up off the ground; just a crazy game we're in and you might as well play to win."

Q145. "The first years are hard years, much more than we know…we'll do all things unknown and new, and one day we'll all say, hey look, we've come through the first years."

A136. *Another Day* (1978)

A137. *Please Stand By* (1978)

A138. *Julie Farr, M.D.* (1978)

A139. *Here's Boomer* (1980)

A140. *Angie* (1979)

A141. *Sweepstakes* (1979)

A142. *Delta House* (1979)

A143. *Good Times* (1974)

A144. *The Roller Girls* (1978)

A145. *The Paper Chase* (1978)

Q146. "Now the world don't move to the beat of just one drum; what might be right for you, may not be right for some..."

Q147. "...and the touch of a breeze gently stirs all the trees and a bird wants to please my ear; [name of show] oh so slowly moves along."

Q148. "How will you make it on your own? This world is awfully big, girl, this time you're all alone...it's time you started living...time you let someone else do some giving."

Q149. "Who can turn the world on with her smile? Who can take a nothing day and suddenly make it all seem worthwhile? Well it's you, girl, and you should know it, with each glance and every little movement you show it."

Q150. "There's a holdup in the Bronx, Brooklyn's broken out in fights; there's a traffic jam in Harlem that's backed up to Jackson Heights."

Q151. "Softness in his eyes, iron in his thighs, virtue in his heart, fire in every part of [name of show]."

Q152. "Look, it's the man who flies around like an eagle...Look, it's the nut who walks around in pajamas. That's no nut boy, that's [name of show]."

Q153. "...stay free where no walls divide you, you're free as the roaring tides so there's no need to hide...and life is worth living, but only worth living if you're [name of show]."

Q154. "You're searching for something or someplace to go; your mind is a landscape, you're traveling for free, so fill it with heroes that you want to be..."

A146. *Diff'rent Strokes* (1978)

A147. *The Long Hot Summer* (1965)

A148. *The Mary Tyler Moore Show* (1970 theme)

A149. *The Mary Tyler Moore Show* (1973 theme)

A150. *Car 54, Where Are You?* (1961)

A151. *The Mighty Hercules* (1960)

A152. *Captain Nice* (1967)

A153. *Born Free* (1974)

A154. *Billy* (1979)

Q155. "Some people got it, some people don't; you'll never know until you try...it could be magic, the way I feel; it could be magic, but it feels so real."

Q156. "So long class of '65, we're all in the world outside, but through all our lives we'll be the class of '65."

Q157. "...The story goes that grandma was best at shootin' buttons off a rustler's vest...Grandpa kept his gun in trim, nobody messed around with him...Every gun in the West would run from [name of show]."

Q158. "Phoebe Figalilly is a silly name and so many silly things keep happening; what is this magic thing about Nanny, is it love or is it magic?"

Q159. "Some people stand in the darkness, afraid to step into the light...don't you worry, it's gonna be all right, I'm always there, I won't let you out of my sight."

Q160. "The miracle of imagination, the marvels of earth, sea, and sky. These wonders untold, are ours to behold in the funny world, the sunny world, the wonderful world of color."

Q161. "Que sera, sera, whatever will be, will be; the future's not ours to see, que sera, sera."

Q162. "Saddle up, saddle up, saddle up. This is the story of [name of show] enforcing law within the territory. Praise be the glory of [name of show] who rode the Arizona territory. Ride on, ride on, ride on."

Q163. "Boy, the way Glenn Miller played, songs that made the Hit Parade; guys like us we had it made, those were the days."

Q164. "...bold and brave and gay; injustice he is fighting to win a better day. Shout a cheer, adventure is near, riding with [name of show]."

A155. *Tabitha* (1977)

A156. *What Really Happened to the Class of '65* (1977)

A157. *Pistols and Petticoats* (1967)

A158. *Nanny and the Professor* (1970)

A159. *Baywatch* (1991)

A160. *Walt Disney's Wonderful World of Color* (1965)

A161. *The Doris Day Show* (1968)

A162. *26 Men* (1957)

A163. *All in the Family* (1971)

A164. *Ivanhoe* (1957)

Q165. "I ride with the wind, my eyes on the sun, my hand on my [name of show]."

Q166. "...they robbed the rich, gave to the poor—except what they kept for expenses. So, when other legends are forgotten, we'll remember that things were rotten; yea for Robin Hood."

Q167. "When he gets into a scrape he makes his escape with his friend, an ape named Ape, then away he'll schlep on his elephant Shemp while Bella and Ursula stay in step..."

Q168. "Yes sir, that's my baby; no sir, I don't mean maybe; yes sir, that's my baby now."

Q169. "...like a beautiful child growing up free and wild; full of hopes and full of fears, full of laughter, full of tears throughout the years in Seattle."

Q170. "He's the boss, he's a V.I.P., he's the championship, he's the most tip-top, [name of show]."

Q171. "Tra-la-la, la-la-la, tra-la-la, la-la-la."

Q172. "Jammin' gears has got to be a fever, a lot of men become addicted to the grind. It takes a special breed to be a truck drivin' man and a steady hand to haul that load behind."

Q173. "...there's Dave Saville and what is more, there's the boy we know as Theodore; now you see, on camera three, the brother known as Simon on the family tree; and here's the star of the show, Alvin, Alvin, Alvin."

Q174. "When criminals in this world appear and break the law they should fear and frighten all who see or hear, the cry goes up both far and near for [name of show]."

A165. *Restless Gun* (1957)

A166. *When Things Were Rotten* (1975)

A167. *George of the Jungle* (1967)

A168. *Mona McCluskey* (1965)

A169. *Here Come the Brides* (1968)

A170. *Top Cat* (1961)

A171. *The Banana Splits Adventure Hour* (1968)

A172. *Movin' On* (1974)

A173. *The Alvin Show* (1961)

A174. *Underdog* (1964)

Q175. "Mars, Saturn, the Milky Way, when they're groovin' who can say...Josie's on a rocket ride, Pussycats are out of sight...Come along and dig the chase..."

Q176. "...wants a gal who's dreamy...wants a gal who's creamy...wants a gal to call his own..."

Q177. "In the world there are many worlds...we all have our secret world...a world that's deep inside, a world we mostly hide from view."

Q178. "Oh [name of show], full of fun seems to be the ideal...lets you hide all the sadness you feel."

Q179. "With a little love, just a little love, open your heart and see where it's headin'...feel it in your heart when you've succeeded, making all the sadness light, gettin' some fun in your life...with a little love, just a little love."

Q180. "Any kind of weather, any time of day, when the rig is ready, he'll be on his way to carry any cargo anywhere; name the destination and brother he'll be there."

Q181. "Primrose Lane, life's a family on Primrose Lane, just a family on Primrose Lane with you."

Q182. "You may think I'm being absurd but how would you like to fly around like a bird, 'cause that's what they're able to do, look at life [name of show]."

Q183. "...so walk hand-in-hand with me, there are love songs to be sung. Say you'll be my girl and we'll show the world, we're [name of show]."

Q184. "It's [name of show], brave and free, fighting evil 'neath the sea. He is a boy, a very special boy...in a flash he foils the foe...loyal friend of the seas is our [name of show]."

A175. *Josie and the Pussycats in Outer Space* (1972)

A176. *Dobie Gillis* (1959)

A177. *Bracken's World* (1969)

A178. *The Good Life* (1971)

A179. *The Debbie Reynolds Show* (1969)

A180. *Cannonball* (1958)

A181. *The Smith Family* (1973)

A182. *From a Bird's Eye View* (1971)

A183. *Never Too Young* (1965)

A184. *Marine Boy* (1966)

Q185. "He's been everywhere, flying through the air; he's everyone's friend. He will always land just to lend a hand. He's a friend to the end."

Q186. "There's a school where the students all major in fun, studyin' the sun...the classes meet on the grooviest beach by the sea, tuition is free down at sunshine Malibu, [name of show]."

Q187. "Dusty's the reason for their plight, thanks to Dusty nothing's right; only the wagon master's hand keeps them a rollin' to the promised land."

Q188. "That Mississippi, she is a mystery, she's just a waitin' to be explored; go get your gear mate, we'll meet you here mate, welcome aboard."

Q189. "Hello, hey, hi, how are you now; want you to know we have so much to do now, a world of adventure is waitin' for you here..."

Q190. "From West Vir-gin-y they came to stay in sunny Cal-i-for-ni-ay, old Grandpappy Amos and the girls and the boys of the family known as [name of show]."

Q191. "The ground just shook and everywhere you look all you see is [name of show]."

Q192. "Who makes the warning bells on the cable cars play 'The Gang's All Here'?...who lights the lights of Chinatown just by walking in view? Who? [name of show], it sure isn't you."

Q193. "Let me hear a melody, a simple sing-along singin' song and I sing, yes I sing along."

Q194. "Rowdy redhead headin' for the big time; lookin' like a Texas sequined star; makin' smiles at every tight-jeaned cowboy; sassin' the good ol' boys around the bar."

A185. *The Peter Potamus Show* (1964)

A186. *Malibu U.* (1967)

A187. *Dusty's Trail* (1973)

A188. *The New Adventures of Huck Finn* (1968)

A189. *The Hardy Boys* (cartoon; 1969)

A190. *The Real McCoys* (1957)

A191. *Babes* (1990)

A192. *Phyllis* (1977)

A193. *Sing Along With Mitch* (1961)

A194. *Flo* (1980)

Q195. "The kite sailing high in the sky; the firehouse band on the Fourth of July. Remember the Main Street trolley, oh by golly, I've got the hometown blues."

Q196. "Poor little girls, now you're trapped in this cruel, crazy world...while other girls make dates you make license plates."

Q197. "What a bright new world, what a wonderful beginning...from two different worlds two kids found each other...together and until forever it's [name of show]."

Q198. "I just saw the most beautiful ghost in the world...and she lived here, she loved here and cried here; she slept here and never really left here [name of show]."

Q199. "Sometimes you wanna go where everybody knows your name and they'll always be glad you came."

Q200. "...By and by they'll come a guy, the lucky guy who'll end up calling her his; for if given half a chance, there is no one who wouldn't go for the kind of girl she is."

Q201. "If you only had a penny to your name you'd go out and buy her a bright and shiny ribbon for her hair—just to see her smile..."

Q202. "Come join the Warner Brothers and the Warner sister, Dot; just for fun we run around the Warner movie lot."

Q203. "Believe it or not I'm walking on air, I never thought I could feel so free, flying away on a wing and a prayer, who could it be, believe it or not, it's just me."

Q204. "Pretty baby, you've got the look. Take your best shot; just one was all it took to see you've got the look. Take your best shot, you've got the look."

A195. *Hizzoner* (1979)

A196. *Women in Prison* (1987)

A197. *Phyl and Mikhy* (1980)

A198. *Jennifer Slept Here* (1983)

A199. *Cheers* (1982)

A200. *Funny Face* (1971)

A201. *The Sandy Duncan Show* (1972)

A202. *Animaniacs* (1993)

A203. *The Greatest American Hero* (1983)

A204. *Living Dolls* (1989)

Q205. "Everytime I turn around I see the girl that turns my world around...her spirit's lifting me right off the ground; what's gonna be, guess we'll just wait and see."

Q206. "We may be less than wealthy, but we're young and healthy and anyone who's young and healthy knows that that's the way the traffic flows; we know this is a living [name of show]."

Q207. "You can count on me, no matter what you do, you can count on me...No one loves you more than I do...You can count on me, no matter what you do, you can count on me."

Q208. "I'm doin' it the best I can, leanin' on nobody but me; seein' it from where I stand, nothing comes easy...I keep doin' it the best I can."

Q209. "There's room enough for two in a place that I know; haven't any view with the blue sky above...there's room enough for you, and I've got room enough for two in my life."

Q210. "You never know how things are gonna turn out...but there's one thing I can count on, that's for sure, the girl I fell in love with is the same as before."

Q211. "Stop all your fussin', slap on a smile...don't hide your feelings, you know you want to have a good time and in my opinionation, the sun is gonna surely shine."

A205. *Punky Brewster* (1984)

A206. *It's a Living* (1980)

A207. *My Two Dads* (1987)

A208. *Just the Ten of Us* (1988)

A209. *My Sister Sam* (1986)

A210. *The New Gidget* (1986)

A211. *Blossom* (1991)

Q212. "And at [name of show], she's a prime-time queen; she struts her stuff on the TV screen; her outlandish charm fills this funny farm that we call [name of show]."

Q213. "Let's give them something to talk about, something extra to figure out; let's give them something to talk about."

A212. *Madame's Place* (1982)

A213. *Women of the House* (1995)

2

THE STAR AND THE THEME

Q214. Many times a song is so associated with a performer that it becomes his or her musical signature. Match the song title (left column) with the star (right column).

1. "Seems Like Old Times"
2. "Life Could Not Better Be"
3. "Melancholy Serenade"
4. "This Could Be the Start of Something Big"
5. "Love in Bloom"
6. "Thanks for the Memory"
7. "Over the Rainbow"
8. "Thanks for Dropping By"

a. Jack Benny
b. Garry Moore
c. Perry Como
d. Danny Thomas
e. Jackie Gleason
f. Vic Damone
g. Lawrence Welk
h. Dinah Shore

9. "The Lively One"
10. "Dream Along With Me"
11. "Holiday for Strings"
12. "See the U.S.A."
13. "Love Is Like a Butterfly"
14. "Bubbles in the Wine"
15. "Danny Boy"
16. "Love Nest"
17. "Love Is All Around"
18. "Que Sera, Sera"
19. "Moon River"
20. "Happy Trails to You"

i. Steve Allen
j. Judy Garland
k. Doris Day
l. Arthur Godfrey
m. Roy Rogers and Dale Evans
n. Andy Williams
o. Mary Tyler Moore
p. Bob Hope
q. George Burns and Gracie Allen
r. Red Skelton
s. Dolly Parton
t. Danny Kaye

A214. 1 and l
2 and t
3 and e
4 and i
5 and a
6 and p
7 and j
8 and b
9 and f
10 and c
11 and r
12 and h
13 and s
14 and g
15 and d
16 and q
17 and o
18 and k
19 and n
20 and m

3

The Singer and the Star

Q215. Sometimes the series star also performs the show's theme song. Match the star (left column) with the title of the theme song (right column) he or she sings.

1. Lee Majors	a. "Shenandoah"
2. Doris Day	b. "I Will Walk With You"
3. Don Durant	c. "Working for a Living"
4. Roy Rogers and Dale Evans	d. "Nice Work If You Can Get It"
5. Tony Randall, Swoosie Kurtz, and Kaleena Kiff	e. "The Eyes of a Ranger"
6. Robert Horton	f. "Sigmund and the Sea Monsters"
7. Cybill Shepherd	g. "Jump Street"
8. Della Reese	h. "The Unknown Stuntman"
9. Christine Ebersole	i. "Que Sera, Sera"

10. Greg Evigan	j. "There's a New Girl in Town"
11. Chuck Norris	k. "Gimme a Break"
12. Kathy Maisnik	l. "Happy Trails to You"
13. David Naughton	m. "Easy Street"
14. Marla Gibbs	n. "Those Were the Days"
15. Linda Lavin	o. "B. J. and the Bear"
16. Loni Anderson	p. "Movin' Along"
17. Carroll O'Connor and Jean Stapleton	q. "There's No Place Like Home"
18. Johnny Whitaker	r. "Friends Forever"
19. Nell Carter	s. "Johnny Ringo"
20. Holly Robinson	t. "Making It"

A215. 1 and h (*The Fall Guy*, 1981)
2 and i (*The Doris Day Show*, 1968)
3 and s (*Johnny Ringo*, 1968)
4 and l (*The Roy Rogers Show*, 1951)
5 and r (*Love, Sidney*, 1981)
6 and a (*A Man Called Shenandoah*, 1965)
7 and d (*Cybill*, 1995)
8 and b (*Touched by an Angel*, 1994)
9 and c (*Rachel Gunn, R.N.*, 1992)
10 and o (*B.J. and the Bear*, 1979)
11 and e (*Walker, Texas Ranger*, 1995)
12 and p (*Star of the Family*, 1982)
13 and t (*Making It*, 1979)
14 and q (*227*, 1985)
15 and j (*Alice*, 1976)
16 and m (*Easy Street*, 1986)
17 and n (*All in the Family*, 1971)
18 and f (*Sigmund and the Sea Monsters*, 1973)
19 and k (*Gimme a Break*, 1981
20 and g (*21 Jump Street*, 1987)

4

Theme Composers

Q216. Match the composer (left column) with the series (right column) for which he wrote the TV theme.

1. Nelson Riddle	a. *The Odd Couple*
2. Henry Mancini	b. *Quantum Leap*
3. David Rose	c. *Shirley's World*
4. Mike Post	d. *The Big Valley*
5. Mike Post (with Pete Carpenter)	e. *Johnny Staccato*
6. Johnny Williams	f. *Cannon*
7. Neil Hefti	g. *Peter Gunn*
8. Quincy Jones	h. *Bonanza*
9. John Barry	i. *The Addams Family*
10. Jackie Gleason	j. *The Honeymooners*
11. Paul and Linda McCartney	k. *M Squad*

12. Elmer Bernstein	l. *Lost in Space*
13. George Duning	m. *The Dick Van Dyke Show*
14. Jack Elliott and Allyn Ferguson	n. *Route 66*
15. John Parker	o. *Honey West*
16. Jay Livingston and Ray Evans	p. *The Rockford Files*
17. Vic Mizzy	q. *Sanford and Son*
18. Count Basie	r. *Charlie's Angels*
19. Joseph Mullendore	s. *The Zoo Gang*
20. Earle Hagen	t. *Highway to Heaven*

A216.
1 and n
2 and g
3 and t
4 and b
5 and p
6 and l
7 and a
8 and q
9 and c
10 and j
11 and s
12 and e
13 and d
14 and r
15 and f
16 and h
17 and i
18 and k
19 and o
20 and m

5

The Spoken Word

Often an announcer or narrator or the star himself uses words to convey the program's theme. Identify the series associated with the spoken word passages below:

Q217. "The study of law is something new and unfamiliar to most of you, unlike any other schooling you have ever known before. You'll teach yourself the law but I'll train your minds. You come in here with a skull full of mush and, if you survive, you'll leave thinking like a lawyer."

Q218. "In the aftermath of the bloodletting called the Civil War, thousands of ruthless, restless, searching men traveled West. Such a man is William Colton. Like the others he carried a blanket roll, a proficient gun, and a dedication to a new chapter in American history, the opening of the West."

A217. *The Paper Chase* (1978)

A218. *The Loner* (1965)

Q219. "In 1972 a crack commando unit was sent to prison by a military court for a crime they did not commit. These men promptly escaped from a maximum security stockade to the Los Angeles underground. Today, still wanted by the government, they survive as soldiers of fortune. If you have a problem, if no one else can help—and if you can find them—maybe you can hire [name of show]."

Q220. "We searched for a man named James Sonnett and the legends folks tell may be true; most call him gunman and killer; he's my son, whom I hardly knew. I raised Jim's boy from the cradle 'till the day he said to me I have to go find my father. And I reckoned that's how it should be, so we ride, Jim's boy and me."

Q221. "Out of the clear blue of the Western sky comes [name of show]."

A222. "This is me, Nicole Bradford. Cute, huh? This is my dad and this is my dad. How did I get two dads? They inherited me...one dad who's down to earth and one dad with his head in the clouds."

Q223. "If sailors' tales to sailors' tombs...and all the old romance retold exactly in the ancient way can please me as they pleased of old, the wiser youngsters of today, so be it!...Arrrrh ha and forlorn!"

Q224. "This is the story of three men who came to be known as [name of show]. Many years later and a half a continent away that name was to win undying glory on the slopes of San Juan Hill. But our story is the beginning of the legend. Three men who came to be known in awe and admiration as [name of show]."

A219. *The A-Team* (1983)

A220. *The Guns of Will Sonnett* (1967)

A221. *Sky King* (1951)

A222. *My Two Dads* (1987)

A223. *Long John Silver* (1956)

A224. *The Rough Riders* (1958)

Q225. "Out of the library of American folklore, those treasured stories such as Huck Finn, Paul Bunyan, and Rip Van Winkle—which have brought us laughter and joy for generations—come the warm and lovable tales of [name of show]; presented by the Blatz Brewing Company of Milwaukee, Wisconsin, on behalf of Blatz dealers everywhere."

Q226. "The swamp is my world. It is where I am; it is what I am. I was once a man. I know the evil men do. Do not bring your evil here. I warn you—beware the wrath of the [name of show]."

Q227. "These are stories of people who have been helped by the many great organizations which are dedicated to bringing truth to those who are fed lies; light to those who live in darkness; protection to those who live in fear."

Q228. "...a shadowy flight into the dangerous world of a man who does not exist. Michael Knight, a young loner on a crusade to champion the cause of the innocent, the helpless, the powerless in a world of criminals who operate above the law."

Q229. "You got big dreams? You want fame? Well fame costs and right here is where you start paying—in sweat."

Q230. "I was born in the Bronx, New York, in December 1941. I've always felt responsible for World War II. The first thing I remember liking that liked me back was food...I decided to move out of the house when I was twenty-four. My mother still considers this the day I ran away from home. Eventually I ran to Minneapolis, where it's cold...and now I'm back in Manhattan. New York, this is your last chance."

A225. *The Amos and Andy Show* (1951)

A226. *Swamp Thing* (1990)

A227. *The Crusader* (1955)

A228. *Knight Rider* (1982)

A229. *Fame* (1982)

A230. *Rhoda* (1974)

Q231. "It's out there, people violating contracts, swindling, trespassing, killing, reusing postage stamps; crimes beyond counting; but come morning, some citizen accused of an interesting one will seek us out."

Q232. "My name is Conrad Steiner, I'm a doctor of medicine...Guardian of birth, healer of the sick, comforter of the aging. To the profession of medicine, to the men and women who labor in its cause, this story is dedicated."

Q233. "The legend of the Baudine brothers has etched itself in frontier history in the last quarter of the nineteenth century. Morgan "Two Persons" Baudine, captured by the Cheyenne and freed eight years later by the army. Quentin Baudine, a young doctor from San Francisco...both join together in a search for their sister, Patricia, still a captive of the Cheyenne...The legend of the Baudine brothers, this is their story, this is [name of show]."

Q234. "At twenty-four he had been the youngest general in the Civil War. Within five years he had been reduced in rank and sent West to be forgotten. But he was not the kind of man to let the world forget. His name, George Armstrong Custer."

Q235. "A gay new comedy about the life and loves of a secretary in Manhattan. It's time to [name of show]."

Q236. "No matter how dark the night there is always a new dawn to come, the sun is but a [name of show], a dramatic serial for those who face today and look forward to tomorrow's promise."

Q237. "From the world's most exotic cities, from Paris, London, Shanghai, New York, the stories of the people who give these cities life on [name of show]."

A231. *Rosetti and Ryan* (1977)

A232. *Medic* (1954)

A233. *The Quest* (1976)

A234. *The Legend of Custer* (1967)

A235. *Meet Millie* (1952)

A236. *Morning Star* (1965)

A237. *Star Theater* (1963)

Q238. "Presenting an unusual story of love and mystery on [name of show] starring Edmund Lowe as the famed newspaper columnist and amateur detective, David Chase. And now for another thrilling adventure as we accompany David Chase and watch him match wits with those who would take the law in their own hands."

Q239. "A fiery horse with the speed of light, a cloud of dust and a hearty Hi-ho Silver! [name of show]. With his faithful Indian companion, Tonto, the daring and resourceful masked rider of the plains led the fight for law and order in the early West. Return with us now to those thrilling days of yesteryear. [name of show] rides again."

Q240. "Chosen from among all others by the immortal elders...Billy Batson and his mentor travel the highways and byways of the land on a never-ending mission to right wrongs, to develop understanding and to seek justice for all. In times of dire need young Billy has been granted the power...to summon awesome forces at the utterance of a single word, [name of show]. A word that transforms him in a flash to the mightiest of mortal beings, Captain Marvel."

Q241. "This is the most danger-packed show on television. Every jump, every aerial maneuver is real, photographed just as it happened without tricks or illusions. All that stands between the jumper and death is his [name of show]."

Q242. "Whatever it is, wherever it is, at home or around the world, you see it here, [name of show]. And here's your host, Jack Smith."

A238. *Front Page Detective* (1951)

A239. *The Lone Ranger* (1949)

A240. *Shazam!* (1974)

A241. *Ripcord* (1961)

A242. *You Asked for It* (1950)

Q243. "These [scenes of destruction] and hundreds of other legitimate claims are paid by insurance companies. Once in a while some joker comes along with an attempt to defraud. By any other name, they're still [name of show]. That's where I come in, I'm John Hunter, investigator for the Eastern Insurance Company."

Q244. "...Operating from his secret mountain headquarters on the planet Earth [name of show] rallies men of good will everywhere. As he rockets from planet to planet let us follow the champion of truth, justice, and freedom throughout the universe. Stand by for [name of show]."

Q245. "At this moment thousands of children are running from their homes, crying out for help, seeking escape from brutality and indifference. One man hears them well: Steve Arizzio, former juvenile officer, now a clinical psychologist, has spent a lifetime answering such calls."

Q246. "Have you ever been certain your telephone would ring in the next ten seconds? Or have you ever walked down a strange street before and had the feeling you knew what laid beyond the unturned corner? Yes? Then you've had a brief encounter with the world of the unknown. You are ready for the actual human experience that follows."

Q247. "Come, you'll witness things strange, unexpected, mysterious, but not to be denied. Join me now and take [name of show]."

A243. *The Cheaters* (1960)

A244. *Captain Video* (1949)

A245. *The Runaways* (1979)

A246. *One Step Beyond* (1959 opening)

A247. *One Step Beyond* (1961 opening)

Q248. "Somewhere on an uncharted portion of the planet Earth stands the laboratory of [name of show]. In this secret location, known only to a few in the outside world [name of show] and his associates experiment in time and space to learn from the past to learn for the future."

Q249. "This is Los Angeles, one of the least corrupt cities in the United States. And its police force is one of the most honest and efficient in the world. But it wasn't always so."

Q250. "Deep in the heart of the Amazon, the Butler family was exploring an uncharted river canyon. Suddenly, caught up in a violent whirlpool, they were propelled through an underground cavern and flung into a hostile world of giant prehistoric creatures—a world that time forgot."

Q251. "Once upon a time there were three little girls who went to work for the police academy. And they were each assigned very hazardous duties. But I took them away from all that and now they work for me. My name is Charlie."

Q252. "When I walk through the streets of [name of show], I see a small but growing town, a busy town with its roots deep in the coal-mined earth. But behind the closed doors and drawn curtains are the secret lives of its people...the truth about this town, about any town. The real stories waiting to be told."

A248. *Captain Z-Ro* (1955)

A249. *City of Angels* (1976)

A250. *Valley of the Dinosaurs* (1974)

A251. *Charlie's Angels* (1976 opening)

A252. *Gibbsville* (1976)

Q253. "For millions of years the earth was fertile and rich. Then pollution and waste began to take their toll. Civilization fell into ruin. This is the world of the twenty-fifth century. Only a handful of scientists remain—men who have vowed to rebuild what has been destroyed. This is their achievement, [name of show], a mobile storehouse of scientific knowledge manned by a highly trained crew of young people. Their mission: to bring the hope of a new future to mankind."

Q254. "This is the landscape of [name of show]. Desert, forest, mountain and plains. It is intense heat, bitter cold, torrential rain, blinding dust; men risking their lives, earning small reward; the life of challenge—[name of show]."

Q255. "Here's adventure. Here's romance. Here's O. Henry's famous Robin Hood of the Old West, [name of show]."

Q256. "There were six people who loved to watch television, but they didn't like what they saw...Armed with determination and a strong will to change the course of television, they wrote their own shows...but that wasn't enough, they had to sell them...they went straight to the networks, but the networks were not ready for them...But did that stop them? No. They built their own network...and they liked what they saw."

Q257. "The story you are about to see actually happened and is completely documented. It's one of those strange events that seem to defy all explanation. They lie beyond the veil of human knowledge, yet they happen."

A253. *Ark II* (1976)

A254. *Rawhide* (1958)

A255. *The Cisco Kid* (1950)

A256. *Second City TV* (1977)

A257. *The Veil* (1958)

Q258. "The forework of liberty, protecting the inalienable rights of free people. Serving unstintingly and without prejudice to maintain the laws of our land [name of show]."

Q259. "My name is Walt. I work as night watchman here at Fred's Wax Museum to put myself through criminology college. I use to be lonely...until I plugged in my crime computer. Suddenly oscillating vibrations brought to life three legendary monsters—Dracula, the Werewolf, and Frankenstein—creatures hated and feared for centuries now determined to make up for their past misbehavings by fighting crime wherever they find it. Together we're [name of show]."

Q260. "Stories of the Old West, stories of hardship and adventure, of dreams and courage; stories of the American pioneer are all a part of our past, our heritage."

Q261. "...his dual identity known only to his secretary and to the district attorney. And now to protect the rights and lives of decent citizens rides [name of show]."

Q262. "Once upon a time...there lived a very nice man and a very nice woman. They were married to each other and they loved each other very much...but they had a problem...they each thought the other had a more interesting life. They wished they could change places with each other and they said it...in front of a statue that had a magic spell and lo and behold his spirit and personality went into her body and hers went into his—and that's the way they are today. Will they live happily ever after? Well, let's see."

A258. *The Grand Jury* (1958)

A259. *The Monster Squad* (1976)

A260. *Death Valley Days* (1969 opening)

A261. *The Green Hornet* (1966)

A262. *Turnabout* (1979)

Q263. "There are those who believe that life here began out there; far across the universe with tribes of humans who may have been the forefathers of the Egyptians or the Tolteks or the Mayans. Some believe there may yet be brothers of man who even now fight to survive somewhere beyond the heavens."

Q264. "A scientist both wise and bold set out to cure the common cold. Instead he found this power pill which he said most certainly will turn a lamb into a lion, like an eagle he'll be flying, solid steel will be like putty; it will work on anybody. But then 'twas found this potent pill made the strongest men quite ill; so the secret search began to find the one and only man. What they found made them squeamish for only Stanley Beemish, a weak and droopy daffodil could take the special power pill...When he took the pill specific, it made him the most prolific, terrific [name of show]."

Q265. "A public defender is an attorney employed by the community and responsible for giving legal aid without cost to any person who seeks it and is financially unable to employ private counsel. It is his duty to defend those accused of crime until the issue is decided in a court of law."

Q266. "Tonight [name of show] presents the top tunes of yesterday and today, America's most popular music as determined by [name of show] survey, featuring the best-sellers in phonograph records, sheet music, the songs most played on automatic coin machines and the songs most played on the air all over America."

A263. *Battlestar Galactica* (1978)

A264. *Mr. Terrific* (1967)

A265. *Public Defender* (1954)

A266. *Your Hit Parade* (1958)

Q267. "March the Fourth, nineteen and thirty-three. Mercy, what times these are. Nobody in this whole country has enough money to buy dirt. Lucky, though, we live here in Kansas City, Kansas, where there is plenty of dirt for free; just everything else we can't afford."

Q268. "Once upon a time, a junkman had a dream [go to the moon and salvage all the junk]. So he put together a team: an ex-astronaut and a fuel expert. They built a rocket ship and they went to the moon. Who knows what they'll do next."

Q269. "This is my boss, Jonathan Hart, a self-made millionaire; he's quite a guy. This is Mrs. H; she's gorgeous; what a terrific lady. By the way, my name is Max, I take care of them, which ain't easy, 'cause their hobby is murder."

Q270. "Our tour of the Pacific was over; we were going home, forty of us, forty kids...the storm was getting worse...then we crashed. The pilots were dead. We were all alone on an island two thousand miles from nowhere. A few hours later we found a town built for an atomic bomb test. The Atomic Energy Commission had cancelled the test and deserted this island. We had food, shelter and one thing more—a frightening realization that we would never leave here...this was our home forever...no more anything; just us—and God are we scared!"

Q271. "The great stars, the excitement, the thrills, the laughter, and the heartbreak of Hollywood's golden era."

A267. *Apple Pie* (1978)

A268. *Salvage 1* (1979)

A269. *Hart to Hart* (1979)

A270. *The New People* (1969)

A271. *Silents Please* (1960)

Q272. "That's me, Sam Hayden. My wife died a couple of years ago...so now there's just me and Jill, that's my little girl. What do I do? Well, I wash dishes, drive cabs...anything to make a buck...Jill and I are hanging in there and it's working out pretty good, well most of the time."

Q273. "If you do not, on a national scale, attack organized criminals with weapons and techniques as effective as their own, they will destroy us...an attack has been mounted from Washington; an undercover team of federal agents is the spearhead of that attack—[name of show]."

Q274. "This is the year two thousand and twenty. The place is the Challenger Sea Mount, the top of an underwater mountain, a complex beneath the sea. Two hundred and fifty men, women, and children live here. Each of them a scientist pioneer. For this is our last frontier, a hostile environment which may hold the key to tomorrow."

Q275. "Home, home on the range, where the deer and the antelope play. And who could be more at home on the range than [name of show] with his thrilling adventures of the great outdoors; his exciting experiences rivaling those of Davy Crockett, Daniel Boone, Buffalo Bill, and other pioneers of this wonderful country of ours."

Q276. "There are eight million stories in the Naked City. Some are violent, some sad, but one of them is just plain cuckoo. This is a modern fable about two young people who make a bargain only to find out they were going to get a lot more than they bargained for. We call our fable [name of show] and it stars Michael Callan and Patricia Harty."

A272. *Sunshine* (1975)

A273. *The Silent Force* (1970)

A274. *Sealab 2020* (1972)

A275. *The Range Rider* (1951)

A276. *Occasional Wife* (1967)

Q277. "...champion of the people, defender of truth and guardian of our fundamental rights to life, liberty, and the pursuit of happiness."

Q278. "On November thirteenth Felix Unger was asked to remove himself from his place of residence. That request came from his wife...with nowhere else to go, he appeared at the home of his childhood friend, Oscar Madison. Sometime earlier, Madison's wife had thrown him out requesting that he never return. Can two divorced men share an apartment without driving each other crazy?"

Q279. "What you are about to see is a real-life story taken from the files of police racket and bunco squads, business protective associates and similar sources all over the country. It is intended to expose the confidence game, the carefully worked out frames by which confidence men take more money each year from the American public than all the bank robbers and thugs with their violence."

Q280. "Lost in the Devil's Triangle, trapped in a dimension with beings from the future and from other worlds, a party of adventurers journeys through zones of time back to their own time."

Q281. "Space, the final frontier. These are the voyages of the starship *Enterprise.* Its five year mission: to explore strange new worlds, to seek out new life and new civilizations, to boldly go where no man has gone before."

A277. *Mr. District Attorney* (1951)

A278. *The Odd Couple* (1970)

A279. *Racket Squad* (1950)

A280. *The Fantastic Journey* (1977)

A281. *Star Trek* (1966)

Q282. "The year is 1987 and America launches the last of its deep space probes. In a freak accident, *Ranger 3* and its pilot...are blown out of their trajectory and into an orbit which freezes his life support systems and returns [him] to earth five hundred years later."

Q283. "What if you could find a brand new world right here on Earth where anything's possible. Same planet, different dimension. I found the gateway."

Q284. "Democracy is a very bad form of government but I ask you never to forget it; all the others are so much worse."

Q285. "This old album makes me remember so many things in the past. San Francisco and the house on Stinner Street where I was born. It brings back memories of my cousins, aunts, and uncles; all the boys and girls I grew up with. And I remember my family as we were then. My brother Nels, my little sister Dagmar, and of course, Papa. But most of all when I look back to those days so long ago, most of all [name of show]."

Q286. "We travel through time to help history along, give it a push where it is needed. When the Omni is red it means history is wrong. Our job is to get everything back on track."

Q287. "This man has a singular advantage over other men...Ben Richards is immune to every known disease, including old age. Periodic transfusions of his blood will give other men a second, a third lifetime, perhaps more..."

Q288. "Man lives in the sunlit world of what he believes to be reality. But there is unseen by most an underworld, a place that is just as real, but not as brightly lit, a dark side."

A282. *Buck Rogers in the 25th Century* (1979)

A283. *Sliders* (1995)

A284. *Slattery's People* (1964)

A285. *I Remember Mama* (a.k.a. *Mama*, 1949)

A286. *Voyagers* (1982)

A287. *The Immortal* (1970)

A288. *Tales From the Darkside* (1988)

Q289. "This is where the wealthy and the powerful rule [scenes of Manhattan]. It is her world. A world apart from mine. Her name is Catherine. From the moment I saw her she captured my heart with her beauty, warmth, and courage. I knew then as I know now she would change my life forever."

Q290. "...an innocent victim of blind justice, falsely convicted for the murder of his wife, reprieved by fate when a train wreck freed him on route to the deathhouse, freed him to hide in lonely desperation, to change his identity, to toil at many jobs, freed him to search for a one-armed man he saw leave the scene of the crime, freed him to run before the relentless pursuit of the police lieutenant obsessed with his capture..."

Q291. "It began with a closed, deserted diner and a man too long without sleep to continue his journey. It began with the landing of a craft from another galaxy. Now David Vincent knows [name of show] are here, that they have taken human form. Somehow he must convince a disbelieving world that the nightmare has already begun."

Q292. "Extraordinary crimes against the people and the state had to be avenged by agents extraordinary. Two such people are John Steed, top professional, and his partner, Emma Peel, talented amateur, otherwise known as [name of show]."

Q293. "An actual account from the pages of my newspaper, the *Tombstone Epitaph*. This is the way it happened in the town too tough to die."

A289. *Beauty and the Beast* (1987)

A290. *The Fugitive* (1963)

A291. *The Invaders* (1967)

A292. *The Avengers* (1966)

A293. *Tombstone Territory* (1957)

Q294. "Nothing travels faster than news. An electronic impulse splinters distance at one hundred and eighty-six thousand miles a second. From Tokyo, from London, from Rio, from New York, an age of speed and curiosity. The news probes and the probe is truth. I'm Catherine Wells, wire service reporter, *Trans Globe News*."

Q295. "There is nothing wrong with your television set. We are controlling transmission...Sit quietly and we will control all that you see and hear. You are about to participate in a great adventure. You are about to experience the awe and mystery which reaches from the inner mind to [name of show]."

Q296. "This is the Yankee Doodle Society, a secret organization like those that operated during the American Revolution; young patriots determined to help mold their own future by fighting for freedom behind British lines."

Q297. "He journeyed the earth battling his wicked stepmother Hera, the all-powerful Queen of the Gods. But wherever there was evil, wherever an innocent would suffer, there would be [name of show]."

Q298. "I am [name of show] and I know many things for I walk by night. I know many strange tales hidden in the hearts of men and women who have stepped into the shadows. Yes, I know the nameless terrors of which they dare not speak."

A294. *Wire Service* (1956)

A295. *The Outer Limits* (1963)

A296. *The Young Rebels* (1970)

A297. *Hercules, the Legendary Journeys* (1994)

A298. *The Whistler* (1954)

Q299. "From Hollywood, the glamour capital of the world, join us in a make-believe search for the most beautiful girl on earth...and although this is not a real contest, we will bring you our version of the all-American beauty, that one-of-a-kind girl who not only has personality and poise, but beauty and talent as well...And now, here's the host and star of the show, Mr. Beauty himself, Rip Taylor."

Q300. "Up, up, rockets blazing with white hot fury, the man-made meteors ride through the atmosphere, breaking the gravity barrier, pushing up and out, faster and faster, than outer space for [name of show]."

Q301. "Peter Murphy, American secret agent marked for death, meets a bizarre destiny. As his pursuers close in he comes face to face with his exact double, multimillionaire Mark Wainwright. The millionaire takes the bullet meant for the spy and Murphy finds the perfect cover. He steps into the shoes and life of the man with his face and Peter Murphy, now alias Mark Wainwright, becomes [name of show]."

Q302. "High adventure in the wild, vast regions of outer space. Missions of daring in the name of interplanetary justice. Travel into the future with Buzz Corey, commander-in-chief of the [name of show]."

Q303. "There is a fifth dimension beyond that which is known to man. It is a dimension as vast as space and as timeless as infinity. It is the middle ground between light and shadow, between science and superstition and its lies between the pit of man's fears and the summit of his knowledge. This is the dimension of imagination, it is an area which we call [name of show]."

A299. *The $1.98 Beauty Show* (1978)

A300. *Rod Brown of the Rocket Rangers* (1953)

A301. *The Man Who Never Was* (1966)

A302. *Space Patrol* (1950)

A303. *The Twilight Zone* (1959 opening)

Q304. "You're traveling through another dimension, a dimension not only of sight and sound but of mind, a journey into a wonderous land whose boundaries are that of imagination. There's a signpost up ahead, your next stop [name of show]."

Q305. "...with Yukon King, swiftest and strongest lead dog, breaking the trail in the relentless pursuit of law breakers in the wild days of the Yukon."

Q306. "The immortal pen of James Fenimore Cooper brings you thrilling tales of excitement; blazing action on the early American frontier; stirring adventures filled with the daring and courage of Hawkeye, first of the long rifles, and his blood brother, Chingachgook, [name of show]."

Q307. "This is Buddy Overstreet. He's wanted by the head of the most powerful crime syndicate in the country. In a steamroom Buddy overheard their vital secrets and the mysterious words 'Chicken Little.' Now he knows too much. These are the orders given to all members of the syndicate from one end of the country to the other—'Get him, get him, get him.'"

Q308. "Dr. David Banner, physician, scientist, searching for a way to tap into the hidden strengths that all humans have. Then an accidental overdose of gamma radiation alters his body chemistry. And now when David Banner grows angry or enraged, a startling metamorphosis occurs...the creature is driven by rage...David Banner is believed to be dead and he must let the world think that he is dead until he can find a way to control the raging spirit that dwells within him."

A304. *The Twilight Zone* (1961 opening)

A305. *Sergeant Preston of the Yukon* (1955)

A306. *Last of the Mohicans* (a.k.a. *Hawkeye and the Last of the Mohicans*, 1957)

A307. *Run, Buddy, Run* (1966)

A308. *The Incredible Hulk* (1978)

Q309. "Ladies and gentlemen, the story you are about to see is true, the names have been changed to protect the innocent."

Q310. "The one absolute unselfish friend that a man can have in this selfish world, the one that never proves ungrateful or treacherous, is his dog."

Q311. "Bull's-eye! [name of show] hits the entertainment bull's-eye every week with her hard riding, straight shooting, and suspense."

Q312. "Whenever the laws of any state are broken, a duly authorized organization swings into action. It may be called the state police, state troopers, militia, the Rangers, or the [name of show]. These are the stories of the men whose training, skill, and courage have enforced and preserved our state laws."

Q313. "Long ago, a lone explorer named Arnie Sacnuson made a fantastic descent to the fabled kingdom of Atlantis at the earth's core. After many centuries his trail was discovered...by me, Professor Oliver Lindenbrook, my niece Cindy, student Alec McQuen, our guide Lars, and his pet duck Gertrude. But we were not alone. The evil Count Sacnuson, last descendant of the once noble Sacnuson family, followed us to claim the center of the earth for his power mad schemes. He ordered his...servant Tor to destroy our party, but the plan backfired, sealing the entrance forever. And so for us began a desperate race to the earth's core, to learn the secret of the way back. This is the story of our new [name of show]."

A309. *Dragnet* (1952)

A310. *Sam* (1978)

A311. *Annie Oakley* (1954)

A312. *Highway Patrol* (1955)

A313. *Journey to the Center of the Earth* (1967)

Q314. "This is [name of show]. They play movie stars who are husband and wife. Starring Ida Lupino and Howard Duff; and in real life they are actually husband and wife. It's [name of show]."

Q315. "Anne Jeffreys as Marian Kerby, the ghostess with the mostess. Robert Sterling as George Kerby, that most sporting spirit. And Leo G. Carroll, host to said ghosts as [name of show]."

A314. *Mr. Adams and Eve* (1957)

A315. *Topper* (1953)

6

THEME SONG HAPPENINGS

The following deal with theme song changes or events that occur in the theme itself.

Q316. Before *Happy Days*, the 1974–84 series about the Cunningham family, used a theme song called "Happy Days," a 1958 (to 1966) show about the Stone family used a similarly-titled theme. Name that series.

Q317. Any fan of TV knows that the Brady Bunch Kids (Marcia, Jan, Cindy, Greg, Peter, and Bobby) sang the opening theme song for *The Brady Bunch*. This, however, is only true from the second through the fourth seasons. What group sang the song during the first one?

Q318. The Hoagy Carmichael standard "Georgia on My Mind" has been used thus far as the theme song for two different TV series. One was *Designing Women* in the eighties. What was the other one (from the seventies)?

A316. *The Donna Reed Show*

A317. The Peppermint Trolley Company

A318. *Lobo*

Q319. Mindy Sterling and Dennis Tufano originally sang the theme to *Family Ties* ("Without Us"). What two well-known singers replaced them beginning with the tenth episode?

Q320. Frankie Laine first sang the theme to *The Adventures of Champion* in 1955, then the one to *Rawhide* in 1958. Name either of the other two theme songs Laine performed.

Q321. The theme from *The Andy Griffith Show* is perhaps the best known example of a series that used whistling in its signature song. Five other series also used whistling; three of them are *The Whistler, Tombstone Territory*, and *Major Dad*. Name either of the other two.

Q322. *Family Matters* began as a simple sitcom about incidents in the lives of the Winslow family. The character of Steve Urkel was added to save the floundering show and its theme song was changed to "As Days Go By." What was the original sentimental song, performed by Louis Armstrong, used as the show's theme?

Q323. *Get Christie Love* was a series about a beautiful black female detective for the L.A.P.D. As the theme song concluded, Christie turned to the camera and said what became her catch phrase. What were her words?

Q324. When *The Adventures of Superman* switched from black-and-white to color, what very noticeable opening graphic also changed with it?

Q325. In the opening to *Colt .45*, star Wayde Preston approaches the camera then draws his guns. What results when he fires them?

A319. Johnny Mathis and Deneice Williams

A320. *Rango* (1967); *The Misadventures of Sheriff Lobo* (1979)

A321. *Leave It to Beaver* (1957); *Camp Runamuck* (1965)

A322. "What a Wonderful World"

A323. "You're under arrest, Sugah!"

A324. A steam locomotive is seen in black and white episodes; a diesel engine in color episodes.

A325. The show's title appears as he fires.

Q326. When a theme song has lyrics and it tells of the show's main character, the words often praise the star, telling of his or her joys or sorrows. We learned, for example, that Mary Richards "Could turn the world on with her smile" and that Jim Bowie was a "mighty adventuring man." What 1977 series took the opposite approach and degraded the star with these final words: "It sure isn't you"?

Q327. In the opening to *The Rifleman*, Chuck Connors approaches the camera to demonstrate his skill with his .44-40 rifle. How many shots does he fire?

Q328. The 1988 series *Nightingales* dealt with the struggles of a group of student nurses. While its theme music is easily forgettable, some of its visuals were unique (and blasted by critics). What were they?

Q329. *Police Squad* told the story of a crack (pot) lieutenant named Frank Drebin. The theme spoofed other theme songs. Name one of the two unusual things that happened in the opening.

Q330. When *The Abbott and Costello Show* returned for its second season in 1953, it changed somewhat, using a different laugh track and a different theme song. Besides dropping Costello's "Hey, Abbott!" yell from the original theme, the new opening one was unique for what reason?

A326. *Phyllis*

A327. Twelve

A328. The nurses in their sexy lingerie

A329. The guest star was bumped off and as the announcer intoned the episode's title, a different one appeared in graphics.

A330. It encompassed all the normal closing theme credits thus eliminating an ending theme song.

7

First Line/Second Line

The first or the most familiar line of a theme or opening narration is presented here. Supply the line that follows.

Q331. *The Brady Bunch* (1969): "Here's the story of a lovely lady who was bringing up three very lovely girls..."

Q332. *Love, American Style* (1969): "Love, American Style, truer than the red, white, and blue..."

Q333. *Texas John Slaughter* (1958): "Texas John Slaughter made 'em do what they oughter..."

Q334. *Davy Crockett* (1954): "Born on a mountain top in Tennessee, greenest state in the land of the free..."

Q335. *The Mickey Mouse Club* (1955): "Who's the leader of the club that's made for you and me..."

Q336. *Swamp Fox* (1959): "Swamp Fox, Swamp Fox, tail on his hat, nobody knows where the Swamp Fox at..."

Q337. *Sigmund and the Sea Monsters* (1973): "Now Sigmund the Sea Monster and Johnny and Scott are friends..."

A331. "All of them had hair of gold like their mother, the youngest one in curls."

A332. "Love, American Style, that's me and you."

A333. "'cause if they didn't they die."

A334. "Raised in the woods so he knew every tree, kilt him a b'ar when he was only three."

A335. "Hey there, hi there, ho there, you're as welcome as can be."

A336. "Swamp Fox, Swamp Fox, hidin' in the glen, he runs away to fight again."

A337. "The finest of friends that ever could be on the land or the sea."

Q338. *Howdy Doody* (1947): "It's Howdy Doody time, Bob Smith and Howdy too, say Howdy Doo to you..."

Q339. *Blondie* (1968): "Blondie, so soft, so bouncy...that super perfect wife..."

Q340. *Astro Boy* (1963): "...crowds will cheer you, you're a hero..."

Q341. *Electra Woman and Dyna Girl* (1976): "Electra Woman and Dyna Girl fighting all the evil thieves..."

Q342. *The Road Runner Show* (1971): "If you're on a highway and a Road Runner goes beep beep..."

Q343. *Happy Days* (1974): "Sunday, Monday, Happy Days. Tuesday, Wednesday, Happy Days..."

Q344. *The Adventures of Superman* (1953): "Faster than a speeding bullet. More powerful than a locomotive. Able to leap tall buildings in a single bound..."

Q345. *The King Kong Show* (1966): "King Kong, you know the name of King Kong..."

Q346. *Ruff and Ready* (1957): "Get set, get ready, here come Ruff and Ready..."

Q347. *Mister Ed* (1961): "A horse is a horse of course, of course, and no one can talk to a horse, of course..."

Q348. *H. R. Pufnstuf* (1969): "H. R. Pufnstuf, who's your friend when things get rough..."

Q349. *The Ice Palace* (1971): "Skating is beginning, things are swinging at the Ice Palace..."

Q350. *I Married Joan* (1952): "I Married Joan, what a girl, what a whirl, what a life..."

A338. "Let's give a rousing cheer, 'cause Howdy Doody's here; it's time to start the show, so kids let's go."

A339. "Dagwood, so brave, so noble; Dagwood, my all together life."

A340. "Go, go, Astro Boy."

A341. "Each writes for a magazine, hiding the life she leads."

A342. "Just step aside or you might end up in a heap."

A343. "Thursday, Friday, Happy Days; Saturday, what a day, groovin' all week with you."

A344. "Look up in the sky. It's a bird! It's a plane! It's Superman!"

A345. "You know the name of King Kong, ten times as big as a man."

A346. "They're tough but steady, always Ruff and Ready."

A347. "That is, of course, unless the horse is the famous Mister Ed."

A348. "H. R. Pufnstuf, can't do a little 'cause he can't do enough."

A349. "Love and laughter is what we're after at the Ice Palace."

A350. "Oh, I married Joan, what a mind, love is blind, what a wife."

Q351. *Where the Action Is* (1965): "Oh baby come on let me take you where the action is..."

Q352. *The Huckleberry Hound Show* (1958): "The biggest show in town is Huckleberry Hound for all you guys and gals..."

Q353. *The Addams Family* (1964): "They're creepy and they're kooky, mysterious and spooky, they're altogether ookey, the Addams Family..."

Q354. *The Mighty Mouse Playhouse* (1955): "Mr. Trouble never hangs around when he hears this mighty sound..."

Q355. *Zorro* (1957): "Out of the night when the full moon is bright comes the horseman known as Zorro..."

Q356. *Lidsville* (1971): "Lidsville is the kook-kook-kookiest..."

Q357. *Spider-Man* (1969): "Spider-Man, Spider-Man, does whatever a spider can..."

Q358. *Beany and Cecil* (1961): "...so come on kids, let's flip our lids higher than the moon..."

Q359. *The Flintstones* (1960): "Flintstones, meet the Flintstones, they're a modern stone-age family..."

Q360. *WKRP in Cincinnati* (1978): "Baby, if you've ever wondered, wondered whatever became of me..."

Q361. *Hullabaloo* (1965): "Feel that beat comin' strong, feel like you wanna come along..."

Q362. *Hong Kong Phooey* (1974): "Hong Kong Phooey, number one super guy..."

A351. "It's so nice to meet you baby where the action is."

A352. "The biggest clown in town is Huckleberry Hound with all his cartoon pals."

A353. "Their house is a museum, when people come to see 'em, they really are a screa-um, the Addams Family."

A354. "Here I come to save the day. That means that Mighty Mouse is on his way."

A355. "This bold renegade scars a Z with his blade, a Z that stands for Zorro."

A356. "Lidsville is the groove, groove, grooviest; Lidsville is the living end, friend."

A357. "Spins a web any size; catches thieves just like flies; look out—here comes the Spider-Man."

A358. "'Cause now it's Beany and Cecil in a whole half-hour of Bob Clampett Cartoo-OOO-ooons."

A359. "From the town of Bedrock, they're a page right out of history."

A360. "I'm living on the air in Cincinnati, Cincinnati, WKRP."

A361. "Then jump for joy, we're tellin' you it's Hullaballoo."

A362. "Hong Kong Phooey, quicker than the human eye."

Q363. *The Adventures of Robin Hood* (1955): "Robin Hood, Robin Hood riding through the glen; Robin Hood, Robin Hood with his band of men..."

Q364. *Green Acres* (1965): "Green Acres is the place to be, farm living is the life for me..."

Q365. *Johnny Ringo* (1959): "Ringo, Johnny Ringo, his fears were never shown..."

Q366. *The Jetsons* (1962): "Meet George Jetson, his boy Elroy..."

Q367. *Bat Masterson* (1958): "Back when the West was very young, there lived a man named Masterson..."

Q368. *The Jeffersons* (1975): "We're movin' on up to the East Side..."

Q369. *Have Gun—Will Travel* (1957): "Have Gun—Will Travel reads the card of a man, a knight without armor in a savage land..."

Q370. *The Pruitts of Southampton* (1966): "The Pruitts of Southampton live like the richest folk..."

Q371. *Felix the Cat* (1960): "Felix the cat, the wonderful, wonderful cat..."

Q372. *Love Thy Neighbor* (1973): "Love thy neighbor, follow the golden rule..."

Q373. *Gilligan's Island* (1964): "Just sit right back and you'll hear a tale, a tale of a fateful trip..."

Q374. *The Roy Rogers Show* (1951): "Happy trails to you until we meet again..."

Q375. *The Beverly Hillbillies* (1962): "Come and listen to my story about a man named Jed, a poor mountaineer barely kept his family fed..."

A363. "Feared by the bad, loved by the good, Robin Hood, Robin Hood."

A364. "Land spreading out so far and wide, keep Manhattan, just gimme that countryside."

A365. "Fastest gun in all the West, the quickest ever known."

A366. "Daughter Judy; Jane, his wife."

A367. "He wore a cane and derby hat, they called him Bat, Bat Masterson."

A368. "To a deluxe apartment in the sky."

A369. "His fast gun for hire heeds the calling wind, a soldier of fortune is the man called, Paladin."

A370. "But what the folk don't know is that the Pruitts are flat broke."

A371. "Whenever he gets in a fix, he reaches into his bag of tricks."

A372. "Love thy neighbor, you'll find that it's really cool."

A373. "That started from this tropic port aboard this tiny ship."

A374. "Happy trails to you, keep smilin' until then."

A375. "And then one day he was shooting at some food and up through the ground came a bubbling crude."

Q376. *Chico and the Man* (1974): "Chico, don't be discouraged at the man, he ain't so hard to understand..."

Q377. *Get Christie Love* (1974): "What a face, just dig her walking, Christie Love..."

Q378. *Shotgun Slade* (1959): "Shotgun Slade of the two-barreled gun, you're afraid that someday you'll be won by a woman..."

Q379. *Scooby-Doo, Where Are You?* (1969): "Scooby dooby doo, where are you? We got some work to do now..."

Q380. *The Love Boat* (1977): "...The Love Boat soon will be making another run..."

Q381. *Andy's Gang* (1955): "I got a gang, you got a gang, everybody's gotta have a gang..."

Q382. *Married... With Children* (1987): "Love and marriage, love and marriage go together like a horse and carriage..."

Q383. *Three's Company* (1977): "Come and knock on our door, we've been waitin' for you..."

Q384. *The Rebel* (1959): "Johnny Yuma was a rebel, he roamed through the West..."

Q385. *Friends* (1994): "...It's like you're always stuck in second gear and when it hasn't been your day, your week, your month or even your year..."

A376. "Chico, if you try now, I know you can lend a helping hand."

A377. "If it's trouble, she's your girl. Get Christie Love, Get Christie Love."

A378. "A dreamin' woman, a schemin' woman, maybe someone like me. Better run, Shotgun Slade. I'm the one, Shotgun Slade."

A379. "Scooby dooby doo, where are you, we need some help from you now."

A380. "The Love Boat promises something for everyone."

A381. "But there's only one gang for me—good old Andy's Gang."

A382. "This I tell you brother, you can't have one without the other."

A383. "Where the kisses are hers and hers and his, Three's Company, too."

A384. "Johnny Yuma, the Rebel, he wandered alone."

A385. "I'll be there for you, I'll be there for you."

8

Male Vocalists

Q386. Match the male vocalist (left column) with the series (right column) on which he performed its theme song.

1. Waylon Jennings	a. *Jennifer Slept Here*
2. Leon Redbone	b. *The Rebel*
3. Johnny Western	c. *Freebie and the Bean*
4. Joey Scarbury	d. *Hi Honey, I'm Home*
5. Jack Jones	e. *The Six O'Clock Follies*
6. José Feliciano	f. *Teech*
7. Harry Nilsson	g. *Mr. Belvedere*
8. Johnny Cash	h. *Going Places*
9. Ronnie Milsap	i. *Welcome Back, Kotter*
10. Rupert Holmes	j. *Nanny and the Professor*
11. Bobby Hart	k. *Snoops*
12. Joe Cocker	l. *Chico and the Man*

13. Frankie Laine
14. B. B. King
15. Louis Armstrong
16. Mark Lennon
17. Eddie Money
18. Al Jarreau
19. Ray Charles
20. John B. Sebastian

m. *Moonlighting*
n. *The Rousters*
o. *Hardball*
p. *Designing Women*
q. *Have Gun—Will Travel*
r. *Rawhide*
s. *The Love Boat*
t. *The Dukes of Hazzard*

A386.
1 and t
2 and g
3 and q
4 and a
5 and s
6 and l
7 and j
8 and b
9 and n
10 and d
11 and c
12 and e
13 and r
14 and f
15 and p
16 and h
17 and o
18 and m
19 and k
20 and i

9

Female Vocalists

Q387. Match the following female vocalist (left column) with series (right column) on which she performed its theme song.

1. Linda Ronstadt	a. *Bare Essence*
2. Carly Simon	b. *Sunday Dinner*
3. Amy Grant	c. *Fay*
4. Kim Carnes	d. *The Hogan Family*
5. Phoebe Snow	e. *The Trials of Rosie O'Neill*
6. Nell Carter	f. *Working Girl*
7. Sarah Vaughan	g. *Tabitha*
8. Reba McEntire	h. *Pete Kelly's Blues*
9. Jaye P. Morgan	i. *Dorothy*
10. Jeannie C. Riley	j. *You Take the Kids*
11. Roberta Flack	k. *New Attitude*

12. Dionne Warwick
13. Connee Boswell
14. Melissa Manchester
15. Charlotte Rae
16. Lisa Hartman
17. Dorothy Loudon
18. Sheryl Lee Ralph
19. Aretha Franklin
20. Queen Latifah

l. *The Facts of Life*
m. *Grace Under Fire*
n. *9 to 5*
o. *Living Single*
p. *Delta*
q. *The Love Boat* (last season)
r. *Harper Valley*
s. *Headmaster*
t. *Sister Kate*

A387. 1 and s
2 and f
3 and t
4 and b
5 and n
6 and j
7 and a
8 and p
9 and c
10 and r
11 and d
12 and q
13 and h
14 and e
15 and l
16 and g
17 and i
18 and k
19 and m
20 and o

10

Groups

Q388. Match the musical group or duo (left column) with the series (right column) on which they performed its theme song.

1. The Beach Boys	a. *China Beach*
2. The Ken Darby Singers	b. *Down the Shore*
3. The Supremes	c. *The Brady Bunch* (first season)
4. R.E.M.	d. *Here We Go Again*
5. The Waitresses	e. *Three's Company*
6. Barbi Benton, Didi Carr, and Marianne Black	f. *Baywatch* (closing theme)
7. The Rembrandts	g. *The Torkelsons*
8. Southside Johnny and the Asbury Jukes	h. *Square Pegs*
9. Oingo Boingo	i. *Karen*

10. The Peppermint Trolley Company	j. *I Married Joan*
11. Holly Robinson and Dawnn Lewis	k. *Family Ties*
12. Carol Sager and Peter Allen	l. *Fast Times*
13. The Roger Wagner Chorale	m. *Texaco Star Theater*
14. Julia Rinker and "the other" Ray Charles	n. *P. S. I. Luv U*
15. David Hasselhoff and Laura Branigan	o. *The Adventures of Jim Bowie*
16. Johnny Mathis and Deneice Williams	p. *It Takes Two*
17. Crystal Gayle and Paul Williams	q. *Sugar Time*
18. Greg Evigan and Suzanne Fountain	r. *Hangin' With Mr. Cooper*
19. Naomi and Wynonna Judd	s. *Friends*
20. The Merry Texaco Star Men	t. *Get a Life*

A388. 1 and i
2 and o
3 and a
4 and t
5 and h
6 and q
7 and s
8 and b
9 and l
10 and c
11 and r
12 and d
13 and j
14 and e
15 and f
16 and k
17 and p
18 and n
19 and g
20 and m

11

Put on the Thinking Cap

The following themes are designed to test your memory of shows that you have probably seen, but whose signature songs have been locked away in the deep, unexplored areas of your mind.

Q389. "They crash him and his body may burn; they smash him, but they know he'll return to live again, [name of show]."

Q390. "Hello, Mac, you've got a heart of gold so be good to yourself tonight...you're on a winning streak, you're favored to win and you might...hang on, Mac."

Q391. "If you've got a case that needs super detection...we never lose...we're four in a war in the war against crime."

Q392. "Looking for an old car, found a funny schlep car, let's make him ours. Found a magic horn, a new car was born."

A389. *Captain Scarlet and the Mysterons* (1967)

A390. *The McLean Stevenson Show* (1976)

A391. *The Kids From C.A.P.E.R.* (1976)

A392. *Wonderbug* (1976)

Q393. "Where is the world that they use to know? How will they ever return? Now they have a home where the strangest creatures roam."

Q394. "Do you believe you believe in magic; 'cause I believe...that I do; yes I can see I believe that it's magic when your mission is magic and love will shine through."

Q395. "Kind of dusty, the earth beneath my feet. Kind of dusty as I ride through the burning heat...I have a dream when the sun goes down...'cause I'm Oregon bound."

Q396. "Pieces of an old life; reflections of a past. Mom and Dad are gone, Nick and Muggsy left alone, time for movin' on."

Q397. "Rest the dial for a while; have a laugh and a smile...you'll begin with a grin when you first tune us in on [name of show]."

Q398. "Say hey today, my friend's here to stay, and what could be sweeter than [name of show]."

Q399. "There is nothing else in my heart more beautiful to me; what more could I want from my love, you are all I need."

Q400. "Look around and see, what still is here; the world is a place for love and laughs; we're [name of show]."

Q401. "We never know what fate has planned, so what's wrong with giving love a helping hand? Electronically, let's see if we can see [name of show]."

Q402. "Meet the sulky, overbulky, kind of hulky super heroes, not too distant and electronically transistored super heroes."

A393. *Far-Out Space Nuts* (1975)

A394. *Mission Magic* (1973)

A395. *The Oregon Trail* (1977)

A396. *Muggsy* (1976)

A397. *The Tom and Jerry Cartoon Show* (1966)

A398. *Salty* (1974)

A399. *We've Got Each Other* (1977)

A400. *On Our Own* (1977)

A401. *The Perfect Match* (1967)

A402. *The Marvel Super Heroes* (1965)

Q403. "There are lots of funny animals in all this world, but have you ever seen a panther that is pink? Think! A panther that's positively pink!"

Q404. "[name of show] is like no place you've ever known; let me tell you [name of show] has a character all its own...[name of show] is a Doodletown town dream come true."

Q405. "I must explore what's on my mind...No time to be alone, comin' into my own."

Q406. "Look at you now, you're on your way, things are getting better every single day..."

Q407. "In a magic place there's a princess caught in a chase and no matter how fast she goes, right on her heels it goes [name of show]."

Q408. "Jambo, Jambo means hello in a happy kind of African way. Jambo, Jambo means let's go in a happy kind of an African way."

Q409. "Now if you have the feelin' there is something you missed, you dig that dancin' then you can't resist, 'cause we dance them all from the rock to the twist on the Lloyd Thaxton hop."

Q410. "Hey baby doll, mama's got a job today, and it's the best job anywhere; hey baby doll, mama's got a job today..."

Q411. "Big John has a problem as you can plainly see. One minute he's forty, the next he's thirty-three. Big John keeps a changin' before your very eyes."

Q412. "The state gives us jobs and look at our luck—Papa is a head waiter and Mama drives a truck."

A403. *The Pink Panther Show* (1969)

A404. *Our Place* (1967)

A405. *Fay* (1975)

A406. *One in a Million* (1980)

A407. *Here Comes the Grump* (1969)

A408. *Jambo* (1969)

A409. *The Lloyd Thaxton Show* (1964)

A410. *The Shari Lewis Show* (1975)

A411. *Big John, Little John* (1976)

A412. *Ivan the Terrible* (1976)

Q413. "[name of show] he's a mad man with an evil mind...he's as crazy as you'll ever find."

Q414. "Half dog, half ghost, he's the most; he's my friend; he speaks the words of the birds and the bees..."

Q415. "Come along now and join the party, come along now and have some fun; the show will start in just a moment; you're gonna laugh until it's done."

Q416. "There's a boy in me who comes alive each summer. Won't you come play ball with me? Let's have fun and not keep score...that's what I'm playing ball for."

Q417. "When tomorrow comes, what will it bring? Will it be winter or will it be spring? Will a prayer be answered? Will the sun rise for you?"

Q418. "From time to time we all get our problems, that's part of life you can't ignore. Sometimes you need somebody to solve them, that's what I'm here for."

Q419. "The night was his companion, the dream his guiding light, and freedom kept it burning between the wrong and the right...destiny is calling a man named [name of show]."

Q420. "[name of show] starting out alone; what kind of world will they create...for each of them, time has just begun."

Q421. "...but never mind you three, there's the wizard as you can see; he'll fix that one, two, three in the funny place called [name of show]."

Q422. "Come gather around me, space travelers surround me, hark now to the ballad of [name of show]. I may well confound you, astound you, spellbound you with heroes and villains the bad and the good."

A413. *Dr. Shrinker* (1976)

A414. *McDuff, the Talking Dog* (1976)

A415. *The New Casper Cartoon Show* (1963)

A416. *Ball Four* (1976)

A417. *Search for Tomorrow* (1975 theme)

A418. *Mulligan's Stew* (1977)

A419. *Young Dan'l Boone* (1979)

A420. *The New People* (1969)

A421. *The World of Oz* (1962)

A422. *Rocket Robin Hood* (1967)

Q423. "Stronger than a whale he can swim anywhere; he can breathe underwater and go flying through the air...so be wary every demon, for the savior of Atlantis is the Prince of the Deep."

Q424. "Tony Stark makes you feel he's the cool exec with the heart of steel and [name of show] all gets the praise; he fights and fights with repulsive rays..."

Q425. "When [name of show] throws his mighty shield; all those who chose to oppose his shield must yield...and the red, the white, and the blue will come true when [name of show] throws his mighty shield."

Q426. " 'Cross the rainbow bridge of Asgard, where the blooming heavens roar, you'll behold in breathless wonder, the God of Thunder, [name of show]."

Q427. "People say God looks out for the working man, sure hope he's looking out for me; these empty pockets need a helping hand..."

Q428. "Wake up in the morning, feeling shy and lonely, gee I gotta go to school. I don't think I can make it, don't think I can take it, I'm wondering what I'm gonna do."

Q429. "Learning to master the fears, learning to fight through these tears...learning that first Golden Rule, knowing that anything is possible, 'cause nothing's gonna keep us from [name of show]."

Q430. "When we go from [name of show] all your wishes permanently come true and it's a new beginning of chances of winning; this time we can't lose [name of show]."

Q431. "Nary a cop, nary a road, nary a soul in sight to help us lighten our load; but there's that voice loud and clear sayin' 'Welcome Pioneer,' [name of show]."

A423. *Sub Mariner* (1965)

A424. *Iron Man* (1965)

A425. *Captain America* (1965)

A426. *Mighty Thor* (1965)

A427. *The Torkelsons* (1991)

A428. *Degrassi Junior High* (1987)

A429. *Learning the Ropes* (1988)

A430. *Rags to Riches* (1987)

A431. *Guestward Ho* (1960)

Q432. "I use to buy a pickle, it only use to cost a nickel, and a bus ride only use to cost a dime. These days can be forgotten, the world has gotten rotten...so in order to survive, what you really need today is [name of show]."

Q433. "She's a new livin' girl...just a new livin' girl with a special way of knowing everything is gonna be all right."

Q434. "You are so beautiful to me. Can't you see, you're everything that I hoped for, you're everything I need. You are so beautiful to me."

Q435. "We're off to outer space, we're leaving Mother Earth to save the human race, our [name of show]."

Q436. "The seasons change the colors of the leaves like time can color your memories. But with every change, I still feel the same, I keep coming back to you..."

Q437. "The people in the street or the pouring of the rain; is it a feeling in your heart or is it something you can't name? Oh, James."

Q438. "There's a lot to discover...got your bridges to build, your dreams to fulfill. It's all out there waiting for you to find."

Q439. "When the sun sets on the inner city, there's a million stories you never know. When the streets sing, it's great folk music and you play along or it's down you go."

Q440. "Hey, won't somebody listen, let me say what's been on my mind. Can I bring it out to you; I need someone to talk to and no one else will spare me the time."

A432. *Lotsa Luck* (1973)

A433. *Stockard Channing in Just Friends* (1980)

A434. *Struck by Lightning* (1979)

A435. *Star Blazers* (1976)

A436. *Married: The First Year* (1976)

A437. *James at 15* (1977)

A438. *James at 16* (1978)

A439. *Flatbush* (1979)

A440. *Matt Lincoln* (1970)

Q441. "Hello golden school days, so long old Broadway, I've got some girls I'm teachin' a brand new act today..."

Q442. "Sierra majesty beneath the sky; Sierra wilderness where eagles fly; she is my life to me, she is my home."

Q443. "Get on board, come and join the double-deckers; take a ticket for a journey on a double-decker London bus."

Q444. "I can run through fire and come out grinning; toss a few dice and wind up winning, but I feel kind of funny taking orders from women."

Q445. "Take a trip with us today, don't get left behind; take a trip with us today, we will lead you to a land of dreams."

Q446. "When he walks down the street he smiles at everyone; everyone that he meets calls him [name of show]."

Q447. "No one can compare to the prince who wears a medallion on his chest. Using all his might, changing wrong to right. [name of show] he's the best."

Q448. "Sometimes it's honey and sometimes it's brine, learning to be a family isn't easy."

Q449. "We have this dream, America, a vision bright and clear...we have planted ourselves here. In the rain, in the sunshine, we will make this land our home."

Q450. "In the Everglades there's a way of life; it's a way of peace without stress or strife; there's a fellow there who protects these rights. Lincoln Vail of [name of show], the man on patrol in [name of show]."

A441. *Dorothy* (1979)

A442. *Sierra* (1974)

A443. *Here Come the Double-deckers* (1970)

A444. *Szysnyk* (1977)

A445. *The Krofft Supershow* (1976)

A446. *King of Kensington* (1977)

A447. *Prince Planet* (1966)

A448. *We'll Get By* (1975)

A449. *The New Land* (1974)

A450. *The Everglades* (1961)

Q451. "Your money is nice, but easily spent. Pretty soon we're just shaking our heads wondering where it all went."

Q452. "Looking to the left, looking to the right, looking all day, looking all night, looking for the one who's gonna be right."

Q453. "Baby you know it, you can count on me; baby you know it, you showed me how good love can be."

Q454. "People make the world go round; beautiful people, famous faces, fancy places; uptown, downtown; how the sun comes pouring down on beautiful people."

Q455. "All you're gonna find are hard times for hard crimes; who's life will be taken or are you gonna let me take a piece of you."

Q456. "Stop, look, and listen to us, 'cause we're happiness bound. Take a trip to the stars without fuss on our merry, merry-go-round."

Q457. "During the eighteen-seventies, the wildest spot in the United States was the desolate region west of the Pecos River...It was said that civilization stopped at the east bank of the Pecos. It took one man...who was sick of the lawlessness to change all this. His name was [name of show]."

Q458. "...I've been both mother and father to her since she was born. She's grown up now...When she was little I could spank her and make her mind me...When she disobeyed, I took her roller skates away for a week. What can you do when a girl reaches this age [twenty-one]. She's completely out of hand. I've got a problem, believe me, I've got a problem."

A451. *Working Stiffs* (1979)

A452. *Joe and Valerie* (1977 theme)

A453. *Joe and Valerie* (1978 theme)

A454. *People* (1978)

A455. *David Cassidy—Man Undercover* (1978)

A456. *The Jean Arthur Show* (1966)

A457. *Judge Roy Bean* (narration opening, 1955)

A458. *My Little Margie* (narration opening, 1952)

12

Themes Like Old Times, the Forties and Fifties

Q459. Match the song or melody (left column) with the series (right column) on which it was used as a theme.

1. "Manhattan Serenade"
2. "Donna Diana Overture" by Von Reznicek
3. "Emblem"
4. "The Ballad of Paladin"
5. "Happy Trails to You"
6. "Blue Star"
7. "Bubbles in the Wine"
8. "You're My Greatest Love"

a. *Medic*
b. *The Honeymooners*
c. *Life With Luigi*
d. *The Roy Rogers Show*
e. *The Californians*
f. *Have Gun—Will Travel*
g. *Shirley Temple's Storybook*
h. *Leave It to Beaver*

9. "Home Sweet Home"
10. "The Land of the Pecos"
11. "Oh Marie"
12. "Friendship"
13. "I've Come to California"
14. "The Toy Parade"
15. "Dreams Are Made for Children"
16. "My Calico Gal"
17. "Twenty Mule Team"
18. "San Francisco Blues"
19. "Parade of the Chessmen"
20. "Riff Blues"

i. *Buckskin*
j. *The Line-Up*
k. *Easy Aces*
l. *Death Valley Days*
m. *The Lawrence Welk Show*
n. *Racket Squad*
o. *My Friend Irma*
p. *The G. E. Theater*
q. *Judge Roy Bean*
r. *Jackson and Jill*
s. *Mike Hammer*
t. *Sergeant Preston of the Yukon*

A459. 1 and k
2 and t
3 and p
4 and f
5 and d
6 and a
7 and m
8 and b
9 and r
10 and q
11 and c
12 and o
13 and e
14 and h
15 and g
16 and i
17 and l
18 and j
19 and n
20 and s

13

Themes Like Old Times, the Sixties

Q460. Match the song or melody (left column) with the series (right column) on which it was used as a theme.

1. "High Wire"	a. *Dr. Kildare*
2. "For Those Who Are Young"	b. *The Law and Mr. Jones*
3. "Put on a Happy Face"	c. *Hong Kong*
4. "That's Life"	d. *The Jean Arthur Show*
5. "When the Saints Go Marching In"	e. *The Bill Dana Show*
6. "Nervous"	f. *Peyton Place*
7. "Three Stars Will Shine Tonight"	g. *Johnny Midnight*
8. "The Enchanted Melody"	h. *The Green Hornet*

9. "Evan's Theme"
10. "Wild Honey"
11. "Assembly Stomp"
12. "José Olé"
13. "The Ballad of Jed Clampett"
14. "Flight of the Bumble Bee"
15. "Merry-Go-Round"
16. "Lullaby of Broadway"
17. "Robin's Theme"
18. "Best Friend"
19. "With a Little Love"
20. "The Fishin' Hole"

i. *The Bing Crosby Show*
j. *The Debbie Reynolds Show*
k. *The Courtship of Eddie's Father*
l. *Danger Man*
m. *The Andy Griffith Show*
n. *Mr. Novak*
o. *The Dick Powell Show*
p. *Honey West*
q. *The Case of the Dangerous Robin*
r. *The Hollywood Palace*
s. *The Beverly Hillbillies*
t. *The Shirley Temple Show*

A460. 1 and l
2 and f
3 and r
4 and i
5 and b
6 and o
7 and a
8 and t
9 and c
10 and p
11 and n
12 and e
13 and s
14 and h
15 and d
16 and g
17 and q
18 and k
19 and j
20 and m

14

Themes Like Old Times, the Seventies

Q461. Match the song or melody (left column) with the series (right column) on which it was used as a theme.

1. "Love Is All Around"	a. *All in the Family*
2. "When We're Singing"	b. *The Bob Newhart Show*
3. "Girls, Girls, Girls"	c. *The Jeffersons*
4. "Keep Your Eye on the Sparrow"	d. *M*A*S*H*
5. "There's a New Girl in Town"	e. *The Sandy Duncan Show*
6. "Those Were the Days"	f. *Angie*
7. "Different Worlds"	g. *Tabitha*
8. "Happy Days Are Here Again"	h. *The Mary Tyler Moore Show*
9. "Home for Emily"	i. *The Dukes of Hazzard*

10.	"I Want It All"	j.	*Laverne and Shirley*
11.	"Movin' on Up"	k.	*Sugar Time*
12.	"Making Our Dreams Come True"	l.	*Headmaster*
13.	"Suicide Is Painless"	m.	*Fay*
14.	"We've Gotta Stick Together"	n.	*Adam's Rib*
15.	"Good Old Boys"	o.	*The Partridge Family*
16.	"Coming Into My Own"	p.	*Mulligan's Stew*
17.	"The Kind of Girl She Is"	q.	*Alice*
18.	"Two People"	r.	*Blansky's Beauties*
19.	"Could It Be Magic"	s.	*Apple Pie*
20.	"He's a Man"	t.	*Baretta*

A461. 1 and h
2 and o
3 and k
4 and t
5 and q
6 and a
7 and f
8 and s
9 and b
10 and r
11 and c
12 and j
13 and d
14 and p
15 and i
16 and m
17 and e
18 and n
19 and g
20 and l

15

Themes Like Old Times, the Eighties (Part I)

Q462. Match the song or melody (left column) with the series (right column) on which it was used as a theme.

1. "You Can Count on Me"	a. *My Sister Sam*
2. "Room Enough for Two"	b. *What a Country*
3. "Nothing's Gonna Stop Me Now"	c. *Punky Brewster*
4. "Brand New Life"	d. *My Two Dads*
5. "There's No Place Like Home"	e. *Bare Essence*
6. "Then Came You"	f. *Freebie and the Bean*
7. "I Want to Be an American"	g. *Roomies*
8. "One in a Million"	h. *Growing Pains*

9. "Swingin' on a Star"
10. "Everytime You Turn Around"
11. "Looking for Some Answers"
12. "Tough Enough"
13. "You and Me, Babe"
14. "Shine on Me"
15. "In Finding You I Found Love"
16. "Believe It or Not"
17. "My Life"
18. "We've Got Each Other"
19. "Ain't That the Way"
20. "Together Through the Years"

i. *The Greatest American Hero*
j. *Cagney and Lacey*
k. *Perfect Strangers*
l. *The Hogan Family*
m. *Webster*
n. *The New Gidget*
o. *Bosom Buddies*
p. *The Rousters*
q. *Who's the Boss*
r. *227*
s. *Amen*
t. *Out of This World*

A462. 1 and d
2 and a
3 and k
4 and q
5 and r
6 and m
7 and b
8 and n
9 and t
10 and c
11 and g
12 and p
13 and f
14 and s
15 and e
16 and i
17 and o
18 and h
19 and j
20 and l

16

Themes Like Old Times, the Eighties (Part 2)

Q463. Match the song or melody (left column) with the series (right column) on which it was used as a theme.

1. "Doin' It the Best I Can"	a. *Melba*
2. "Along Comes a Friend"	b. *Star of the Family*
3. "Ob-La-Di, Ob-La-Da"	c. *Doctor, Doctor*
4. "Friends Forever"	d. *Family Ties*
5. "Is It Because of Love"	e. *Just the Ten of Us*
6. "We're Sisters"	f. *Snoops*
7. "Where Everybody Knows Your Name"	g. *The Golden Girls*
8. "Good Lovin'"	h. *Me and Maxx*

9. "Sure Beats Working for a Living"
10. "As Days Go By"
11. "Without Us"
12. "Everywhere You Look"
13. "Thank You for Being a Friend"
14. "When Everyone Cared"
15. "Where Love Spends the Night"
16. "The Edge of the Sky"
17. "Happy Together"
18. "Goodbye Blues"
19. "Curiosity"
20. "Movin' Along"

i. *It Takes Two*
j. *Family Matters*
k. *Live-In*
l. *Kate and Allie*
m. *Hawaiian Heat*
n. *Jesse Hawkes*
o. *Life Goes On*
p. *The Goodtime Girls*
q. *Cheers*
r. *The Duck Factory*
s. *Full House*
t. *Love, Sidney*

A463. 1 and e
2 and l
3 and o
4 and t
5 and h
6 and a
7 and q
8 and c
9 and r
10 and j
11 and d
12 and s
13 and g
14 and p
15 and i
16 and n
17 and k
18 and m
19 and f
20 and b

17

Themes Like Old Times, the Nineties (Part I)

Q464. Match the song or melody (left column) with the series (right column) on which it was used as a theme.

1. "Thank God for a Friend Like You"
2. "Rescue Me"
3. "Some Day My Prince Will Come"
4. "Workin' for a Living"
5. "We Are a Family"
6. "All the Time in the World"
7. "The Second Time Around"

a. *The Royal Family*
b. *Step by Step*
c. *Top of the Heap*
d. *The Trials of Rosie O'Neill*
e. *Sweating Bullets*
f. *You Take the Kids*
g. *Baby Talk*

8. "Any Way the Wind Blows"	h. *Hope and Gloria*
9. "Finish What Ya Started"	i. *Cybill*
10. "Puttin' on the Ritz"	j. *Princesses*
11. "Everything Will Be All Right"	k. *Working Girl*
12. "I Wish I Knew"	l. *Walker, Texas Ranger*
13. "It's Never Too Late for Love"	m. *The Torkelsons*
14. "Let the River Run"	n. *Harry and the Hendersons*
15. "Nobody's Got It Easy"	o. *Touched by an Angel*
16. "Nice Work If You Can Get It"	p. *Rachel Gunn, R.N.*
17. "I Will Walk With You"	q. *Scorch*
18. "Bread and Butter"	r. *Sydney*
19. "Your Feet's Too Big"	s. *Pacific Station*
20. "The Eyes of a Ranger"	t. *Walter and Emily*

A464. 1 and h
2 and s
3 and j
4 and p
5 and a
6 and q
7 and b
8 and e
9 and r
10 and c
11 and m
12 and d
13 and t
14 and k
15 and f
16 and i
17 and o
18 and g
19 and n
20 and l

18

Themes Like Old Times, the Nineties (Part 2)

Q465. Match the song or melody (left column) with the series (right column) on which it was used as a theme.

1. "Climb That Mountain High"	a. *Hangin' With Mr. Cooper*
2. "A Million Miles Away"	b. *Twin Peaks*
3. "Love Begins at Home"	c. *Get a Life*
4. "Blood Is Thicker"	d. *Max Monroe, Loose Cannon*
5. "I Don't Wanna Go Home"	e. *Man of the People*
6. "Why Should I Worry?"	f. *Man in the Family*
7. "Pipeline"	g. *Mad About You*
8. "Celebrate Life"	h. *Baywatch*

9. "Love Crazy"
10. "Way Cool"
11. "Wild Thing"
12. "Calling You"
13. "I'm Always Here"
14. "Final Frontier"
15. "When You're Smiling"
16. "I'm the Man"
17. "Tied Up"
18. "Stand"
19. "Falling"
20. "Soul Man"

i. *Bagdad Cafe*
j. *Charlie Hoover*
k. *Clarissa Explains It All*
l. *His and Hers*
m. *Good Grief*
n. *Camp Wilder*
o. *The Fanelli Boys*
p. *Down the Shore*
q. *Sibs*
r. *Sunday Dinner*
s. *Flying Blind*
t. *Delta*

A465. 1 and t
2 and s
3 and r
4 and q
5 and p
6 and o
7 and n
8 and m
9 and l
10 and k
11 and j
12 and i
13 and h
14 and g
15 and f
16 and e
17 and d
18 and c
19 and b
20 and a

19

Closing Themes

Many times a series has two different theme songs—one for the opening cast credits and one for the closing production credits. Identify the following end themes from these lyrics:

Q466. "A man who rides all alone and all that he'll ever own is just a badge and a gun and he's known as the [name of show]."

Q467. "Prohibition and bathtub gin, if Benny sent you, you'd walk right into a speakeasy, speakeasy; come along to the song of [name of show]."

Q468. "Soft guitars under the palms will gently lead you to a lover's arms; see the waves kissing the shore while you are kissing someone you adore."

Q469. "In our little house there's dad and mother, and of course there's sister and brother, and sometimes there is another sister or brother. In our little house there's always [name of show]."

A466. *Lawman* (1958)

A467. *The Roaring Twenties* (1960)

A468. *SurfSide 6* (1960)

A469. *Room for One More* (1962)

Q470. "Who is the tall dark stranger there [name of show] is the name, ridin' the trail to who knows where; luck is his companion, gamblin' is his game."

Q471. "I'm closing this case now, but they'll be others, because that's the way the world is built. Remember, there are people who can slap you on the back with one hand and pick your pocket with the other—and it could happen to you."

Q472. "The street that wears the fancy label, that's glorified in song and fable; the most exciting people pass you by, including a private eye."

Q473. "The soft island breeze brings you strange melodies and they tell of exotic mysteries under the tropical spell of the [name of show]."

Q474. "They've got the fever, got the fever, gold fever. Got the fever, got the fever, gold, gold, gold."

Q475. "Carefree as the tumbleweeds, a joggin' along with a heart full of song and a rifle and a volume of the law."

Q476. "Show me a gal who's kissed him once, I'll show you a gal who's kissed him twice; once any gal has kissed him twice, she's dreamin' of shoes and rice."

Q477. "In the avenues and alleyways, where the soul of a man is easy to buy, everybody's wheelin', everybody's stealin'...every city's got 'em, can't we ever stop 'em, some of us are gonna try."

Q478. "Now listen to my story, yes listen while I sing of days old in England when Arthur was the king. In days of old when knights were bold, his stories told of Lancelot."

A470. *Maverick* (1957)

A471. *Racket Squad* (1950)

A472. *77 Sunset Strip* (1958)

A473. *Hawaiian Eye* (1959)

A474. *The Alaskans* (1959)

A475. *Sugarfoot* (1957)

A476. *Bronco* (1958)

A477. *The Protectors* (1972)

A478. *The Adventures of Sir Lancelot* (1956)

Q479. "Sundance, Sundance, anywhere you wander, my heart's riding with you…just beyond the sunset love is waiting for you…"

Q480. "Hey baby, I hear the blues a-callin', tossed salad and scrambled eggs…"

Q481. "Good night, sleep tight, and pleasant dreams to you; here's a wish and a prayer that every dream comes true…"

Q482. "I wish I was a spaceman, the fastest guy alive, I'd fly you 'round the universe in [name of show]; way out in space together, conquerers of the stars…"

Q483. "In a moment of crises you have to believe in yourself; though you may be frightened, you know there is nobody else…"

Q484. "Well now it's time to say goodbye to Jed and all his kin; they would like to thank you folks for kindly droppin' in…"

Q485. "On the inside the stars still shine and the rain falls down; but the sun and rain are prisoners too when morning comes around."

Q486. "When I look all around, I can't believe the things I've found. Now I need to find my way. I'm lost, I'm lost, find me, livin' in the [name of show]."

Q487. "He's the greatest man we know; say he's not and you'll be walking the plank, sir. Let's go a roaming, a roaming across the ocean, oh, let's go a roaming with [name of show]."

Q488. "They will be here with all of us, dodging a taxi, a car, a bus; where will they go, what will they do in this strange place where everything is new."

A479. *Hotel De Paree* (1959)

A480. *Frasier* (1993)

A481. *The Lawrence Welk Show* (1955)

A482. *Fireball XL-5* (1963)

A483. *Baywatch* (1994 theme)

A484. *The Beverly Hillbillies* (1962)

A485. *Prisoner: Cell Block H* (1980)

A486. *Land of the Lost* (1974)

A487. *The Buccaneers* (1956)

A488. *It's About Time* (1967 theme)

Q489. "Her brand of charm is so disarming, frowns turn upside down. We owe a debt to Sweden, she's just what we've been needin', so glad [name of show] came to town."

Q490. "No phone, no lights, no motor cars; not a single luxury; like Robinson Crusoe, it's primitive as can be."

Q491. "Marina, I want Marina, what are these strange enchantments that start whenever you are near?"

Q492. "Dust over the prairie, dust everywhere. Dust covers your face and your hair; gold is what we carry, stop we don't dare, for Wells Fargo must get it there."

Q493. "Now with his horse and with his guns he's not afraid of anyone...he's the son of a son of a gun, [name of show]."

Q494. "Someday maybe Fred will win the fight, then that cat will stay out for the night..."

Q495. "...the mailman, the grocer, and even schoolkids know, it's worth their while to stop and watch that smile when [name of show], that [name of show] says hello."

Q496. "Dawn spreads its paint brush on the plain, spilling purple upon sleepers of the [name of show]."

Q497. "With faith and understanding our quarrels all will cease; we'll walk the land together and learn to live in peace. On this [name of show] let us find the pathway to friendship and love."

Q498. "There was a gun that won the West; there was a man among the rest; the fastest gun or man alive, a lightning bolt when he drew that [name of show]."

A489. *The Farmer's Daughter* (1963)

A490. *Gilligan's Island* (1964)

A491. *Stingray* (1965)

A492. *The Tales of Wells Fargo* (1957)

A493. *Buffalo Bill, Jr.* (1955)

A494. *The Flintstones* (1960)

A495. *Hazel* (1961)

A496. *Wagon Train* (1957)

A497. *Broken Arrow* (1956)

A498. *Colt .45* (1957)

Q499. “Yesterday’s sorrow and hope for tomorrow all meet to the beat of [name of show].”

Q500. “Move along [name of show] next pasture’s always so green; driftin’ on [name of show] don’t forget the things you have seen and when you settle down, where will it be [name of show].”

Q501. “Friendship, friendship, just the perfect blendship. When other friendships have been forgot, theirs will still be hot.”

A499. *Bourbon Street Beat* (1959)

A500. *Cheyenne* (1955)

A501. *My Friend Irma* (1952)

Arhionvar, the dread magic, was coming, and the city was in terrible danger. Arhionvar had been behind the device that the traitor-wizard Pettivox and the former Underlord, Crowe, had built to confine Wellmet's magic, and it had preyed on the desert city of Desh until that city's magic had nearly been destroyed. Now it was coming to Wellmet. We had to be ready when it got here, or our city, and its magic, would die, sure as sure.

Nevery had a plan, one based on his long-ago experiments with pyrotechnics, the ones that'd blown the middle out of his mansion house, Heartsease. He knew that setting off an explosion while doing a magical spell enhanced the effect of the spell. He'd been doing research in the academicos library, looking at old grimoires to find the right spell to enhance, something that would force Arhionvar to leave Wellmet alone. We thought a banishing spell might work, if we set explosive traps all around the city to make it stronger. My part of the plan was to help with the pyrotechnics and to scout the city for good places to set the traps.

"All right, boy?" Nevery asked sharply.

"All right, Nevery," I said.

"A delight to read, sure to draw avid fans back for more." —*The Bulletin of the Center for Children's Books* (starred review)

"I couldn't put it down. Wonderful, exciting stuff!"
—Diana Wynne Jones,
author of *Howl's Moving Castle*

"A fun read for fans of fantastic adventures."
—*School Library Journal*

"What works wonderfully well here is the boy's irresistible voice."
—ALA *Booklist* (starred review)

"Conn, equally gifted at picking locks and being a thorn in the side of all, remains a vivid, memorable lead." —*Kirkus Reviews*

FOUND

BOOK THREE

BY SARAH PRINEAS

ILLUSTRATIONS BY
ANTONIO JAVIER CAPARO

HARPER
An Imprint of HarperCollins*Publishers*

The Magic Thief: Found
 For information address HarperCollins Children's Books, a division of HarperCollins Publishers, 195 Broadway, New York, NY 10007.
www.harpercollinschildrens.com

Library of Congress Cataloging-in-Publication Data
Prineas, Sarah.
Found / by Sarah Prineas ; illustrations by Antonio Javier Caparo. — 1st ed.
p. cm. — (Magic Thief ; bk. 3)
Summary: Connwaer, the young thief-turned-wizard's apprentice, escapes from prison and follows the call of magic to the distant and mysterious Dragon Mountain on a quest to save Wellmet from Arhionvar, a dread magic that can destroy the city.
ISBN 978-0-06-137595-8
[1. Magic—Fiction. 2. Wizards—Fiction. 3. Apprentices—Fiction. 4. Fantasy.] I. Caparo, Antonio Javier, ill. II. Title.
PZ7.P93646Fou 2010 2009023977
[Fic]—dc22 CIP
AC

Typography by Sasha Illingworth
15 LP/BR 10 9 8 7 6 5 4
❖
First paperback edition, 2011

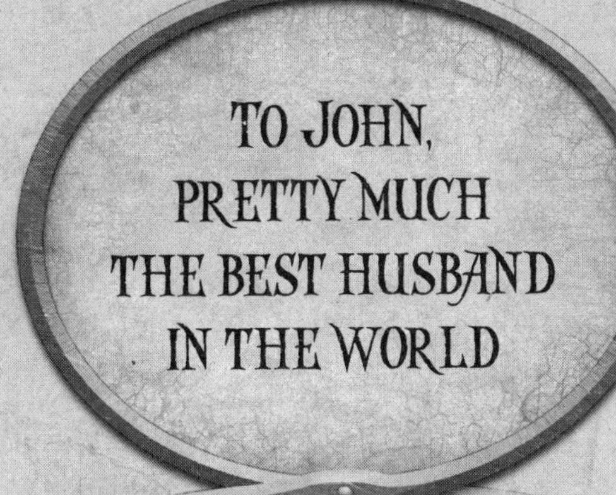
TO JOHN,
PRETTY MUCH
THE BEST HUSBAND
IN THE WORLD

WELLMET

THE RIVER
1. Heartsease
2. Academicos
3. Wizards' houses
4. Magisters Hall
5. Night Bridge
=== tunnels under river to islands

THE TWILIGHT
6. Sark Square
7. Dusk House ruins
8. Factories and warehouses
9. Half Chick Lane
10. Strangle Street
11. Sparks's house

N
W
E
S
12
THE SUNRISE
12. Dawn Palace

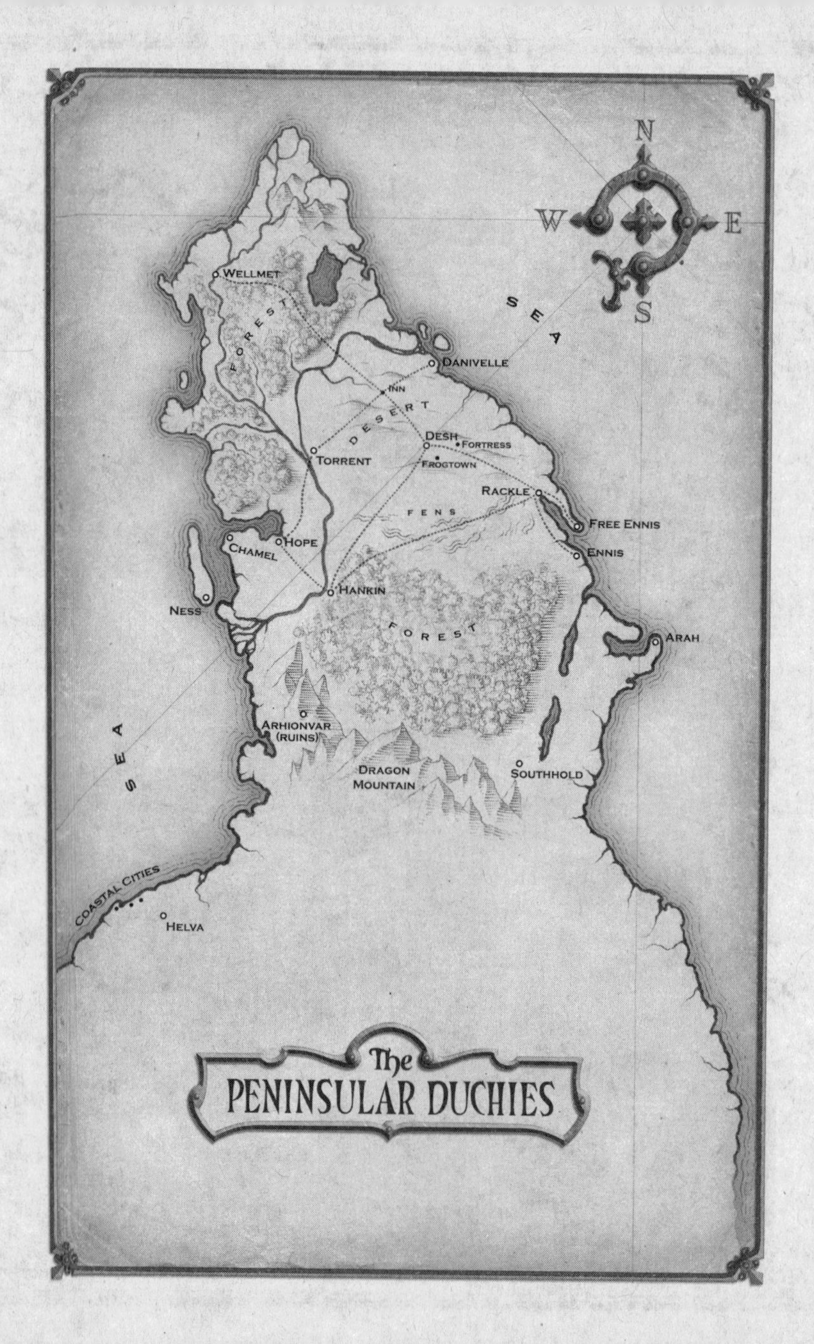

N
W
E
S
SEA
WELLMET
FOREST
DANIVELLE
INN
DESERT
DESH
FORTRESS
FROGTOWN
TORRENT
RACKLE
FENS
FREE ENNIS
ENNIS
HOPE
CHAMEL
HANKIN
NESS
FOREST
ARAH
ARHIONVAR
(RUINS)
DRAGON
MOUNTAIN
SOUTHHOLD
SEA
COASTAL CITIES
HELVA
The
PENINSULAR DUCHIES

A wizard is a lot like a thief. If a wizard has quick hands, he can make things disappear. He can even make himself disappear.

I lurked in my alley shadows, waiting for the wizard. Winter was just beginning, and the air had a sharp edge of cold. The night was thick with river fog and factory soot, and it was quiet, nobody about. A good night for minions and misery eels.

I shivered and hunched into my coat. What was taking him so long?

Then I heard it.

Step step tap.

Step step tap.

Nevery, wizard and city magister, was coming up the steep street toward me. He paused, peering into the shadows with his keen-gleam eyes. Fog smoked around him.

He couldn't see me. For melting into shadows I wore dark brown trousers and the black sweater Benet had knitted for me. My black, shaggy hair hung down in my eyes. Over it all I had on my black coat with the shabby velvet collar, the one Nevery'd given me when I'd been in the Dawn Palace jail cells, a place I'd spent too much time in lately. He'd hidden lockpick wires in the collar, and I'd used them to escape. That'd been almost ten days ago.

On Nevery went, *step step* and then *tap* with his cane past my dark alley.

As he passed, I darted feather-foot out of the shadows and—*quick hands*—lifted the purse string out of the pocket of his cloak, then stepped back into the alley. His locus magicalicus was in his pocket, too, but I knew better, now, than to nick it.

He went on, and I padded after him, sticking to the edge of the street where I could duck into a doorway to hide if he looked back. He went 'round a corner onto Half-Chick Lane and stopped. The tumbledown houses on each side of the street were dark shadows leaning against each other, with slices of dark narrow alley between them.

"Well, boy?" he said, his voice loud in the quiet street. "Aren't you going to pick my pocket?"

I stepped out of the shadows. "Nevery, I already did."

He whirled around and leaned on his cane, scowling at me.

"You were distracted," I said. "You have to pay attention."

"Curse it, Connwaer," Nevery said. "Now, give the money back."

"If you want it back, you'll have to pick it from my coat pocket." Carefully, so he couldn't see, I slid his purse string up inside the sleeve of my sweater. Distraction, that was the key.

"Learning to pick locks was easier," Nevery grumbled. He'd been better at it, too. He was a wizard, but he was good at thinking like a thief. I'd taught him lockpicking back when we'd lived together at Heartsease, his mansion house. He handed me my knapsack, which he'd been carrying. It was full of food, biscuits from Benet, packets of bacon and cheese, apples, and wax candles.

I nodded toward the street where it led down the hill. "I'll walk with you back to the bridge, all right? And you can try me on the way."

"And you'll be distracted, will you, boy?"

I grinned. "I'll pretend I am, Nevery."

I slung the knapsack onto my back and we headed down Half-Chick Lane and turned onto Strangle Street. I kept my eyes on the shadows just in case anyone was following us.

"Hrm," Nevery said after a short while. "Have you, ah, read that treatise about Arhionvar?"

Arhionvar, the dread magic. I didn't need to read about Arhionvar—I had enough experience with it. At the same moment, I felt his hand grope in my coat pocket. Good try. I stepped sideways and glanced at him, shaking my head.

"Curse it," he muttered.

We turned another corner, onto Shirttail Street, which led straight down toward the bridge. From here, as we walked, we had a view across the rushing black river to the Sunrise, the nice part of the city, where the rich people lived and the streets were lit up with werelights, and the Dawn Palace glowed pink against the night sky.

"I gave you the Arhionvar treatise back when we were having those troubles with Underlord Crowe, boy. I suppose you didn't bother to read it," Nevery said.

I didn't answer him. He knew I hadn't.

A chilly wind blew off the river, bringing with

it the smell of mud and dead fish. Nevery paced alongside me, his cane going *tap tap* against the cobblestones.

"Watch out for that pothole," he said, bumping my arm and then dipping into my empty pocket.

"You're not very good at this," I said, pulling away. "What you need is an incentive."

"Indeed?" Nevery said.

"Yes," I said. "If you're a gutterboy and you don't pick a pocket, you don't get dinner, but if you try it and get caught, you end up in a guard cell or somebody beats the fluff out of you. So you have to get very good at it."

"I see," Nevery said. He cast me a sharp look. "And you are very good, are you, boy?"

"I have quick hands, Nevery," I said. But I had gone hungry often enough, and I'd gotten caught more than once, even apart from the time Nevery had caught me stealing his locus magicalicus. After I'd picked his pocket, everything had changed. I wasn't a gutterboy anymore; I was a wizard.

We came down to the bridge across the river; the houses built on it were closed up night-tight. Nevery paused. From behind us I heard the *skff skff* of foot-steps sliding along an alleyway, then silence. Drats. We were being followed.

Nevery leaned on his cane. "Don't forget, boy. We'll meet at the chophouse in four days."

I wasn't likely to forget that. Arhionvar, the dread magic, was coming, and the city was in terrible danger. Arhionvar had been behind the device that the traitor-wizard Pettivox and the former Underlord, Crowe, had built to confine Wellmet's magic, and Arhionvar had preyed on the desert city of Desh until that city's magic had nearly been destroyed. Now it was coming to Wellmet. We had to be ready when it got here, or our city and its magic would die, sure as sure.

Nevery had a plan, one based on his long-ago experiments with pyrotechnics, the ones that'd blown the middle out of Heartsease. He knew that setting off an explosion while doing a magical spell enhanced the effect of the spell. He'd been doing research in the academicos library, looking at old grimoires to find the right spell to enhance, something that would force Arhionvar to leave Wellmet alone. We thought a banishing spell might work, if we set explosive traps all around the city to make it stronger. My part of the plan was to help with the pyrotechnics and to scout the city for good places to set the traps.

"All right, boy?" Nevery asked sharply.

"All right, Nevery," I said.

"Well then, good night," he said, turning toward the Night Bridge.

Not a very good night, no. Out of the corner of my eye, I caught a quick-look of a darker shadow in an alley, then another scuff of a footstep from the street behind us. Not Dawn Palace guards on this side of the river. Minions, then. They'd warned me off the streets of the Twilight, and if they caught me they'd beat the fluff out of me, or worse.

"I will send a bird tomorrow," Nevery went on,

"with a copy of the Arhionvar treatise, if I can lay my hands on it."

I didn't answer. If I could get into the alleys I might be able to get away from them. "'Night, Nevery," I whispered, and ran.

To: Willa Forestal, Duchess of Wellmet, Dawn Palace

Yes, I received your letter about the cursed order of exile that has again been passed against my apprentice. No, I will not tell you where he is hiding. And you may tell Captain Kerrn that I have no further comments about Conn's means of escape from the Dawn Palace prison cells. I would be appalled by your stupidity on this subject, except that I already know your opinion of magic—and those who practice it.

It is thanks to my apprentice that we know the nature of the dire threat facing us. The predator magic, Arhionvar, was indirectly responsible for creating the device that weakened our magic, nearly destroying the city last winter. Because my apprentice defeated Arhionvar at Desh, it is surely seeking its next prey—Wellmet. Willa, it is coming. If we are not ready to defend ourselves, Arhionvar will devour our magic and the city will be destroyed. Pretending this threat does not exist will not make it go away.

The other magisters are fools and will not act. With some assistance, I have been preparing defenses for the city.

Wellmet is approaching its darkest hour. I know you have been ill since the Shadow attack, and I am sorry to hear it. Yet I ask again for your help.

NEVERY FLINGLAS

Magister

CHAPTER 2

I skiffed off Shirttail Street and headed into the maze of twisty, narrow streets that made up the Deeps, the part of the Twilight that rubbed up against the mud-flats south of the bridge. Down in the Deeps, the alleys were clotted with mud and trash, and patches of chill fog hung in the air.

I stumble-ran through the alleys, hearing pounding footsteps from behind. Then a shout from off to the left, and I took the next right, turning 'round a corner and racing up a stone stairway between two tall, dark buildings. At the top I paused to catch my breath and heard, from the darkness below, another shout and footsteps coming up the stairs. Drats, they kept coming!

If I was lucky, I could make it to my hiding place in Rat Hole, the worst part of the Twilight, where the houses were in rot-ruins and nobody lived, except me. They'd never find me in those dark and tangled streets.

I rounded a corner and stumbled into wide, cobbled Sark Square, the marketplace. Curse it, they'd herded me in this direction; out in the open was not where I wanted to be. The square was empty and dark, the cobblestones slick and wet.

"Got him!" a man shouted, and ahead of me dark figures burst from the mouths of the streets and alleys that led into the square.

I skidded to a stop and whirled 'round to go back the way I'd come. More men came from that direction, closing in, shouting. I flung myself at an opening between two of them, and a big hand grabbed me by the scruff of my neck.

I struggled and kicked, and then a bag came down over my head.

The minions shoved me ahead of them down a stone stairway; I took two steps, tripped, and bounced the rest of the way down. Ow, ow, ow. I wriggled out of the bag and crouched in the middle of the room, catching my breath and looking around. I knew at once where they'd brought me, to the cellar of a building on Clink Street that had once been a guard station. But the guards didn't bother with the Twilight anymore, so the minions had taken it over.

The room was long, with a low ceiling and shadows and spiderwebs lurking in its corners. Along one wall were flickery lanterns hung on nails, and along the other were prison cells, heavy doors with barred windows and pickable locks, where guards had once kept the bagmen and pickpockets they caught on the streets of the Twilight.

I got stiffly to my feet. The room was crowded, minions leaning against the damp walls, giving me their best menacing looks. One of them tossed my knapsack onto the floor. I started toward it, and the minion glared at me and showed me his fist.

I recognized him. He was big and burly, with a bumpy nose and just one eyebrow. His name was Fist. Standing beside him was his partner, Hand.

"Warned you off once," Fist said.

He had, true.

Fist took a heavy step forward; I stepped back, away from him. "An' now here you are again," he said.

Hand came around behind me and grabbed my

shoulders; I tried to squirm away, but he held me too tight.

Fist stepped forward again and, moving slowly, rested the rough knuckles of his fist on my face, right under my eye. I held my breath.

"What're you up to, little blackbird?" he growled.

I didn't say anything. Fist and the minions thought I was making a bid to be Underlord, like Crowe, my mother's brother, to run the Twilight, the rundown, rotten side of the city. But being Underlord was the last thing I wanted.

Fist grabbed me by the front of my coat and drew back his fist to hit me.

"I'm not up to anything!" I gasped, and gritted my teeth, ready for the blow.

"You've been warned off," Fist said again, leaning over me. His breath was hot and smelled like fish. "Why'd you come back to the Twilight?"

Because I had nowhere else to go, that was why. I couldn't stay with Nevery and Benet because the Dawn Palace guards were watching all the time. I was under an order of exile. If Kerrn, the captain of the Dawn Palace guards, caught me, she'd drag me back to one of her prison cells and fill me up with truth-telling phlister until I told her what I was up to. And then she'd throw me out of the city.

But Fist wouldn't care about any of that, so I kept quiet. The flames in the lanterns flickered, sending little shadow mice scurrying along the edges of the floor.

"Nothing to say?" Fist asked. He gave me a little shake and let me go and, behind me, Hand let me go, too. I ducked around them both and skiffed toward the door. I got two steps and felt Fist's big hand on the scruff of my neck.

He jerked me back. "Not done with you yet," he growled. Keeping his grip on me, he nodded at a short, big-eared minion with a bushy mustache. "Tell what you found in his place."

Big-ears nodded. "Papers with writing on 'em. Books with writing in 'em. Things for writing with."

Drats, they'd found my Rat Hole attic room.

"What're you up to, little bird?" Fist asked.

Right. I took a deep breath. "I'm a wizard," I said.

The minions lined up against the wall growled at that. "He's a lying gutterboy, he is," one of them said, shaking his head.

"Crowe's," said another minion.

"I'm not Crowe's," I said.

"Maybe you are, and maybe you aren't," Fist said. He looked down at his rough-knuckled hand. "Maybe you'll end up at the bottom of the river tonight, blackbird, and maybe you won't."

I clenched my teeth to hold in a shiver of fright. What did he want with me, anyway? "Fist, I really am a wizard," I said.

He nodded. "Twilight needs a wizard," he said.

I stared at him. I'd heard that once before, when I was buying blackpowder explosives from a pyrotechnist called Embre. Had Fist been talking to Embre? "What d'you want, exactly?" I asked.

"Something's going on," Fist said. Along the

walls, the minions nodded; a couple of them looked twitchy, as if they were afraid.

"What?" I asked.

"You say you're a wizard," Fist said. "You're going to tell us. Something's happening. Something with the magic."

Asked boy again where staying in Twilight; would not say, curse him. Have sent Benet to look for his bolt-hole, but boy very good at hiding, and Twilight slums difficult to search.

On way home from Twilight stopped at Heartsease to check rebuilding project. Despite cold, workers have set new foundations, walls, steps leading to door. Window glass goes in tomorrow. Boy's cat there, prowling around the island.

A distraction. Must focus on essentials. Tests show magic of Wellmet remains weak—damaged, we now think, by the Underlord's prisoning device. Prey, as boy says, for Arhionvar. Must also continue research to find appropriate spells for defense of city.

No reply from duchess. Will make last appeal

to magisters, but expect more waffling. They cannot believe that the magic is a living being; they still think it is simply a substance to be used. In this way the magisters are like thieves, stealing the substance of the magic, controlling it with a few spellwords, without considering the consequences of their actions. Because they feel safer ignoring the truth about the magic, they continue to deny that Arhionvar is threat. Fear boy and I must act alone. At dinner tonight at Twilight chophouse discussed Jaspers's second treatise on pyrotechnics, which boy read in sorcerer-king's library. Implications for defense of Wellmet.

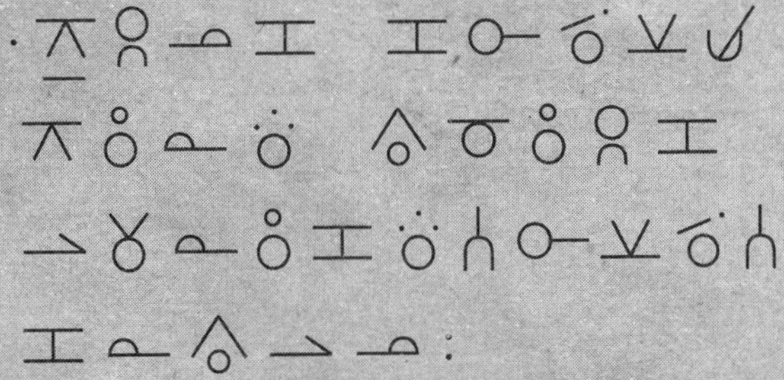

The minions didn't bother checking me for lockpick wires; they just tossed me in one of the basement cells and set two men to watching me all night. I did have wires. I also had

Nevery's purse string. I felt up my sweater-sleeve for it. Nothing; it was gone. Had the dratted minions taken it off me?

I thought back. No, clever-Nevery had. He'd picked his purse string out of my sleeve when he'd bumped my arm and pretended to pick my pocket. He was probably laughing at me right now. Wrapped in my coat, I lay down on the cold stones and went to sleep.

In the morning, Fist and Hand dragged me out of the cell and up to the streets. The sun was barely up. The rain had stopped, and a fog had risen up from the river and hung in the air like a sooty, yellow curtain. I hunched into my coat and shivered. We headed up the hill, then through Sark Square, which was just stirring, a few shops opening up.

I followed them onto Wyrm Street, which snaked up through the steepest part of the Twilight, where the houses had once been the most grand but were now falling to pieces. Only one place this road would take us.

Dusk House. Where the Underlord Crowe and his wizard, Pettivox, had built their device. It'd been a terrible machine built to imprison all of Wellmet's magic. The device had almost succeeded and now the magic was weaker than it'd been before.

When Nevery and I had destroyed the device, Dusk House had been blasted to pieces. Out in front of its ruins was a shattered stone gateway, the iron gates rusting and hanging off their hinges, and a jagged stone wall like a row of broken teeth. Inside the wall were big chunks of stone, scattered about from when the house had exploded. Snakes of fog slithered around them. Our footsteps sounded loud on the gravelly ground, *crunch*, *crunch*.

Fist stopped at the edge of the pit where Dusk House had once stood. "Here," he said, pointing down.

The pit was steep-sided, hewn out of the rock. Down there was where I'd lost my locus magicalicus. It'd been destroyed, blown into sparkling green dust when I'd released the magic from the device.

I looked down into the pit. It was half filled with sooty fog. “I don’t see anything,” I said.

“Wait for it,” Fist muttered, and backed away from the edge of the pit.

I waited. My stomach growled and I told it to be quiet. Behind me, one of the minions shifted; stones grated under his shoe.

Then everything fell silent. In the pit, the fog rose higher, like a cup filling up with milk, until it overflowed past me, up to my knees, and then it was all around me, damp and smother-white and silent.

I blinked, and the fog was gone. I looked down. Where the fog had been, darkness was filling the pit, shifting and velvety black. The air tingled, stretched like a rope pulled too hard and about to snap. Silence pushed against my ears. Tiny bolts of lightning crackled at the edges of the pit. The blackness welled up, rushing all around me, and my skin prickled as if I was filled with pins. My feet left the ground. I held my breath and looked at the magic all around me, and it was like looking into a night sky full of stars.

The magic knew me. It'd always protected me, even before I'd become a wizard. It'd chosen me because it knew that I would protect it, if I could. *What d'you want?* I shouted at it.

But I didn't have a locus magicalicus, so it couldn't hear me. The magic felt wound tight, frightened—it was worried about Arhionvar, I figured. *I'm doing all I can*, I wanted to tell it. But it wouldn't understand.

The velvety, star-filled blackness held me for another long, waiting moment. It turned me, like it was examining me, trying to figure out what I was. In my bones I felt a deep, rumbling hum. Then the giant hand of the magic dropped me and I crashed to the ground. Like water rushing down a drain, the magic swirled away into the bottom of the pit.

The air went *pop* and I could hear again. Fog settled into the pit.

I got to my feet and looked over my shoulder.

Fist and Hand stood near the smashed Dusk House gates, watching me. Time to get away.

Running as fast as I could, going 'round the edge of the pit, I got halfway to the back gate leading away from Dusk House before Hand caught up to me and tripped me. I went down hard, then rolled over.

"Still not done with you, blackbird," Fist said, catching his breath. He reached down and jerked me to my feet, then pushed me toward the front gate. His hand gripped my coat collar. "It picked you up," Fist said. "Never seen it do that before."

I shrugged.

"It's strange, right?" he asked.

It was more than strange. Wellmet's magical being was worried, clear as clear. But why was it in the pit where Dusk House had been?

"There's somebody wants to talk to you about it," Fist said; behind him, Hand nodded.

Who? I wondered.

They led me down the hill and along the rutted

road past the mudflats and along the curve of the river to a shack way outside the city.

I'd been there before. Sparks, the pyrotechnist, lived there with her nephew, Embre.

Well. I'd been wanting to talk to Sparks, anyway, and Embre, too. Once Nevery and I figured out what explosive devices we'd use for the traps, we'd need pyrotechnic materials, and we'd have to buy them from Sparks and Embre.

Their shack was long and had tar paper nailed up all over it, and a scrawny apple tree grew beside the front door. Behind it was a backyard that looked like a mud farm—furrows with a white, limey crust on them, like snow.

Sparks was there, digging.

Embre was there, too. He was a boy a lot older than I was, with black hair, dark eyes, and a sharp, pale face covered with soot smudges from working with blackpowder ingredients. He sat at the end of a mud row in a wooden wheelbarrow with a ragged blanket covering his stick legs.

I squelched through the mud to Embre's wheelbarrow.

"Hello," I said.

He scowled at me.

"Hello, Sparks," I called.

She bustled back along the row, and when she reached us she leaned on her shovel and grinned. She wore a holey gray dress and had her ashy hair tied up in a kerchief; her face was red from working hard. "Here," she said, handing her shovel to me. "Have a go at this." She nodded at her mud garden. "Just turn the dirt."

Turn the dirt, right. I went down the row to where Sparks had left off, stuck the shovel in, and lifted. As the dirt came up, so did the sharp-sour smell of old cesspools. I turned the dirt and dug up another shovelful, then another; as I worked my way down the row, Sparks stayed beside me, watching.

"Steady as you go," she said.

"What is this stuff?" I asked. The dirt was wet and smelly and had straw mixed in with it.

"Niter beds," Sparks said. She gave me her gap-toothed grin again. "Piss and straw, wood-ash and horse manure. We make our own saltpeter, we do, for the pyrotechnics." She pointed with her chin at Embre, down at the other end of the row in his wheelbarrow. "Come to talk to Embre, have you?"

I shrugged. Had I?

"Better come inside, then, before he takes a chill."

Down at the house, while Sparks bustled off to make tea, Embre climbed out of his wheelbarrow, dragged himself across the floor to his high stool at the table, and pulled himself up.

I stayed by the doorway. "What d'you have to do with the minions?" I asked him.

"Nothing," he said. He fixed me with his dark stare. "Why'd you come back here?" he asked. "From what I hear, the minions warned you out of the Twilight once, but you didn't listen. Are you making a bid to be Underlord?"

"No," I said. "They think I am, but I'm not."

Embre narrowed his eyes. "They don't believe you. Your name, Connwaer, is a true name, a blackbird name, just like Crowe's. You're his nephew. And he trained you to become Underlord after him, didn't he?"

He'd tried to. But I'd run away from Dusk House to live on the streets of the Twilight. "I was never Crowe's," I said. "I'm a wizard."

"If you really are a wizard, maybe you're making the magic do strange things in the Dusk House pit," Embre said. "You're making people afraid so they'll accept you as Underlord."

I stared back at him. "Embre, this has nothing to do with Crowe, or any Underlord business. The magic's doing strange things because it's afraid. The city's in danger. Both sides of it, the Sunrise and the Twilight." The minions had done me a favor, I realized, bringing me to see Embre. Maybe he would help me and Nevery.

"What kind of danger?" Embre asked.

"A bad magic is coming here," I said.

He frowned. "*Bad magic?* You're going to have to do better than that."

Right. I'd have to start at the beginning. I went to the table and sat down on a stool, across from him. "Remember when I got pyrotechnic materials from you?"

Embre nodded. "You and your friend, that red-haired girl. Sparks sold you blackpowder materials and I gave you a recipe for controlled explosions."

"That's right," I said. "I needed the blackpowder so I could do magic, because I don't have a locus stone." Most wizards hadn't figured out what, exactly, pyrotechnics and magic had to do with each other. Neither had I, but I did know that the magical being of Wellmet liked it when things blew up, and that I could do magical spells if I created a pyrotechnic explosion at the same time. "When I did the controlled explosion, it didn't work. I blew up Heartsease." My home, and Nevery's home. I'd hurt Benet, too, and even though he was all right, and Heartsease was being rebuilt, I still wasn't sure as sure that Nevery'd forgiven me for it.

"I know about this," Embre said. "You were exiled. And now you've come back because you want to be Underlord."

"No!" I shook my head, frustrated. "When I was exiled I went to Desh, the desert city. It was being attacked by a magic called Arhionvar, and now that magic is coming here, to Wellmet."

"What d'you mean, coming?" Embre said.

"It's like a—" What was the word? "When an animal hunts another animal to eat it, you know?"

Embre gave me a sharp smile. "A predator."

"Right. Arhionvar is a predator magic, and Wellmet's magic is its prey. But we can't get anybody to believe us about how dangerous Arhionvar is. The duchess is ill and won't do anything, and the wizards can't understand what the magic really is."

"What is it, then, *really*?" Embre asked.

I nodded. It was a good question, one I wished the magisters would think more about. "The magic is a being. It lives here. Every city is built on the place where its magical being lives, and the magic helps the city and protects it."

"Except for this predator magic, Arhionvar," Embre said.

"Right," I said. "Arhionvar tried to kill the Desh magic, and it's attacked the Wellmet magic before. If it comes here and we don't defend the city, I think it'll kill Wellmet's magical being and the city'll be destroyed. It will die."

Embre's gaze sharpened. "The people will die?"

I shook my head. "I don't know. Some of them might. They won't be able to stay here if Arhionvar takes over." I paused. "We're trying to stop it, me and Nevery. He's a wizard, and I'm his apprentice. We might be able to use pyrotechnics to set some traps, but we'll need a lot of blackpowder and slowsilver." I leaned across the table. "Wellmet's in big trouble, Embre. Will you help us?"

He looked down and rubbed at a patch of soot on the palm of his hand. "I don't know." He frowned. "Maybe. Maybe not. I'll think about it."

On the way back to my attic room in the Rat Hole, I thought about skiffing off to pick a pocket or steal something to eat, but every time I started down an alley or tried to turn onto

another street, a minion stepped out and glared at me. Right. Straight back to my room, it was, with no stops for anything else. The minions following was their way of saying they knew where to find me, that I was free only because they let me stay free, and I still had my fluff because they'd decided not to beat it out of me yet.

The alleys grew narrower and more rutted; the houses on either side were soot-stained brick, with empty, broken windows or missing roofs, or front doors hanging off their hinges. Nobody lived here in the Rat Hole anymore. It was the oldest part of the city, the area where the artists and potters and glass-blowers and carpet weavers had lived a long time ago, before the factories were built and the workers had moved into tenements to be close to their work.

I turned off the alley into a dark space between two brick buildings only as wide as my shoulders. Then through a backyard full of rotted barrels and rusting metal hoops, and across another alley to my hiding place.

Once it'd been a tall town house in a row of town

houses like books lined up on a shelf. I went up the narrow stone steps to the front door, which was missing. The doorway was framed by stone doorposts shaped like dragons, but worn down so they were barely recognizable. But I knew what they were. A dragon was etched faintly into the stone doorstep, too.

I stepped in. Beside the door, under a piece of plaster that'd fallen from the ceiling, I'd stashed a candle and a striker. Rat Hole was full of misery eels, not just in the midnight-dark cellars, but in the rotted houses, too. The light would keep them away if they came after me. The candle had little toothmarks on it; rats had been at it. I struck a spark and lit it.

The building was just one room wide. With a faint circle of light around me, I went through the dark, empty downstairs, creaking over rotted floorboards to a rickety stairway, and up three more floors. I'd found a ladder and used it to climb up to the attic because the stairs there had rotted all away.

I pulled up the ladder behind me. Safer that way.

My room was narrow, with two windows in the

slanted ceiling, both of them patched with brown paper and stuffed with rags around the frames to keep out the wind and rain. Rats lived in the walls. The air was chill and damp and smelled like mold and rot and smoke.

When I'd left, my room had been tidy.

In the flickering candlelight I looked it over. The minions wanted me to know they'd been there. My bed-blankets were kicked into a corner, my pile of books and grimoires had been thrown around the room, and some torn-out pages were stuffed into the fireplace. My shelf of food—biscuits and half a sausage wrapped up in paper—was empty. They'd thrown a jar of jam against a wall; it looked like a jam star splashed across the cracked plaster.

Drats. I took a deep breath and went to the hearth to pull the pages out. One by one, I flattened them on the floor and piled them together. Most of them weren't burnt, just crumpled and smudged with ash.

Fist had taken my knapsack of food, so I had nothing to eat. My stomach felt hollow with hunger.

I dug around in some of the things the minions had thrown against the wall. My teakettle, dented, and in the corner, a cracked teacup. I found half a biscuit, too, dusty and rat-gnawed.

I went down to the pump in the house's kitchen, climbed back up, and made tea from the scraps of tea leaves I swept up from the floor.

Drinking dusty tea, eating the half biscuit, and wishing for a better breakfast, I thought about what Fist had told me. Something going on with the magic, he'd said. I knew the Wellmet magic was frightened of Arhionvar. Even without a locus magicalicus, I could feel the magic hanging over my head like a storm cloud. The magic's watchers, its black birds, watched me all the time and flew down to sit on my shoulder and say *krrrr, krrrr* into my ear.

The magic wanted me to do something. It knew as well as I did that Arhionvar was coming. The knowing made me feel like mingled slowsilver and tourmalifine—about to explode. But what more could I do than I was already doing?

Tap, *tap*, *tap* at one of the slanted windows in the ceiling. I creaked up out of my blankets, still sore from falling down the stone steps in the minions' place, went over to the window, and cracked it open.

A black bird hopped in, shaking drops of misty rain from its wings.

"Hello," I said to it. A quill was strapped to its leg, a message from Nevery. The letter was written on a long, narrow piece of paper rolled up tight and tied with a piece of thread. Not a letter, I saw when I unrolled it, but the treatise on the lost city of Arhionvar.

I'd read it, but first I had a note to write back. While the bird hopped around on the floor, I dug around in the mess the minions had made. They'd taken my paper and pens and ink bottle, and all my notes about pyrotechnics, but I found a rat-nibbled stub of pencil to write with and a blank space on one of the pages the minions had ripped out of a book.

I tried to write neatly, because Nevery hated it when he couldn't read my handwriting.

Nevery,

I need to talk to you, and to Rowan, if you can get her. The magic is doing something strange in the Twilight. If you send Benet with the boat we can meet at Heartsease tonight.

—Connwaer

I folded up the torn-out book page and slid it into the quill.

"Off you go," I said to the bird, and opened a window so it could fly away. It flapped off into the fog.

After it was gone, I stuffed rags back into the cracks around the window frame and started cleaning up the mess the minions had left. It didn't take long. Then I sat down against the wall, wrapped in my damp blankets, and read the Arhionvar treatise.

Nevery'd told me about this treatise before, when I'd first become a wizard, but I'd been too distracted by Crowe's device to read it.

According to the treatise, Arhionvar had once been a city far away in the southern Fierce Mountains. For some reason the city had died. All the people had fled. It wasn't in the treatise, but I could guess the rest: The city's magic had left the mountains and had become a predator magic—a magic called Arhionvar after the city where it'd lived. I didn't know why it had left its proper place to wander around attacking other cities, as it'd attacked Desh, and as it was about to attack Wellmet. It'd already partly succeeded against Wellmet; the magic was weaker now than it'd been before the device, Nevery said. Prey for the predator.

After a while, the bird came back, *tap tap tapping* at my window. I creaked it open and the bird hopped onto my shoulder. In the quill, a message from Nevery.

Not tonight. Meeting with magisters later. Meet Benet at Tryworks warehouse dock tomorrow night just after dark. Don't be late.

And don't tear pages out of books to write on, boy. If you need money for paper, ask for it.

—N

Drats. I wrote him a quick note back saying I would meet Benet where he said, and that I had received the Arhionvar treatise he'd sent, and then I sent the bird off again.

CHAPTER 5

Late in the afternoon, as the clouds crowded in over the city for the night's rain, I heard the clump-clump of heavy feet coming up the stairs. The footsteps stopped under the hole in my floor where the stairs had been.

"Hoy there, blackbird!"

The minion Fist. No point in pretending I wasn't there. I put down the roll of paper with the Arhionvar treatise written on it, climbed out of my nest of blankets, and went over and lay down on my stomach so I could look through the hole in the floor.

"You're here, are you?" Fist asked, looking up at me.

Where else would I be? I nodded.

"Got something for you." He held up a big, square package wrapped in brown paper. "Come down and get it."

Unless it was food, I didn't want it. I shook my head.

"No harm," Fist said. "Just some books."

"Leave them there," I said.

Fist shrugged and, very gently, set the package on the floor. Then he turned and clump-clumped back down the stairs.

I waited until I heard him go out of the house,

then got the ladder and skiffed down for the package and lugged it back up to my room. The light had gotten too dim to see much, so I lit a nub of candle, set it on the hearth, and unwrapped the stack of books. A slip of paper was wrapped up with them. I recognized the neat handwriting; it was a note from Embre.

These books were found last winter in a cellar in the Twilight. You might find them interesting.

Embre

The books were old and spotted with mildew, and they had titles like **Pyrotechnics for Industrial Purposes** and Further Notes on Explosive Ratios. The book on the bottom of the stack was covered with crumbling black leather, and even though some of the letters had flaked off, I could make out the title, printed in gold:

TH
GRIM   RE
OF
A
NAM LE S
ZARD
AND
ANON MOUS
PYRO   NIST

My hands shaking a little from excitement, I opened the book. The binding cracked, and more bits of leather flaked off the cover. The pages inside were yellowed, and the tiny, messy handwriting had faded to gray. Holding the book closer to the candle, I peered at the words. Magic spells and strange ideas about pyrotechnics, it looked like.

I started reading. In the second chapter, at the top of the page, was written *Some Notes on Finding Spells w/ Absolute Stoichiometrical Pyrotechnic Effect.*

Stoichiometrical. What did that mean, exactly?

One of my torn-up books was a lexicon. I looked up the word, but it wasn't there. Nevery would know, though. I went back to the book.

A long time later, my last candle guttered and went out. I sat up, blinking. The room was completely dark. The book. It was full of information. I didn't understand any of it.

Except that in chapter two were special pyrotechnic instructions and a spell for finding a locus magicalicus. A finding spell!

I stood up and stretched. Carefully, I felt my way to a shelf and set down the book so the rats couldn't get at it. Words from the book swirled around in my head.

Magical interference effects.

Metal jelly.

Absolute stoichiometric control must be maintained!

Solution will be vertuminous blue.

Hot filament ignition.

I was too excited to sleep. This was a lot more complicated than making blackpowder, or combining slowsilver and tourmalifine. But the results! What if I could do this spell? I might find a new locus magicalicus in a few days! Then I'd be able to do a lot more to protect the Wellmet magic from Arhionvar.

For the rest of the night I paced in my black-dark room, listening to the rats scrabble in the walls, waiting for daylight so I could see to read. As soon as the sky turned glimmer-gray, I stood by the window with the book open, reading.

All day I read, getting hollower with hunger, but filling up with ideas.

When I finished the book, I lay on the floor and stared up at the slanted ceiling. Rain pattered on the roof and leaked in through the windows. So many instructions. And a list of ingredients, and things called *solutions* and *reagents*. Words that weren't in my lexicon. Maybe Nevery would understand it.

The sky outside my attic window was dark gray.

Dark gray.

Meet Benet at Tryworks warehouse dock tomorrow night just after dark.

Drats, I was going to be late.

Quickly I put on my coat. One of its pockets was ripped on the inside, so I slid the book in so that it went down through the pocket into the lining of my coat, where it would be safe.

As darkness fell over the Twilight, I ran through puddles until I arrived at Ten Crane Street, panting, my head spinning from having nothing to eat except half a biscuit for two days. Down here the air smelled like the river, fishy and muddy. Thunder grumbled overhead and the rain got heavier, running down my neck like cold fingers.

There, the Tryworks warehouse, looming out of the mist and rain like a barge on the river. 'Round the back on the side nearest the river was a doorway where I could wait for Benet. As I rounded the corner, a big hand reached out from the shadows and grabbed me by the scruff of my neck.

"You're late," a rough voice said.

I caught my breath. "Hello, Benet."

Benet was Nevery's bodyguard, and his cook and housekeeper. He was big and broad, with bristly brown hair, a face like a fist full of knuckles, and a scar across his forehead. He wore a plain brown suit and a red waistcoat he'd knitted himself.

He kept ahold of me, glaring. "What're you up to?"

I grinned. "I found a spell in a book."

"Spells, is it?" He let me go. "Come on, you. Boat's tied at the end of the dock."

I followed him out to the dock and into the rowboat he'd tied up there.

"Underneath," he said, pointing with an oar.

I crawled under a sheet of canvas to hide, just in case anybody was watching from shore. It was dark under there and smelled like rotten fish, but it was out of the rain.

The boat jerked as Benet pushed us away from the dock, and I heard him drop the oars into the oarlocks, and the squeak and splash as he started to row. We had to go upstream for a while to get to Heartsease.

I settled down against the curve of the boat, my warm coat wrapped around me, and closed my eyes. As long as I was with Benet I was safe. The river wavelets lapped against the boat, and the rain went *patter-pat* on the canvas just over my head.

I woke up with Benet poking my shoulder with the oar. He stood on the rocky shore of Heartsease island, glowering down at me.

I rubbed my eyes and sat up, then stood up, the boat tipping as I stepped onto one of the slippery black rocks that lined the island. For just a second my head felt light, with hunger most likely, and I wobbled a little. Benet grabbed my arm and pulled me to shore, then gave me a sharp look. "Come on, you."

Once Heartsease had been Nevery's home, and the home of his family for years and years. But I'd blown it up. The explosion was where Benet had gotten his scar. Nevery was trying to rebuild Heartsease to be a home again. Maybe it'd be my home again, too, someday.

I could see that the workers had put up a foundation and four brick walls with rows of tall windows.

"In here," Benet said. He led me through an empty doorway into a room scattered with piles of brick and canvas bags of dry mortar, and slabs of slate for the floors, and builders' tools. In one corner Benet had rigged up a canvas roof, and in the new hearth he'd lit a fire.

Nevery was there, a shadow in the firelight,

sitting on a barrel of nails. "There you are," he said. "You're late."

"Sorry," I said. "I was reading."

"Ah." Nevery nodded. He understood how hard it was sometimes to stop reading.

Benet set down the lantern and leaned against a wall with his burly arms crossed. I sat down on the dirt floor with my back against the wall. "Nevery, d'you have anything to eat?" I asked. I'd been hoping for a pan of bacon sizzling in the hearth, three or four fried eggs with pepper, maybe some biscuits dripping with butter.

"Set aside your preoccupation with food, boy," Nevery said. "What is the trouble with the magic you had to tell me about on this miserable night?"

Drats. My stomach gave a hopeless growl. "The magic's at Dusk House," I said. I stared at the glowing-gold embers in the hearth. And Embre. I needed to tell Nevery about the book Embre had given me.

"And?" Nevery said.

Right. "It's at Dusk House," I said. Had I said that already?

"Boy . . . ," Nevery began.

"Should've realized, sir," Benet said, from where he was leaning against the wall. "He looks peaky."

"Hmmm," Nevery said, and then he reached down and took my chin in his hand, turning my face so he could see me. "Benet is right, my lad. What's the matter?"

I shrugged.

Nevery knew me well enough to wait for an answer.

"I'm having a little trouble with the minions," I said.

"Curse it," Nevery said fiercely. He let me go and looked across at Benet, who nodded and went out. "What kind of trouble, boy?"

"They found out my hiding place," I said.

Nevery muttered angrily into his beard.

"They showed me the magic thing," I said.

"Magic thing?" Nevery asked. "At Dusk House, I assume."

I told him about the magic welling up from the pit and lifting me off the ground, then draining away.

"Hmmm," Nevery said, and stared into the fire. "Extraordinary. Never heard of magic behaving so strangely. Not a pyrotechnic effect, clearly. Nothing to do with a locus magicalicus. Very odd."

A chilly wind from off the river swirled through the open door. I edged closer to the fire. Inside the lining of my coat the book Embre had given me bumped against my leg. I pulled it out. "Here, Nevery," I said, holding it out to him.

He glanced at the title, then opened the book to the first page. "Where did you get this, boy?"

"From Embre."

Nevery shot me a glare from under his bristly eyebrows. "A friend of yours?"

I wasn't sure if Embre was a friend or not. "He's

a pyrotechnist in the Twilight. His aunt's name is Sparks."

"Ah." Nevery nodded. I wondered if he knew Sparks from when he'd done his own pyrotechnic experiments. He turned a page. "Hmmm," he muttered, and turned another page.

"Look at chapter two," I said. Then I put my head down on my knees and closed my eyes.

"Hello, Connwaer," Rowan said.

I looked up. Rowan was tall and had a proud face, gray eyes, and red hair that was sparkling with raindrops and floating around her head like wild fluff. Across her cheek she had a thin scar, fading from pink to white, got from her fight with the sorcerer-king's Shadows and guards. She was the duchess's daughter and she was my best friend, and, except when she was furious with me, I was hers. She wore an embroidered black wormsilk dress with a green woolen cloak over it and black button-up boots. She stood beside Nevery, who glanced up at her, nodded, and went back to the book.

"I can't stay long." She sat on the floor next to me and rested her elbows on her knees. "Argent rowed me across from the Sunrise. He's tying up the boat now."

Argent. Or *Sir Argent*, as he liked to be called. Rowan's friend.

Nevery looked up from the book. "This finding spell," he said, tapping the page.

"Can you make sense of it, Nevery?" I asked.

He nodded, pulling at the end of his beard. "I can, yes. But I am not sure that working with pyrotechnics is a good idea at this particular moment."

Because of our other pyrotechnic preparations, he meant. But we had to do the finding spell. We *had* to. "I can fight Arhionvar a lot better with a locus stone than without one," I said.

"You're talking about doing a pyrotechnic spell to find your locus magicalicus?" Rowan asked. She leaned forward, her eyes gleaming in the firelight. "Don't be stupid, Connwaer. It's too dangerous.

What if you're caught? You fought Arhionvar in Desh, and you did it without a locus stone."

True, I had. But the dread magic had almost gotten me then. It wanted me to be its wizard, to take me over as it'd done to the wizard it'd found in Desh—Jaggus. The sorcerer-king had been lost to Arhionvar because he'd been alone, with no one to turn to for help. Arhionvar had corrupted Jaggus until he'd attacked his own city's magic. Arhionvar wanted to do the same to me so it could attack Wellmet's magic. I'd fought it off once because I knew I had friends and I wasn't alone, but I'd need a locus magicalicus if I was going to face it again.

"Nevery—" I said. My voice shook a little bit.

"All right, boy," Nevery interrupted. "But you won't be able to work this spell in some Twilight attic. We'll have to use a workroom."

We, he'd said. So he would help me.

"Some of the techniques described here . . ." Nevery shook his head. "Stoichiometry, hmmm," he muttered. "Hot filament ignition. Have to tune the dock pendulum." He went back to the book.

"What exactly is a finding spell?" Rowan asked me.

I turned to her. "A spell I can use to find my locus magicalicus. Nevery can't cast a finding spell for me because it's my stone we have to find. I have to do it."

"I see," Rowan said. "And your locus stone is somewhere in Wellmet?"

I glanced at Nevery to see what he would say.

"It is, almost certainly," Nevery said without looking up from the book.

"It won't be one of my mother's jewels again, will it, Connwaer?" Rowan asked, smiling.

"No," I said. Probably not. Hopefully not. A wizard's locus magicalicus called to him or her. It could be anything, a pebble on the road, or a rounded river stone, or a piece of gravel. My first locus stone had been a leaf-green jewel, the center jewel in the necklace of Rowan's mother, the duchess of Wellmet. To get my hands on it, I'd stolen it.

This time, finding my locus magicalicus was not going to land me in trouble, or in jail.

Rowan Forestal

Captain Kerrn's guards are watching me all the time, waiting for me to lead them to Conn. Kerrn has asked me several times if I know where to find the thief. I don't know where he is staying, so I can say with perfect truthfulness that I do not. I think she suspects me of helping Conn escape from the Dawn Palace. I didn't, but I wish that I had. I have tried to tell my mother and Kerrn that Conn had to return to Wellmet from exile, that in defeating Arhionvar he showed more bravery than any palace guard, but they both still see him as the thief who stole the most valuable jewel in the city from the ducal regalia.

Sneaking out of the palace tonight wasn't easy, but I got out, through the Sunrise, and down to the river without being seen. Argent was at the riverbank with a boat and a flask of hot tea. He was trying very hard to be noble about waiting in the rain.

Poor Argent; he does not know what to make of Conn. He sat uncomfortably on a pile of bricks while

we talked, and then he grumbled all the way home about Conn's terrible manners. It bothers him that Conn does not call me Lady Rowan. Then Magister Nevery's manservant cooked up potatoes and bacon in a pan, and Conn fell on it like a pack of ravening dogs, eating with his fingers because the servant, Benet, hadn't brought a fork. Argent has a point about the manners.

While Argent sat scowling, Conn and Magister Nevery and I talked about the Wellmet magic and the threat of Arhionvar. Conn told us about the strange behavior of the magic at the Dusk House pit. Magister Nevery said he did not know what it meant, and Conn said maybe Nevery should go and try to get the magic to talk to him. After that, they argued about magic and talked about magical spells in great technical detail. Conn seems wound very tightly. I think he is more worried about Arhionvar than he lets on. He's always been quiet. I expect that's because he spent so much of his

childhood alone, on the streets of the Twilight, so he's not used to telling people how he feels. But when he's worried about something, he gets even quieter.

Conn asked about my mother. She isn't any better. I'm afraid she is worse. She sits in her chair, so still and silent, like a pale marble statue. When I kiss her cheek, her skin is like cold stone. Magister Trammel says it is the wound given her by the Shadows that pains her. He works healing spells, but they don't seem to make a difference.

This morning at breakfast I tried to tell her about the magic in the Dusk House pit, but she wouldn't listen. Instead, she told me to cancel my swordcraft lesson so I could attend a meeting with the factory owners, then another meeting with her council, and then yet another meeting with the leaders of the city's chimney swifts.

While she is ill she is asking me to take over more and more of her duties. I'm glad she trusts me, but I'm afraid it means she is not going to recover from her wound.

Connwaer,

As discussed, we must do finding spell right away, get your locus magicalicus, then continue with preparations to defend city from Arhionvar.

For finding spell will need following materials:

Magnetic rust (very little amount) (difficult material to work with; store in folded paper sealed with wax)

Rock salt (crushed, one small sackful)

Ingredients for blackpowder (ratio 15:4:3)

Atriomated water (several cups full) (must be boiled before distilling, note)

Viperic acid (one small-ish bottle)

Mineral spirits (one small bottle sealed with wax) (do not open bottle, boy!)

Copper wire

Cannot buy materials myself in Sunrise; magisters, palace guard watching, will be seen as suspicious activity. However, will prepare abandoned workroom in Academicos for our purposes.
—Nevery

Nevery,

Can you send Benet with more money? I can meet him in the morning at Sark Square.

I got the rock salt and the blackpowder ingredients and the copper wire from Embre. He wants two more silver faces to pay the man who makes the atriomated water, and he says he can't get that much viperic acid for any price.

Nevery, are you sure you should do this if the guards are watching you? I want to find my locus stone, but I don't want you to get into trouble. If you tell me what the words mean, I can do it myself.

—Conn

Boy, I can adjust the stoichiometrics, so we can do with less acid. Get as much as you can. What about the mineral spirits and the rust?
—N

Nevery, I'm going to need more money. Embre says the man who makes the atriomated water wants four silvers now. Sparks says the rust has to be scraped from a lightning-struck rock a day's walk outside the city, so she's going to fetch it tomorrow, unless it's too rainy. I'm not having any luck with the mineral spirits.

Nevery, what is stoichiometry?

—Conn

Dear Nevery,

Even though it was raining, Sparks got the rust and she is trying to dry it, but it keeps sticking to things. Embre is making the viperic acid himself but he says he needs more snakes, so I have been hunting them by the river. Thank you for the money.

Is stoichiometry something about the mixing?

–C

Boy, stoichiometric control has to do with the meticulous measurement of materials needed for the spell. It also has to do with patience, which you don't seem to have developed yet. This pyrotechnic finding spell calls for exactly 495 grains of blackpowder at that ratio, and 53 flakes of magnetic rust, and so on. Also, the timing and order in which the materials are combined must be precisely controlled, hence need for dock pendulum, carefully calibrated.

My preparations here are almost complete.

Write when you are ready.

—Nevery

N—

I'm ready.

—C

Benet came to Sparks's house to fetch the materials for Nevery. That night he came back for me, rowing me across to the academicos. I scrambled out of the boat and waited for Benet to climb out onto the dock.

"Not staying for this part," Benet said.

I didn't blame him; the last time I'd done pyrotechnics,

Benet had gotten his skull cracked open.

"Be careful, you," he said gruffly.

"I'll try," I said. But if I was too careful, I'd never find my locus magicalicus.

With an oar, Benet pushed off from the dock and floated into the darkness.

I turned to look at the academicos. It was a shadow against the lighter night, a big central building with four square, spired towers at its corners, and four-story wings flanking a slate-paved courtyard. Only a few wizards and magisters had rooms here, so it was mostly dark; two lights shone from windows on the ground floor, where the school's master, Brumbee, lived.

I headed across the courtyard toward one of the side entrances. Then I stopped. Strange shadows like dark lumps were clustered on the windowsills and on the wide stairs leading up to the double front doors. The shadows shifted and rustled like leaves blowing in the wind.

Not leaves. They were black birds, the magic's

watchers. Waiting to see what would happen when I did the spell, maybe. One of them swooped down from a windowsill, circled 'round my head, and flapped back to perch with the other birds.

I went on across the courtyard, picked a lock to get in a side door, and went cat-footed up the dark stairs to the room Nevery'd told me to go to. Not his own room, just in case, but the workroom of a wizard who'd died a long time ago.

I knocked softly on the door. After a few moments, it cracked open and Nevery peered out. Without speaking, he opened the door wider to let me in, then closed the door.

"Were you seen?" he asked.

I shook my head.

"You have the rust?"

I pulled the paper packet out of my pocket to show him. My hands were shaking just a little.

Nevery studied me. "You're very quiet, boy, even for you. Nervous?"

I nodded. I had a lump of worry stuck in my

throat, stopping my voice. What if this didn't work? What would we do then?

"Hmph. I need some time before we begin." Turning away, Nevery went to the table and peered down at his grimoire, muttering. He'd recopied the finding spell and the directions and had to read it over again before we started.

I looked around the room. It was more like a study than a workroom. Werelight glowed from lanterns set on the table. Books and papers were piled against a wood-paneled wall, and some more furniture was pushed into a corner and covered with bedsheets. Dusty velvet curtains were pulled across the windows. Nevery'd nailed up rugs and blankets on the walls, to muffle any sounds, I figured.

On the table were the things we needed to work the finding spell. At one end stood a polished dock pendulum, gleaming in the werelight; next to it was a saucer of sparking blackpowder emulsion, a couple of glass stirring rods, some clean rags, two mortars with crystal pestles, a metal bowl full of crushed rock salt, a brass trivet, a fat candle with three wicks, and stoppered vials of measured atriomated water, viperic acid, and mineral spirits.

"You've read over the notes I sent you, boy?" Nevery asked, glancing up from his grimoire.

I cleared my throat. "Yes, Nevery."

"Getting the timing right is absolutely crucial in a stoichiometric spell," he said.

Yes, I knew that. Nevery's notes, written on one long, narrow roll of paper and sent with one of the black birds, had listed everything we had to do, step by step, before I said the finding spell. One thing I was good at was reading something once and then remembering it. I wasn't going to forget anything.

Nevery nodded toward the door. "Put that on."

My ragged, scorch-marked, gray-wool apprentice robe hung on a hook beside the door. I put the robe on over my black sweater, then went back to the table. My breath fizzed a little as it went down into my chest. If this worked, I would find my locus magicalicus *tonight*.

"Fifty-three flakes of the magnetic rust, Connwaer," Nevery said, still looking at his grimoire. "In a mortar. Wipe it out first."

I rolled up the sleeves of my robe, then cracked open the wax-sealed paper. The rust was greeny-black, the tiny flakes clinging together in a crease of the paper. I pulled over a mortar and wiped it out with one of the clean rags, then fished in the collar of my shirt for a lockpick wire.

The rust stuck itself to everything. With an end of the wire I teased out a greenish flake, then tapped it from the wire into the mortar. *One.*

Nevery closed his grimoire. He came to the table and used his locus stone to light the three wicks of the candle, then he moved the trivet over the flames and set his mortar on it. "Almost ready, boy?" he asked.

I nodded. *Forty-nine, fifty . . .*

"Good," Nevery said. He leaned across the table and drew the dock pendulum up to its calibration. He glanced at me and raised his eyebrows.

Fifty-three. "Ready," I said, and my voice cracked.

"Begin," he said, and let the pendulum fall.

While Nevery measured and mixed the aqueous solution, I dissolved the magnetic rust in a threefold concentration of viperic acid, mixing with a glass rod. While it bubbled, I took out the rod and cleaned it off and waited.

"Count two," Nevery said, watching the pendulum. It ticked over twice. "Now."

Quickly I added a fizzing drop of mineral spirit. A puff of blue smoke swirled from the surface of the mixture in my mortar.

Nevery stirred his mortar, watching the pendulum. "The atriomated water should be boiled off in five," Nevery said. "Be careful, boy; the smoke is poisonous."

I nodded, watching the pendulum. Ten more counts and my mixture would turn to metal jelly.

"Has it turned blue?" Nevery asked.

I leaned over to peer at my mixture. Yes, it was

turning blue-green around the edges, and starting to bubble.

"Stir it," Nevery said.

Right. I cleaned off a pestle and poked the jelly; it bubbled up, and I poked it down again. Bubble-poke, bubble-poke.

Nevery lifted his mortar off the trivet, set it into the bowl of rock salt, and started to stir it. "Is your solution ready?" he asked, watching the pendulum.

Almost. The jelly crackled; in a few swing-tocks of the pendulum it would dissolve into a red powder in the bottom of the mortar.

But it didn't. Instead, the pestle cracked in my hand and a thick cloud of choke-black smoke billowed up from the mortar. It went into my lungs like a breath full of feathers; I backed away from the table, coughing. More smoke billowed up and spread out over the ceiling like a thick layer of clouds on a rainy day. Nevery, coughing and holding his arm over his face, jerked aside the curtain and flung the window open.

As a damp breeze blew in from outside, the smoke swirled around below the ceiling and grew thicker, then clumps of sizzling black soot started falling like black snowflakes. A soot-flake landed on my hand, and it burned like a hot ember. More soot-flakes drifted down.

Still coughing, I scrambled under the table. Nevery crawled in after me.

"You all right, boy?" Nevery asked.

I caught my breath. "Yes"—I coughed again—"Nevery." I coughed the last of the black feathers out of my lungs, then we sat watching the soot-flakes pile up on the slate floor, sizzle, and then cool.

"One of your reagents must have been tainted," Nevery said, frowning. "The rust, perhaps, though that doesn't seem likely. Perhaps one of the stirring rods."

Tainted? Oh. How could I have been so stupid? "Nevery, I counted out the magnetic rust with a lockpick wire." And I hadn't cleaned it first.

"Curse it," Nevery muttered.

"Can we try again?" I asked.

"Strict stoichiometric control, boy," Nevery said. Brushing soot-flakes out of the way, he crawled out from under the table and got to his feet. "It means exact measurements, exact timing, and absolutely pure materials."

Coughing up the smoke, I'd coughed up the knot of worry in my throat. "And stoichiometry means patience, right?" I said. That's what he'd told me, anyway. I crawled out and stood up. The soot covered everything in the room like a fall of new snow, except black.

"Yes, boy," Nevery said, looking at me and pulling at the end of his beard. "Patience. Something I never needed until you became my apprentice." He turned to survey the room. "Well, it's not too late, and we have enough materials. We can clean everything and try again."

By *we can clean everything* Nevery meant that *I* could clean everything. I was the one who'd made the stupid mistake, he said. Then he pulled a sheet off a comfortable chair, got a book from the pile of books by the wall, and sat down to read. While he did that, I closed the window, brushed the soot-snow off the table, set out the materials again, and carefully cleaned every speck of soot from the mortars and the stirring rods. When I was almost finished, Nevery put his book aside and came to the table to take the dock pendulum apart and recalibrate it.

We prepared the spell again. This time, when I stirred the metal jelly, it dissolved into a pile of red powder so fine, it swirled like blood in the bottom of the mortar.

Nevery's aqueous solution had turned to powder, too. Now we had to wait fifty counts for it to cool. The dock pendulum ticked over, *tock, tock, tock.*

According to the description in the book, the finding spell would *manifest and point the precise location of the stone, so that the wizard must be prepared to pursue, and thus discover it.* "Nevery?" I said. I wasn't sure what *manifest* meant, exactly.

"What, boy?" He picked up a length of copper wire and held it to the candle flame.

"How will the spell, um, manifest?"

Nevery glanced at me, then back at the wire.

"You only think to ask this now?"

Stupid, I knew. "Well, Nevery—"

"Yes, yes, I know, boy," he said. "We're at twenty-five counts." Without taking his eyes off the candle flame, he went on. "The spell should manifest as a beam of light, which will extend from this room to the place in the city where your locus stone can be found. You know to be ready?"

"I'm ready," I said.

"Count of five," Nevery said. "Four, three, two—"

I picked up my mortar—it was heavy—and dumped my red powder into Nevery's mortar full of blue powder. Even without mixing, the two powders swirled together, repelling each other. Setting the mortar down, I gripped the edge of the table, suddenly nervous again.

"Steady, Connwaer," Nevery said. The end of his copper wire glowed.

I waited.

"Now," Nevery said, and thrust the hot wire into

the mingled powders. Hot filament ignition.

The book had called what would happen a *glowing red wave front*, but I knew a pyrotechnic explosion when I saw one. The mortar filled with ember-gold light. I started the spell. *"Alasanliel-lielalas—"*

"Louder, boy!" Nevery said.

The light burst out from the mortar. I shouted more spellwords—*"eventiensilaollentinumintia—"* The room filled with white-bright fizzing stars.

Nevery, holding up his hand to shade his eyes, went to the window and pulled aside the curtain. "Finish it!" he shouted.

The end of the spell was my name. *"Connwaer!"*

The finding spell gathered itself into a crackling, spinning flower of light just below the ceiling. Vials and the dock pendulum and the mortars were swept off the table and shattered against the walls. Faster and faster the light-flower spun, flinging off sparks; then it slowed, finding its way. Slower, slower . . .

"Be ready, boy," Nevery whispered.

I was ready.

The light-flower drew in its petals, gave a blinding flash, and blasted through the window; shards of glass flew outward, sparkling in the darkness.

Nevery and I leaped for the windowsill to see where the spell pointed.

It blazed a trail from the window, shedding sparks as it flew through the night. South. I got ready to follow it.

"Wait," Nevery said. He grabbed my arm. "It's gone wrong."

The finding spell was supposed to point like a giant finger made of light. But this wasn't a beam of light, it was a blazing knife that sliced through the dark city, cutting a wide scorch line south, through the wizards' houses on one island, through the middle of Magisters Hall on the next island, boiling through the river water and then cutting through the Night Bridge. The spell kept going, blazing a path across a corner of the Sunrise and out of the city.

I saw a glow in the distance as the spell sped away. Then darkness.

For a moment, all was silent. Beside me, Nevery stared out at the city. Then came shouting, and lights blazing up in the sliced buildings. From the first floor of the academicos came the sound of doors slamming, and more shouting.

Nevery went to the door and flung it open. "*Lothfalas*," he muttered, and at the sound of the spell his locus magicalicus flared. He glanced at me over his shoulder. "Go, boy," he whispered, and swept-stepped away, his locus stone filling the stairway with light.

Never went down; I went up.

The stairway was wide and built of soft stone worn down in the middle of the treads from academicos students going up and down to their classrooms. I ran on feather-feet, hearing shouts and running feet from below. Only guards from the Dawn Palace were that noisy; Captain Kerrn must have them stationed nearby.

Up one floor, and I'd need to cut through to another stairway to get off the main level and into one of the towers. I came to a landing lit by a were-light lantern turned low. A door leading off it was locked. I snick-picked the lock and went through. Shelves of rolled-up papers—I was in the scroll room of the academicos library.

I was halfway across the dark-dim room, heading for the door on the other side, when somebody opened it and stepped in.

Plump, wearing a yellow robe, holding an egg-shaped locus magicalicus flaring with light. Brumbee.

I skidded to a stop and stared at him.

He stared back at me. "Oh, dear," he said. "Is that you, Conn?"

Drats!

I whirled and raced back the way I'd come, slamming the door closed and locking it, then standing on the dim stairway, listening. I expected to hear Brumbee shout for the guards, but he didn't.

Quick as sticks I skiffed away, up a narrow, round stairway that snaked up to the very top of one of the four towers on the four corners of the academicos building.

When I reached the roof, I eased the trapdoor closed and stood up, catching my breath. The sky was just turning gray with dawn over the Sunrise part of the city. Where I stood was a flat, square roof covered by lead tiles, with a low wall and clusters of stone spires taller than I was all along its edges.

A black bird perched at the top of each spire.

"Go away, you birds," I whispered. Captain Kerrn knew the magic's birds followed me around. She'd know exactly where to look for me if she saw them up there. I waved my arms at them, but the birds didn't move from their perches.

I edged into the shadows beside one of the spires and crouched down to wait. If I kept quiet, Kerrn and her guards might not find me. I peered around another spire and looked out over Wellmet.

There, the spell-line, a wide burnt-black slash that led from the workroom in the academicos, across the courtyard, and through the islands and the city like a fat line drawn on a map with black ink, headed straight south. The spell-line still smoked.

Across the roof from where I hid, the trapdoor creaked open.

I held my breath.

A pair of black birds spiraled down and landed on the spire I was hiding behind.

"I know you are here, thief," said a low voice.

Captain Kerrn. I pressed myself farther into the shadows.

I heard her climb out the trapdoor and the sliding *skff skff* of her footsteps on the roof.

I glanced quickly around. Nowhere else to hide. Unless . . .

Yes, at the very edge of the tower, between the spires and a five-story drop to the paved courtyard, was a narrow ledge.

Moving slowly, holding tight to the stone spires, I edged from behind my spire hiding place and out onto the ledge; it was just as wide as my foot.

Clinging to the spire, I looked down over my shoulder. The ground was very, very far away. I saw guards crossing the courtyard, and there was small, fat Brumbee in his yellow robes, and small Nevery with guards. None of them looked up.

Part of being a thief meant being good at climbing. I wasn't going to fall.

A black bird landed on the ledge beside me. I kicked at it with my foot and wobbled a little.

Awk, said the bird.

Drats, Kerrn was going to find me. I didn't want her chaining me up in a prison cell and giving me phlister; I *had* to go find my locus stone.

Over the Sunrise part of Wellmet the very edge of the sun peeked up, sending beams of golden light across the city. The beams looked like long arms, reaching out from the sun.

Carefully I turned around until the spire was

at my back. My heels were on the ledge, but my toes rested on nothing but air. I looked down. Way below, the wide courtyard was empty now, except for Nevery. The guards and Brumbee had gone in, probably searching for me. Nevery stood still, gripping his cane, staring up at me. Then he pulled something from his cloak pocket—his locus magicalicus. He held it up, his lips moving, saying a spell, I guessed. He pointed the stone at me, and a flash of white light darted from the stone and over me, then reflected back to Nevery. He turned and pointed the stone at the courtyard stones and said the rest of the spell. An image of me, dark like a shadow, sprang up next to Nevery. He said another word, and the shadow-me started running across the courtyard toward the tunnel entrance.

At the same moment, Brumbee and the guards burst from the academicos door. Seeing the shadow-me, they waved their arms and shouted, and a couple of the guards started across the courtyard.

I heard footsteps clatter across the lead-tiled roof,

then just along the ledge from me, Kerrn poked out her head. If she turned just a little bit, she would see me. I held my breath. The bird on the ledge beside me didn't move.

One of her guards shouted, and the shadow-me disappeared down the tunnel steps.

"*Flaet*," Kerrn said, a curse word in her own language, I guessed, and then she was gone, her footsteps pounding across the rooftiles and the trap-door slamming closed behind her.

Down in the courtyard, Nevery shoved his locus magicalicus into his cloak pocket and headed toward the corner of the building. He was going 'round the back.

Quick as quick I slid off the ledge so the guards wouldn't see me if they looked up, and cat-footed over to the trapdoor.

I skiffed through the shadowy hallways and stair-ways and classrooms of the academicos to a window on the ground floor, unlatched it, and climbed out, and there was Nevery.

We were at the back of the academicos, a narrow strip of deserted courtyard leading to the steep stone bank that ran all around the edge of the island.

"Brumbee saw you, boy," Nevery said.

I caught my breath. "I know."

"I've signaled Benet." Nevery's cloak swirled as he turned away and started toward the stone bank.

"Nevery, d'you know why the finding spell didn't work the way it was supposed to?" I asked, running to catch up.

He didn't answer. "Hurry, boy," he said. His cane went *tap tap* on the paving stones.

We came to the edge of the island. The stone bank where we stood was about Nevery's height above the rough, gray water. Below us, Benet waited in the rowboat, holding on to an iron ring that was set into the side of the wall.

Nevery nodded at the boat. "In you go."

I dropped down into the boat.

"Steady," Benet said. He looked up at Nevery,

standing above us on the wall. "Tonight? Dory-down dock?"

"Yes. Make haste." Nevery looked over his shoulder, back at the academicos.

"Nevery, aren't you coming?" I asked, getting to my feet. The boat sloshed, tipping me back onto my seat. Benet pushed us away from the wall and set his oars in the oarlocks.

Nevery didn't answer; he turned around and swept-stepped away, back toward the academicos.

What was he doing? He needed to come with us or he'd get into trouble. Brumbee had seen me. They'd know Nevery'd been with me. I stood up again.

"Get down," Benet growled. "He can deal with 'em." He pointed with his chin at the canvas tarp I'd hid under before, and took a stroke with his oars. We shot away from the island, headed downstream. I scrambled under the tarp and pulled it over my head. Hidden.

CHAPTER 9

Benet tied the boat to the last falling-down dock in the Twilight before the mudflats began. The air smelled of mud and dead fish, and of dirty drains. He put the oars together and lay them in the bottom of the boat. I started to climb out from under the tarp.

“Stay there,” Benet said. He checked his coat pocket, pulled his truncheon from under one of the boat seats, and climbed onto the dock. He glared down at me.

All right. I pulled the tarp back over my head and settled down in the bottom of the boat to wait. I didn’t want to be there. My feet kept twitching. I wanted to be off, following the finding spell. But Benet had told me to stay, so I would stay.

There was nothing in the boat to eat. The edge of the seat poked into my back. Just after midday the clouds drew in over the city and it started to rain. Not a misty rain, but a hard, straight rain like a curtain across the river. I was glad of my black sweater and apprentice’s robe. I huddled under the canvas tarp, staring at the rain-flattened, gray surface of the river and the mudflats, getting wetter and hungrier. After a while I fell asleep.

When I woke up it was dark and not raining. Benet had tossed a couple of sacks into the boat—*whump*—and climbed in after them. “You all right?”

he asked. His coat had big wet patches on it.

"Yes," I said, pushing the tarp off me. "You?"

"Wet," he said. "You hungry?" he asked.

I grinned at him. "I'm never hungry, Benet."

He gave half a laugh, then put the oars in the oarlocks and untied the rope. He reached into his pocket, pulled out a package wrapped in damp, brown paper, and handed it to me.

As he rowed us out onto the darkening river, I opened the package. Mmmm. A sandwich made of bread and bacon and butter. "Want some?" I asked.

"No," Benet grunted. He looked over his shoulder and took a stroke with an oar to straighten out the boat.

I ate the bread and bacon. "What's going on?" I asked.

"That captain's got her guards out looking for you," he said. "Twilight's crawling with 'em."

"Is Nevery all right?"

"Dunno," Benet said.

While waiting for Benet I'd had plenty of time

to think about what might happen. Nevery'd set it up so we'd done the pyrotechnics in an unused workroom. So even though Brumbee had seen me and he'd told Kerrn that he'd seen me, Kerrn might suspect Nevery was helping me, but she wouldn't *know*. I hoped Nevery was staying quiet. He didn't need to get into trouble over this.

Full night had fallen when Benet rowed us to a shadowy dock on the Sunrise side of the river. He didn't tie up the boat, just held to the side of the dock, ready to push us off if somebody came along. I knew better than to ask what we were doing.

The night grew quiet, the only sound the river wavelets lapping against the side of the boat, and the seat creaking when Benet shifted himself. A fog rose up off the river, surrounding us. I stared at the bank, waiting.

There—a flash of white-bright light cutting through the fog, then another one. "That's the lothfalas," I whispered to Benet; as I pointed, the light flashed again.

"Come on," Benet said. He grabbed the sacks and climbed out of the boat onto the dock, and I followed him. When we reached the street, which was lined by closed-up, dark shops, Nevery was waiting for us, holding a knapsack.

"Ah, good," he said quietly. "Come along." Off he went, *step step tap* along the cobbled street, me and Benet right behind. He led us along the misty, puddled street until we came to the park where Sunrise people came on sunny days to ride their horses and walk on the paths and get their pockets picked. We crunched along one of the gravel paths until we came to an iron-bar fence with a gate in it.

"*Lothfalas*," Nevery whispered. In his hand, his locus magicalicus flared brightly; he whispered another word and it dimmed until it shed a faint circle of light around us. Fog swirled at its edge.

Nevery's eyes were bright. He pointed at the gate. "Pick the lock."

Right. I reached into the collar of my shirt and

pulled out my lockpick wires, then crouched in front of the gate. A simple double-down plunger. One-two and a snick-flick, and I had it open.

"I don't know, boy," Nevery said.

I stood and faced him. He didn't know what?

"I don't know why the finding spell effected the way it did," Nevery said, answering the question I'd asked hours ago. Nevery pulled at the end of his beard, his eyes keen-gleaming down at me. "It is clear that you have some kind of connection to the magic of this city; I suspect that anytime you do a spell, it may have unintended consequences."

Unintended consequences. Trouble, that meant. I'd have to be careful, then, every time I did magic. Once I got back to Wellmet with my locus magicalicus. "Nevery, I need to go," I said. I could feel the spell-line not far away, leading south. It pulled at me like a string.

"Yes, all right, my lad," Nevery said. "Be careful."

"Nevery, I'm always careful," I said.

Benet snorted. He'd taken the knapsack from

Nevery and packed it with the stuff from his sacks; he handed it to me. A blanket was rolled up and strapped to it, too.

"Here," Nevery said. He had my coat, the one with the shabby velvet collar. I took off my apprentice robe, handed it to Nevery, and put on the coat instead. Benet handed me a scarf, one he'd knitted. It was long and nettle-green and had a keyhole shape knitted into each end and a long fringe, and he'd stitched my name on it in runes. The edges were thick enough to hide lockpick wires in, I reckoned.

"It's perfect," I said, stroking the soft wool.

Benet nodded.

"Look, boy," Nevery said. "Stay on the spell-line and it will pull you straight to your locus magicalicus. It cannot be too far away from Wellmet; you'll only be gone for a few days. Send a bird when you've returned and Benet will fetch you, and we'll decide what to do next about that cursed Arhionvar."

I nodded. He was right. I needed to hurry.

Rowan Forestal

I simply do not understand how someone as clever as Conn can be so continually stupid. He's been trying to hide from Captain Kerrn and the guards, yet he has called the worst kind of attention to himself. The Dawn Palace has been in an uproar as the guards have searched the city and come in to report. The magisters sent Nimble to complain about the damage done by Conn's latest pyrotechnic spell, and Magister Nevery stormed in and shouted at my mother behind the closed door of her office until she summoned guards and had him taken away.

Then there was the hearing this morning to determine Conn's punishment for casting a pyrotechnic spell. I don't understand why they call it a *hearing* when no one listened and Conn wasn't there to speak for himself.

I detest the hearing room; it is full of echoes and dark corners. The magisters, dressed in their colorful robes, were sitting at a long table; my mother, wrapped in furs yet still cold as stone, sat at the middle of the table, and I stood

just behind her. Magister Nevery sat to the side on a hard bench, with Captain Kerrn standing behind him.

Magister Nimble began. I have never liked Nimble, and now I hate him. He has a precise voice with a whiny edge, and in this horrid voice he went on about Conn's so-called crimes, how he practiced illegal pyrotechnics and constituted a threat to the safety of the city and all who reside here. Then he ranted about Conn's latest pyrotechnic spell. No one was injured or killed, thank goodness, but several buildings have been damaged and the Night Bridge was sliced in two.

Then Magister Nevery, glaring fiercely, got up from his bench and reminded them all that the dread magic Arhionvar, which had preyed upon Desh, was coming after Wellmet next—had they forgotten that?

The magisters shouted him down—they will not believe, as Conn believes, that the city's magic is a living being, and so they cannot conceive of Arhionvar as a

threat. They said Magister Nevery was exaggerating the danger posed by Arhionvar in order to consolidate his own power. They don't believe that Arhionvar was behind either Jaggus's or Underlord Crowe's attacks on Wellmet; they think they both acted alone, for human reasons, not magical ones. Nimble also accused Nevery of bringing up Arhionvar in order to deflect criticism of his criminal apprentice. Then he accused Nevery of being involved in Conn's latest pyrotechnic disaster.

Nimble is quite right about that, of course.

But Magister Nevery refused to speak further on that subject.

Then Magister Nimble and the other magisters pretended to consult, and Nimble whispered their verdict against Conn into my mother's ear. I protested, but she told me very coldly and stiffly to be silent. Then she pronounced the verdict.

I will never forgive her. Never.

In the morning I woke up under a bush with my stomach growling and frost covering my blanket. The sky was gray, tinged with pink off to the east, and Wellmet was a couple of hours back along the muddy path. The air felt thin, empty of magic.

If I followed the path toward

the south it'd cross the spell-line, I figured, and then I'd follow that, instead, until I found my locus magicalicus. It'd only take a day or two, as Nevery'd said.

I crawled out from under the bush, rolled up the blanket, strapped it to the pack, and put the pack-straps over my shoulder and set off. I'd walk for a bit, and then stop to eat some breakfast. I kept Benet's scarf wrapped warmly around my neck.

I'd seen maps—Rowan had shown them to me. Wellmet was far away from most of the other Peninsular Duchies, the other cities of the land. Right outside Wellmet to the north were fields and pastures; here, to the south, were forests. I'd been out of the city before, when I'd gone to Desh to meet Arhionvar. That muddy road had led through gray, dead forest.

The forest here felt more alive. Winter had begun, and in the morning sunshine the air stayed cold, but the frost sparkled like thousands of jewels on the ground and bare tree branches. Ahead of me I felt the spell-line; if I closed my eyes, it was a silver thread in the darkness, leading from the warm glow that was the magic of Wellmet off into a darker distance.

I walked faster to catch up to it.

At midmorning I stopped to eat. Next to the path was a flat gray rock the size of a door. I climbed up and opened the knapsack to see what Benet had packed for me. Brown-paper-wrapped packages of food, a small canteen full of water, a toothbrush wrapped up in a washcloth, and a flat wooden box with a sheaf of thin paper and three pencils in it. For writing letters.

And a small book that Nevery must've put in, covered with cracked brown leather, a little larger than my hand. *An Advanced Spell Practicum*, it was called. I opened it. The pages were yellow, with black mold spots on them. On the first page was a list of chapters, each one for a different kind of spell.

Transformative
Simulative
Refractoratory

Luminative

Directive

I flipped through the pages to "Simulative." There it was, the remirrimer, the spell Nevery had used to make the shadow-me to distract the guards at the academicos.

I went back to the beginning of the book, and reading the introduction, I ate a biscuit and bacon and some dried apple. When I was done I sat for a minute with my eyes closed. The spell-line was very close. I felt it humming, calling to me.

I packed everything back into the knapsack, hopped off the rock, and headed down the path. Overhead, the sky was bright blue and cloudless. Even though the pack was heavy, and even though the thought of Arhionvar lurked in the back of my head, I felt lighter than a spark given off by a pyrotechnic spell. With a locus stone, I'd be a wizard again, and able to talk to the magic and help protect it, and the duchess and Captain Kerrn and the magisters would see that I belonged in Wellmet and shouldn't be exiled. I'd get to live in the rebuilt Heartsease with Nevery and Benet, where I belonged.

Up ahead, the path curved 'round the base of a low hill covered with bare-branched trees. I followed the path, the tingling from the spell-line getting stronger. Then I saw it.

The finding spell had burned a wide line over the hill, cutting trees in half, leaving branches hanging in tangles. The line rolled down off the hill and, ahead, went across the path. There, three black birds, like black lumps, perched in a tree, watching.

The knapsack bumping on my back, I ran along the path until I reached the spell-line. The black birds flew up squawking. I slung my pack on the ground and crouched down to look.

The spell-line was about as wide as my two arms spread apart, and it'd scorched the ground black like burnt toast. I looked along where it led. Into the forest, away from the path, burning through brown-leafed bushes and trees and snaky vines hanging down. Wide enough for me to walk along.

Testing, I rested my hand on the spell-line.

It was like putting my hand into the river after a heavy rainfall. The line pulled at me and shot tingles of excitement up my arm and into my head. I tugged out my hand and the spell dripped off of it like silver water, shining in the sunlight. I blinked the brights from my eyes and got to my feet.

I looked up into the sparkling blue sky, then into the forest where the spell-line led. "All right, locus stone," I said. "I'm coming."

I picked up my knapsack and got ready to step onto the spell-line.

Then, from behind me, around the low hill, came the jingle-clop sound of horses and voices talking.

Someone was coming.

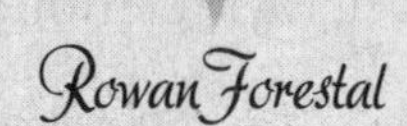

Rowan Forestal

Very early this morning I went to the guardroom to see Captain Kerrn.

You must be very happy, I said to her. You've been waiting to get rid of Conn. You've always hated him.

Captain Kerrn looked troubled and said, I do not hate him. Not at all. But he is a danger to the city.

I do not understand this. Captain Kerrn was with us in Desh, she went to the sorcerer-king's fortress, and she knows about Conn's fight with the dread magic. She must know that we need Conn here in Wellmet to help fight against Arhionvar. Swords alone cannot defend us against magic, and the magisters are no help—Captain Kerrn knows that very well.

She had no answer for this.

My mother will not listen, either; she has been miserably ill for the past few days. She is convinced that Conn is dangerous.

Perhaps he is. He has certainly caused enough trouble to be thought dangerous. But he's faced danger, too, to protect Wellmet. We will need him in the city, when Arhionvar arrives. If we do not defend ourselves against Arhionvar, the dread magic will destroy our magic and, with it, our city.

I have decided what I must do.

Better to hide than meet somebody I didn't want to see. I ducked behind a clump of bushes and a fallen log. One of the black birds spiraled down and perched on a tree branch right over my head.

"Go away," I whispered.

Awk, it said.

The sound of horses

came closer, the clop-clop of hooves on the path and the jingle of bridles. I kept still.

A deep voice said something. Then it said, "I do not know, my lady."

I knew that voice. Drats. And I knew who it was talking to.

I stood up and stepped out from behind the bush. At the same moment, the bird hopped off its branch and flapped in a circle just over my head, squawking.

Rowan reined in her horse and looked down at me from the saddle. She wore a sword in a scabbard on a belt around her waist and had two other horses tethered to her saddle. "Hello, Connwaer," she said. She didn't give me her usual smile. "I thought we'd find you along here somewhere." Her horse shook its head, and she patted its neck.

Argent brought his horse up beside Rowan's. "You don't jump out at horses like that, *boy*," he said, looking down his long nose at me and curling his lip. He looked like a horse himself, doing that.

"Hello, Ro," I said. I glanced at the other two horses. One of them had a saddle on it, and the other was loaded with sacks and leather bags. So they were going on a journey.

Rowan pointed at the spell-line. "Is that what I think it is?" she asked.

"Probably," I said.

"Your finding spell?" she asked. "The one you were talking about with Magister Nevery?"

I nodded.

She climbed down out of the saddle and, holding her horse's reins, stepped up to the spell-line. "It just looks like a burnt path."

"There's magic here, too. It's calling me." I pointed down the burnt trail. "The spell is leading to my locus magicalicus, Ro. That's where I'm going."

"All right." She glanced aside at Argent. "We're coming with you."

I stood in the middle of the spell-line and felt it pulling at me like a river current, bright and shining and icy cold. It was the call of my locus magicalicus, wanting me to come and fetch it. For its call to be this strong, my locus stone had to be close. I took another step along the spell-line.

Night was coming on. But we could walk at night, couldn't we? I needed to get my stone and get back to Wellmet.

Behind me, Rowan said something, but I didn't hear her. All I could hear was the call in my head.

I felt a rough hand on my shoulder, and then Argent spun me around and grabbed my arm. "Lady Rowan said we must stop," he said.

I squirmed out of his grip. "Just a little farther," I said, and headed down the trail again. They could stop for dinner and then catch up.

"It's the spell-trail, Argent!" Rowan called from behind me. "Pull him off the spell or he'll never stop!"

Again the strong hand on my arm, and Argent jerked me off the spell-line and into a prickly bush. It felt like being pulled from a pot of honey; the spell-line held me, and then I popped out of it. The magic dripped and sparked off of me.

"Lady Rowan told you to stop," Argent said to me with a disgusted shake of his head, then turned and walked back to Rowan.

Off to the west, behind the trees, the sun was going down. A cold mist floated low among the trees.

Right. We needed to stop.

I made my way back to Rowan and Argent and the horses. They'd stopped at a clearing covered with damp leaves and wiry yellow grass. A good place to camp for the night. Three black birds perched in a tree at the clearing's edge. Rowan was tying the horses' reins to rope strung between two trees, and Argent was unloading the packs.

"Go find some firewood," he said, without looking at me.

Right, firewood. I headed back into the forest, picking up twigs, stomping on dead branches to break them into pieces.

Somehow I found myself at the edge of the trail again.

Darkness had crept in among the trees; the spell-line rolled out into the night like a wide, black ribbon.

I dropped my armful of wood. I closed my eyes. The spell-line sang in my head. I'd go just a little farther. Rowan and Argent could catch up to me in the morning.

As I stepped into the spell, the night lit up around me. The spell-line glowed like a bright tunnel through the night-dark forest; the call of my locus magicalicus thrummed through my bones and tingled in my fingers.

I'm coming, I told it.

A moment later I felt a hand on my arm and found myself standing in a bush beside the spell-line with magic dripping off me. I blinked the spell-brights out of my eyes. "Idiot," Argent said, panting. "If the trail is pulling at you, then you have to stay off it when we stop for the night." He scowled down at me. "And we *are* stopping for the night."

We made camp and had dinner and tea, and I read in The Advanced Spell Practicum about transformative spells while Rowan did swordcraft drills with Argent, and then we rolled out our blankets to sleep. The fire died down to glowing red embers. The evening mist had faded away, and the night was cool and clear.

I lay in my blanket and looked up at the sky, full of stars like diamonds against black velvet. The sky was never this dark in Wellmet. Off to my left, the spell-line sang to me.

I sat up and pushed my blanket off me.

"Stay off the trail, Connwaer," Rowan said from the darkness, her voice sleepy.

Right. She was right.

The night had gotten colder. I huddled my blanket around me and edged up to the fire, where I threw on another pile of sticks. The embers flared. Beside the firepit, Argent was a long, dark lump with a tousle of blond hair, dead asleep.

Not far away, Rowan sat up from her blankets, rubbing her eyes. "Can't sleep?" she asked quietly.

I shook my head. "The spell is singing to me."

She yawned. Then, clutching her blankets around her, she came and sat beside me.

We were quiet for a while. In the forest, the leaves rustled, and I heard the scurryings of little animals in the underbrush.

"What is it like?" Rowan asked softly. She pointed behind us, at the spell-line.

Hard to explain. "It's very strong," I said.

She gave me her sideways slant-look. "Clearly. Does that mean we'll find your locus stone soon?"

"I hope so," I said, and held my hands up to the fire to warm them.

She moved a little closer, to lean against my shoulder. "I hope so, too."

We sat staring into the fire.

"Conn, there's something else I have to tell you about," Rowan said at last.

I looked over at her.

Rowan used to have short hair, but it had grown out, and she wore it in a stubby horse tail tied at the back of her neck. Some of the hair was still short, though, and got out of the tail to hang down in her face. She pulled on one of the hair ends and nibbled on it.

"Are you listening?" she said.

I nodded.

She sighed. "The magisters and my mother and her council know that you were responsible for the finding spell."

Brumbee had seen me at the academicos after the spell. Of course they knew.

"You're in trouble for it," she said.

Well, that was no surprise. I was always in trouble with the magisters, and with the duchess. "How much trouble?"

Rowan blew out a breath. "A lot. The magisters and my mother have sentenced you to death if you return to Wellmet."

Oh. That would make things complicated when I went back to the city. I thought about it a bit more. "Ro, d'you know if your mother knows you came after me?"

"What do you think, Connwaer?"

I thought the duchess didn't know. That might make things complicated, too.

"I came after you so that when you go back to

Wellmet you'll be with me," Rowan said. "You'll be under my protection. I think that will make things all right."

Maybe it would.

We sat for a bit longer. Then Rowan said she had to sleep, so she woke Argent, tied one end of a rope around his ankle and tied the other end to mine. She understood how the spell-line worked; she knew that if I stepped onto it I wouldn't stop until I reached my locus stone.

Argent wasn't happy about being woken up in the middle of the night. He snorted around like a big yellow horse, then lay down again with his rope-tied ankle sticking out the end of his blankets.

"I'm a light sleeper," he said. He pointed at the rope. "You'd better not wake me up."

I didn't. But I didn't sleep, either. Rowan was worried about the death sentence, and she was right to be. But when I found my locus stone I would go back to Wellmet, no matter what. I would never abandon the magic. Never.

CHAPTER 13

The next day, Rowan said I'd have to ride a horse. So I wouldn't get too tired from walking, she said.

And she wanted to get me off the spell-line, I figured. Going along the trail might be easier if I was high up on the back of a horse instead of right in the pulling river of the spell.

Rowan handed me the horse's reins and told me to get acquainted with it while she finished packing a saddlebag.

My horse was a plain mud-brown color with a mud-brown mane and a splash of white across its nose, like paint. What I knew about horses was that you stayed away from the back end so you didn't get kicked. If you were holding the reins you tried to stay away from the front end so you didn't get bit. The mud-brown horse shook its head, making its bridle jingle. I backed away, and it clopped forward, following me.

"Stop it, horse," I said.

"Mount up," Argent said, swinging onto his tall black horse. I put my foot in the stirrup the way Rowan had shown me, and climbed up into Mud-brown's saddle. Then we set off along the trail.

The blackened spell-line was a long way down

from where I sat, sloshing around in the saddle, gripping the horse's mane and the reins so I wouldn't fall off.

Argent rode just behind me. "Sit up straight, *boy*," he said.

I slouched a bit.

"Keep your elbows in," he said.

Shut up, stupid Argent.

"You ride like a sack of potatoes," Argent said.

I glared at him over my shoulder.

"With wings." He flapped his elbows.

Right, elbows in.

We rode all the morning, stopping for lunch and to rest the horses. When I got down from Mud-brown's saddle my legs felt stiff, but not too bad. We started off again after lunch.

After a little while, Mud-brown stopped in the middle of the trail. Rowan and Argent were ahead, and they kept going.

"Go, horse," I said.

The horse bent its head and snatched at a clump

of brown grass at the side of the burnt trail.

"Rowan!" I called. "This horse is done walking!"

"Just give her a little kick with your heels!" Rowan shouted back.

"Go," I said again, and gave it a little kick.

Mud-brown shook its head but didn't go.

I climbed down out of the saddle. As soon as my feet touched the burnt-black ground, the spell swirled up over my ankles and started pulling at me. I brought the reins over the horse's head, then pulled on them to get it to move. It locked its knees and leaned backward.

I pulled harder, the spell pulling at me. "Come *on*, horse."

It took a quick step forward and pushed me with its nose. I stumbled back, then fell onto the spell-line. The magic washed over me like a shining wave.

I got to my feet. Never mind the stupid horse. It could catch up by itself. Ahead, Rowan and Argent had ridden on. I walked fast.

As I walked past them, Rowan looked down at

me from her horse's saddle. "Conn?" She glanced over her shoulder. "You left your horse!"

That horse was too slow.

Rowan said something to Argent, and he turned his horse and headed back along the spell-line. I kept going.

Rowan let me walk for the rest of the day, leading them along the trail. As the sky darkened, they stopped.

Before Argent could pull me out of the spell, I started running, but his legs were longer than mine. He caught me and jerked me off the path.

The moment my feet touched the ground beside the spell-line, I felt the tiredness of a night without sleep and a day of walking and riding. I stumbled, and Argent grabbed my arm to keep me on my feet.

"Idiot," Argent said.

We traveled like that for four more days through the forest followed by the black birds. My locus magicalicus kept calling me, but it didn't get any stronger. We should've reached it by now. Time was running out—I had to get back to Wellmet!

Rowan was worried about being away from the city for so long. "If you rode," she said, "We could go faster."

True. But I didn't like that horse. So I walked, and walked, and walked.

One evening, after studying the spell-book and memorizing more of the spell-language, I wrote a letter with pencil on one of the papers Nevery'd put into my knapsack.

Dear Nevery,

I haven't found my locus magicalicus yet. It must be farther away than we thought. This is taking too long. Have you seen any sign of Arhionvar yet? Are you working on the pyrotechnic defenses? I will come back as soon as I can.

Rowan's here, too. She brought horses, but they don't work very well.

Rowan told me about the death sentence on me. I'll be careful when I get back. Did you get in trouble because of the finding spell?

Hello to Benet. Thank you for the book. I have been learning the spellwords.

—Conn

I rolled up the paper and tied it with a bit of thread, then tied that onto one of the black bird's legs. It'd fly straight back to Wellmet, to Nevery.

"D'you want to send a letter to your mother?" I asked Rowan.

"No," she said.

"The bird can carry a letter to Nevery," I said, "and he'll send it on."

Rowan folded her arms. "I don't want to write to her."

"She'll worry if you don't," I said.

"Let her worry," Rowan said, and walked away.

I gave the bird a few biscuit crumbs and sent it flapping toward Wellmet.

Nevery's answer came the next day.

I know about the death sentence, boy, and it is a problem, I agree. We must be circumspect.

The aftermath from the finding spell is nothing I cannot manage. Captain Kerrn may suspect all she likes, but she can prove nothing, nor can the duchess or the other magisters, who are fools.

I am more concerned at the moment with Arhionvar. You are right to worry about being gone from the city for so long. The dread magic could arrive at any time.

Make all haste.

—N.

Nevery was safe, then. That was good.

I wasn't sure what *circumspect* meant. Very, very careful, I figured, or I'd end up swinging from Wellmet's gallows tree.

CHAPTER 14

Rowan had a map. She kept it folded inside a square of oiled leather so it'd be dry in case of rain.

Nearby, the burnt-black spell-line cut across a wide trade road, which led through a clearing edged by tall, straight pine trees. Rowan pulled out the map to have a look at where we were. "I think we're about here," she said. She'd put the map on the pine-needly ground and squatted down, pointing. Her gloved finger rested on a line leading to a dot with the word *Torrent* next to it. A city.

"Have we traveled that far south already?" Argent asked, kneeling next to her.

"I think so." She shot me a sideways glance. "We've been making very good time, for some reason."

Because they had to drag me off the trail every night, she meant, and catch up to me in the morning because I'd set off, munching on a biscuit, as soon as the sun came up.

"I didn't think we'd be gone this long," Rowan said. "We didn't pack enough supplies, so we'll have to get more." She stood and, after squinting down at the map once more, folded it into its leather envelope. "We'll follow this road into the city, stock up, and come back to the spell-path."

Leave the spell-line, did she say?

Rowan looked at me and raised her eyebrows. "All right?"

She was right. We needed supplies; we were out of bacon. But leaving the spell-line . . .

"All right," I said slowly.

We mounted up, me on Mud-brown, and pointed the horses down the rutted road toward the city of Torrent. As we clip-clopped away, the spell-line hummed and tugged at me as if it was the line and I was the fish, caught.

I pulled back on the reins, and the horse plodded to a stop. *Call, call, call,* went the spell. I climbed down off of Mud-brown's back.

Rowan turned her horse and brought it to stand next to me. "Can't do it?" she asked.

I shook my head and handed her Mud-brown's reins. "I could wait for you," I said, backing up a step toward the spell-line.

Rowan nibbled her lip. "No, I don't think you can." She stood up in her stirrups and called over her shoulder. "Argent!"

Argent rode back to us. "Yes, Lady Rowan?"

Rowan pointed at me. "Conn can't come along. You'll have to stay here with him."

"Lady Rowan!" Argent protested.

She gave me her sideways smile. "I suspect that as soon as we're gone he'll jump back into the spell, and we'll spend the next four days trying to catch up to him."

She was probably right.

"That would be four days without him," Argent muttered. "We should just let him do it, if he wants to. Or tie him to a tree until we return."

Rowan gave him her most duchess's-daughterly smile. "Oh, I don't think we'll do that. You'll stay with Conn. I'll be back as soon as I can."

Argent tried to tell her she wouldn't be safe going to a city alone, but since she had her sword and was better at swordcraft than he was, he lost that part of the argument. I left them to it, heading back toward the spell-line.

Before I reached it, Argent caught up to me, riding his tall black horse and leading Mud-brown by the reins. Without speaking we went back to the place where the spell-line cut across the road, a wide clearing in the middle of straight, dark pine trees. We took the saddles off our horses, tied their reins to a tree branch, and I put my knapsack and scab-barded sword on the ground.

Argent took out his own sword and started doing practice lunges in the clear area beside the road. I wanted to go over to the humming spell-line, but he stayed between me and it. I went and sat down against a pine tree and watched him parrying an invisible blade and skewering an invisible opponent that I bet looked a lot like me.

After a while he got out of breath. He fetched my sword, then came to where I was sitting and glared down at me. "Come and spar," he said, tossing my sword onto the ground beside me.

With him? With real swords? Not likely. He'd beaten the fluff out of me before, trying to teach me swordcraft.

"Coward," he said. He lifted his sword and pointed at me, sighting down the blade. "You are not fit company for Lady Rowan. You're nothing but a mannerless gutterboy."

"I know what I am," I said.

"Oh, of course." Argent snorted and lowered the blade. "You're a *wizard*."

Right. I nodded.

"You are a wizard's servant boy. If you were a wizard yourself, you would have a locus magicalicus to do magic." He curled his lip. "Go ahead, *wizard*, do some magic."

I got to my feet. Only one way this was going to go, but I didn't want to fight with him. I pointed at the spell-line. That was magic I'd done.

Argent narrowed his eyes. He turned away, walked over to a saddlebag, and took something out, which he held behind him. Then he came back to where I was standing. Slowly he brought up his sword, resting the tip just below my throat. I backed up until I was pressed up against the tree.

"My other idea was a better one," Argent said.

Before I could jerk away, he dropped his sword,

grabbed me, and spun me around, then pressed my face into the rough bark of the tree with a hand on the back of my head. I squirmed a bit to get away, and he pushed harder, mashing my nose. "Stop it," he said. Was he going to slice me open with his sword? I kicked backward with my heels, and he put his leg across my legs to hold them against the tree. He caught one of my hands and, leaning against me to keep me still, tied an end of rope around my wrist. Then he flipped me around, and tied my arms behind the tree.

I blinked bits of pine bark out of my eyes and caught my breath.

"Little squirmer," Argent said, backing away from the tree and dusting off his hands. "Like putting a worm on a fishhook."

I glared at him.

"Wizard your way out of that, *boy*," he said. He went across the clearing and saddled his horse, then came back and fetched his sword and kicked my sword farther from the tree so I couldn't reach it.

Then he swung up into the saddle.

"I am going to join Lady Rowan," he said. "And you"—he pointed at me—"will be here when we return." He kicked his horse into a high-stepping trot down the rutted road.

As he rode away, I heard him laughing.

Am beginning to think I made a mistake allowing boy to leave city. Magic is behaving oddly. Spells are working erratically or not at all. Magisters a quivering mess. People of city nervous. Duchess unresponsive. Have visited Dusk House pit; the magic seems to be focused there. Why? Gathering its strength? In hiding? Can Arhionvar be closer than we realized? I do not quite understand this conflict between magics. The boy has proven well enough that the magics are beings that live—if "live" is truly what they do—in our human cities, but I have not carefully considered what this might mean, and why a living magic such as Arhionvar would seek to kill another city's magic.

I wonder, too, where the magics came from,

what they truly are. Must look into historical grimoires, see if I can find further information. The more we know, the more likely we are to find some way to defeat Arhionvar.

When Argent had tied me to the tree, he'd left a length of rope between my wrists so my arms weren't pulled back too badly. I edged down the trunk until I was sitting on the soft, pine-needly ground.

Across the clearing, Mud-brown was still tied by the reins to a tree branch. The horse stood quietly, ignoring me. In a tree over the horse's head sat the three black birds.

"Come down and peck at these ropes, birds," I called. At the sound of my voice, Mud-brown twitched an ear. A bird sailed down from its branch and landed on the grass beside my leg, then hopped up to my knee.

Awk, said the bird. It cocked its head and looked at me with its yellow eye.

"The ropes," I said.

Awk-awk-awk, it said. Was it laughing at me?

It fluffled its feathers, then hopped off my knee and flapped back to its branch. The other two birds moved over to give it room. They sat there like feathery black lumps, watching me.

Bits of pine needles and bark were stuck in my coat and prickled against my back. I had a lockpick sewn into my shirt sleeve, but that wasn't going to help with knots. I pulled at the ropes for a bit with no luck getting them loose.

Drats. I'd just have to wait until Rowan came back.

I leaned my head against the bumpy bark of the tree, closed my eyes, and listened to the singing of the spell-line. After a while, I fell asleep.

I woke up hearing the cackle-crackle of the birds across from my tree. They muttered to each other and hunched into their wings, looking at the sky.

The sun shone orangey-gold through the trees. Late afternoon. Rowan would be back soon, wouldn't she? My arms were getting stiff.

The birds' chattering grew louder. The horse lifted its head and snorted. In the distance I heard a deep rumble-hum, and then a grating shriek racing up the spell-line toward me; I was halfway to my feet when it slammed into me and echoed around in my skull, making my teeth hurt. I slid back to the ground. A swift black shadow passed over the clearing.

Quick I shook the shriek out of my head and looked up to see what had made the shadow.

Nothing, just late-afternoon sky.

A cloud?

No. No cloud moved that fast.

I pressed my back against the pine tree. Across the clearing, the horse snorted again and lifted its head, looking around with wide eyes. The birds had disappeared. Everything was silent and still.

From the direction of the road came the sound of clopping hooves; after a moment, Rowan rode into the clearing, looking around. Seeing me tied to the tree, she shook her head. She got down from her horse and tied it next to Mud-brown, then headed over toward me and my tree. "Argent told me what he did," she said, taking off her gloves. "He thought it was funny. I sent him on to Torrent to get supplies. I suppose I should have expected it."

Never mind stupid Argent. "Did you see it?" I asked, staring up at the sky.

Rowan frowned. "No. See what?" She pulled her sword from its sheath, to cut the ropes, I guessed.

The spell-line hum-shrieked again, making me squeeze my eyes shut and hunch my head into my shoulders.

When I opened my eyes, something huge and winged, blazing with flames and heat, hurtled across the sky. Then it turned.

Down it swooped. Coming for me.

CHAPTER 16

It roared down over the forest, snapping off the tops of the pine trees as it flew, banking on huge golden wings.

With a crash that shook the ground, it landed in the middle of the road. Its four taloned feet gouged deep ruts into the dirt.

I knew what it was. Nevery'd told me they were extinct, but I'd seen pictures.

Dragon.

It was as if the sun had fallen down from the sky. The spell-line keened a high song. The dragon was as big as a house, with red-gold, liquid-looking scales covering its broad back and muscled legs and tail, smoothing out over its chest and belly. Its head was mostly muzzle and long teeth; it had horns and a spiked crest that ran in a double row down its back to the end of its tail, which ended in a bristle of spikes.

It folded its golden wings and turned its head, glaring around the clearing with flame-bright eyes.

Across from me, Mud-brown the horse was jerking at its tether and making a high whinnying sound, almost like screaming; so was Rowan's gray horse. The dragon cocked its head to look closer, and Mud-brown shrieked and tore loose its reins, then galloped off into the woods followed by Rowan's horse, its tail flying like a flag.

The dragon let them go.

"Conn, is that a dragon?" Rowan whispered. She stood ten paces away from me, gripping her sword, her face white, her eyes wide.

Trying to move slowly, I got to my feet. If the dragon wanted to eat me, I couldn't do anything about it, not with my arms tied behind the tree. Not with them free, either, even with my sword in my hand.

As soon as I moved, the dragon's big head swiveled around and it stared at me, lowering its head, moving closer. I stared back. Its eyes were the deep red-gold of embers in a banked fire. It shifted to the side, its scaled tail sliding over the ground, and raised one of its taloned feet, then brought it toward me. The talon was a curved knife.

Closing my eyes, I pressed myself against the tree, then felt the heat of the talon getting closer.

"No!" Rowan shouted.

My eyes popped open again.

Rowan leaped between me and the dragon, her sword drawn. Her hair had come loose and floated around her head like long, flickering flames. With a quick, silver flash, her sword leaped out and hacked at the dragon's talon. The dragon loomed over her; its claw flinched back. She jumped back, closer to me, and raised her sword again.

"Leave him!" she shouted.

The dragon shifted, then its claw came swooping down to brush her out of the way. Rowan leaped aside, her sword slashing. The blade cut through the dragon's scales, but they healed up again, like water flowing over the wound. She whirled and slashed again. The claw drew back; Rowan watched it, breathing hard, her sword ready. The dragon shifted; I saw it bringing its tail 'round.

"Ro—*watch out*!" I shouted. Too late.

The dragon's tail slithered from behind, knocking Rowan to the ground, then pinning her there, lying across her chest like a heavy log. Her sword lay a pace away from her hand.

She stretched her arm, reaching for the sword. "Conn," she gasped. "Stay still. Don't draw its attention to you."

But the dragon swung its head back to me and raised its claw. It brought the talon forward again. My heart pounded so hard, it was making my whole body shake. The talon went past my face and 'round behind me. A quick slice and it'd cut the ropes tying my hands. I fell forward on my knees onto the pine-needly ground.

I looked up, and the dragon was standing over me, its front legs like two pillars to either side. Before I could scramble away, it lifted a claw and knocked me onto my back, then lowered the claw. One of its talons gouged into the ground next to my neck; the other went through the shoulder of my coat and sweater. I squirmed to try and get away, and the dragon leaned forward, pressing me into the ground.

"All right," I gasped. "I'll keep still."

With its other taloned foot it poked at me, first at my feet, then my shoulder, pushing aside my coat and pulling down the neck of my sweater with a sharp talon-tip.

"Conn, what does it want?" Rowan asked from where she lay under the tail.

It was looking for something. Oh. I was a wizard; it wanted to see my locus magicalicus. "I don't have one," I said softly.

At the sound of my voice, the dragon's head reared back. The talons closed around me, snatching me up, gouging chunks of dirt from the ground. The dragon's other foot grabbed my knapsack. With a thunder-clap of wings, the dragon leaped into the air.

"Conn!" Rowan screamed.

I felt the lurch of the ground pulling at me, and a wild rushing of wind. The dragon beat its wings again, an echoing *whumph*; the land let me go and we whirled upward.

Away we flew, straight toward the dazzling sun.

The dragon circled over the pine forest. I felt when it tracked onto the spell-line leading straight south;

we shot away, faster than falling, the finding spell humming in my bones.

One of the dragon's talons was still stuck through the shoulder of my coat. Just over my face was its foot, like the palm of a giant hand, but covered with smooth scales. I caught my breath and reached up and rested my hand against it. The scales were warm. My hand trembled against them. The dragon's talons went around under my back, holding me tight, the way a bird's foot holds on to a branch. It wasn't going to let me fall. I twisted around to have a look at where we were going.

To the west, at the edge where the land met the sky, the sun was falling down behind low hills. The sky on the other side was turning deep velvet blue, pricked with stars. Below, the land was darkening. I saw a greeny-black blanket of pine forest, then a lighter brown ribbon—a river. Beside it was a wide, soot-smudged clump of houses and streets and towers glinting in the setting sun, the city of Torrent. And straight below us, the scorch-black spell-line.

Rowan hadn't been hurt, that I could see. What would she do when Argent got back with the supplies? She might realize that the dragon was heading down the spell-line. She might try to follow. Or they'd turn and go back to Wellmet.

The sun flung a few last beams of light across the sky, then sank out of sight. The land below grew dark. An icy-cold wind whistled past, but the dragon's foot kept me warm. I leaned to the side and looked up between the talons that curled around me. The stars hung down so low and bright, I could have reached up and brushed them aside with my hand to see into the deep, velvet-black sky.

The dragon flew straight through the night. I had time to tease out the knots and get Argent's rope off my wrists. And to think about what the dragon wanted me for.

Clear as clear, it'd come down the spell-line, and it was bringing me back up the spell-line. It could've killed Rowan, but it hadn't; I didn't think it meant me any harm, either. It might have some other reason for coming to fetch me, but we were flying toward my locus magicalicus, and that was reason enough for me.

"Fly faster, dragon," I said.

It wouldn't hear me, even if it did have ears among all the spikes on its head.

I lay still and listened to the wind rushing past and the *whumph-whumph* of the dragon's wings beating overhead. When I got cold, I curled against the hearth-warm foot and watched the darkness flow by outside my talon-cage.

What would Nevery think if he could see me now?

Curse it, boy, he'd say. *Be careful.*

Right, Nevery. I'd be as careful as I could.

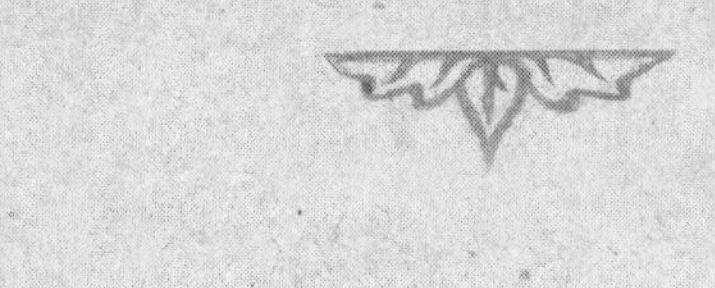 

Magister Nevery,

Conn said one of these black birds would carry this message to you. We were attacked by a dragon, which has taken Conn away with it. It flew along the finding spell-line. We think it must be taking Conn to his locus magicalicus, but we cannot be sure. Sir Argent and I are returning to Wellmet as fast as we can ride, for I have been away too long.

Sir, if you can, will you tell my mother to expect my return? She will be very angry with me. I followed Conn, hoping that if he returned to Wellmet with me he would not be punished for returning from exile. I know Conn well enough to know that he'll come back to Wellmet, no matter what.

Magister Nevery, I have been taught that dragons once lived in the Peninsular Duchies but that they've been extinct for hundreds of years. Something very strange is going on. I suppose neither of us should

be surprised that Conn is at the center of whatever it is.

I am making all possible haste.

Very sincerely yours,

Rowan Forestal

CHAPTER 17

Morning came. First the sky turned metal-gray, then lighter at the eastern edge. The air was thin and icy cold; I shivered in my sweater and coat and huddled closer to the warmth of the dragon. I peered down between the talons to see where we were.

I'd never seen mountains before, but Rowan had shown me pictures, so I knew what I was seeing. We flew over mountains with shadowy pine forests around their knees giving way to broad snowfields glimmering pink in the dawn light, then steep walls and crevices thrusting up to peaks so high that clouds streamed from them like gray-white banners.

The dragon flew among the peaks, deeper into the mountains. The morning sun gleamed off the jagged rock faces; the valleys stayed dark.

The dragon banked, making my stomach lurch, gliding 'round the shoulder of one mountain, and I caught a glimpse of the tallest cloud-wrapped mountain yet, straight ahead of us, and then the dragon folded its wings and plunged down.

The wind screamed past, and I clung to a talon with both hands. Outside was a whirl of gray rock face, a flash of bright blue sky, and then a snowfield racing past just below me, smooth and white.

With a clap of its huge wings, the dragon made

a sharp turn, flinging me against the side of my claw-cage; then the claw opened and I dropped like a bundle of sticks through the air and—*flumph*—landed in the snow.

I heard something else fall into the snow not far away, and then I ducked my head as the dragon swept up its wings and climbed back into the sky.

Lying in the snow, blinking ice crystals out of my eyes, I watched it go. Up the slope it flew, then 'round the side of the mountain, the sun gleaming off its ember-gold scales.

I sat up and looked around.

After the rushing of wind and pumping of dragon wings all night, everything seemed very quiet. I heard the wind whispering across the snow. And something else.

Shedding snow, I stood up, blinking away the white-bright light, and shaded my eyes with my hand to look. All I could see was a snowfield sloping up to a rock ridge that led like a staircase up and around the side of the mountain, where the dragon had gone. I turned and saw the tree line far below, pine trees and piles of gray rocks. I closed my eyes against the dazzle-bright snow and listened.

Yes, coming from higher up the mountain, the singing of the spell-line.

The other *flumph* sound had been the dragon dropping my knapsack. I clumped through the snow, picked it up, and slung it on my back.

The snow was cold, creeping into my boots and making my toes numb; the wind rushing over the snow was cold. But the morning sun lay warm on my black coat.

The spell-line wasn't far away.

I headed toward it. Toward my locus magicalicus.

From far away, the stone stairs leading 'round the side of the mountain had looked like ordinary stairs, but when I got up close I saw that they weren't. I stood at the bottom of the staircase, knee-deep in snow, and looked up. The stairs had been cut out of the side of the mountain, and each step was as high as I could reach. Steps for giants. They led to the spell-line.

I took off the knapsack and tossed it up onto the first step. Standing on my toes, I got my fingers over the edge and pulled myself slowly up, finding cracks for my feet in the stone. I picked up the knapsack and tossed it to the next step, and the next, and the next, and climbed up again and again, until my arms were quivering with tiredness and I had a scrape on my chin and bruised knees from trying to scramble up the rock face. Catching my breath, I stood and looked back, over the snowfield to jagged snowy peaks and brilliant blue sky.

The spell-line was pulling at me, but it was far enough away that I could take time for a rest. I sat down on the stone step and checked my knapsack. Four stale biscuits as hard as rocks, a packet of dried apples, a canteen half full of water, my pencils and paper, a tin cup, a block of cheese about as big as my fist, and the spell-book Nevery'd given me. Enough to eat for a few days, anyway. I ate a few pieces of dried apple and, still chewing, lay down. The stone was like the old, pebbly, wrinkled skin of the mountain under my back. I closed my eyes and felt the sun on my eyelids. The air was cold, but the rock beneath me felt warm.

A shadow passed over the sun; I felt it on my face and heard a *whoosh* of wind. I opened my eyes and sat up.

The flame dragon. It crouched four steps above me, its wings outspread, watching me.

I felt like a mouse about to be pounced on by a hawk.

"All right, I'm coming," I said, getting to my feet. Keeping an eye on the dragon, I picked up my knapsack and threw it onto the next step. My fingers were cold and scraped from clinging to the rock. My neck was warm, though, wrapped in the scarf Benet had knitted for me. I started pulling myself up the step when the dragon dropped from its perch, flying right over my head in a rush of wind. It banked and went around the shoulder of the mountain, where the stairs led.

I climbed until the sun was perched on the mountains to the west, and the snowfield was rosy-gray with the coming night, and the wind off the peaks had grown teeth that nibbled at the back of my neck. The air felt thin, making my breath come in quick gasps. I'd come 'round the side of the mountain. Looking over my shoulder, I saw the blackened path, where the finding spell had burned its way through the snow, leading from Wellmet, far away, to this place. Ahead the spell-line joined the stone stairs and scorched straight to an opening in the side of the mountain that looked like a wide, dark mouth. A cave.

Over the cave perched the flame dragon, clinging with three of its clawed feet to a spire of rock. It gazed down at me with its fire-bright eyes.

On the next step, I climbed into the spell-line.

It wrapped itself around me so I couldn't feel the

wind or my tired arms. The spell dragged me up the last few steps until I stood with my knapsack at my feet on the wide stone step before the cave, where the scorch-mark ended.

The call of the spell-line flickered like a guttering candle and went out.

Everything was quiet. The sky had turned dark blue-black and the full moon had risen behind the mountain, sending sharp shadows and milky white light down to splash across the cave's doorstep.

The finding spell had led here. Sure as sure, somewhere in that cave was my locus magicalicus.

Lady Rowan—

During the past two days I have sent two letters to my apprentice and have had no response; now you tell me about this dragon. As you say, dragons were thought to be extinct. But where Conn is concerned, I have come to expect the unexpected.

It is very urgent that you return with all speed to Wellmet, and if you find my apprentice, bring him with you, whether or not he has found his locus magicalicus. You are both needed here immediately.

—Nevery F.

I picked up my knapsack and stepped into the dark cave. The stone under my feet trembled. Or maybe it was me trembling with tiredness from a whole day of climbing up the side of the mountain.

I knew how to find my locus magicalicus. I took a deep breath.

"*Lothfalas*," I said. The word fell out of my mouth and landed *splat* on the floor. Nothing happened.

"*Lothfalas!*" I shouted, and *lothfalas* went deep into the cave and bounced back to me—*falas—alas—alas* . . .

Nothing.

Maybe there was no magic here, so my locus stone, wherever it was in the cave, wouldn't light up when I said the lothfalas spell. But that couldn't be right. I could feel magic here. Not the same as in Wellmet, not that warm, protecting feeling, and nothing like the cold, stony dread of Arhionvar, but the prickling at the back of my neck and the watchful feeling of the cave felt like magic. Like a magical being was here.

Maybe I was too far away from my locus magicalicus.

The cave was black-dark. I shuffled farther in, my hands held up to stop me from bumping into anything, sliding my feet just in case the ground fell away. My feet kicked small stones that went rattling away over a floor that felt rough, but not too bumpy.

"*Lothfalas*," I said. The dark stayed dark.

My foot knocked against something else. I stretched out my hands until they found a tumbled heap of stones, all the size of my fist or smaller. My locus magicalicus might be in the pile. "*Lothfalas*," I said again. I climbed onto the pile and pushed aside some of the stones.

Late into the night I climbed that pile of rocks and then other piles, saying the lothfalas spell until my voice got hoarse.

I woke up in the morning sprawled out on a pile of stones, my knapsack under my head for a pillow. The ground had been shivering again. A cold breeze trickled in from outside. I sat up, rubbing my eyes, squinting at the morning light. I looked around at the cave.

It was even bigger than the courtyard outside Heartsease, maybe as big as the whole island, a huge hollowed-out space inside the mountain. The walls and ceiling were lost in the dim darkness, but they seemed patchy and shiny in places, as if water was dripping down. The air was warmish, but it made goosebumps prickle on the back of my neck. The air smelled, just a little, of the smoke after a pyrotechnic explosion. The cave floor was flat, chiseled out of the mountain just as the stairs had been. The floor was covered with stones; stones glittery and pebble-dull, big and small, scattered and heaped up in piles; thousands of stones.

I looked down at the pile of stones I'd been sleeping on. It was as high as my chest and as wide as a street in the Twilight. The stones were jumbled together. Some were smooth and brown like river stones; others were weatheredy-gray like the mountain and bigger than my fist; some were shards of shiny black rock; some were lumpy gray gravel. They hadn't all come from the mountain. They must've been gathered here.

"*Lothfalas*," I said loudly. None of the stones lit up. I dug into the pile, shoving the rocks and stones out of the way. They went tumbling and rattling onto the cave floor. "*Lothfalas*," I said again. Still nothing.

I didn't have time for this. I needed to find my stone and get back to Wellmet.

My stomach growled. Right. I did have time for breakfast.

I opened my knapsack and dug inside. Water canteen. Packet of cheese. One, two, three biscuits. Hadn't there been four? Maybe I'd miscounted. I poured some water into the battered tin cup and dunked one of the rock-hard biscuits in to soften it. I ate that, and a piece of cheese, then wrapped up the food and put it away.

Then, leaving my knapsack, I went back to searching. The mouth of the cave grew brighter as the midday sun shone down on the cave's doorstep. Inside stayed dark-dim. I gave up on the pile I'd slept on and moved to the next pile. I climbed onto it and started pushing some of the rocks aside, when I caught a glimpse of something glitter-bright. There, right under two plain brown stones. I picked it up and polished the dust off it with the hem of my sweater. It was about as big as a hen's egg, and deep blue.

I caught my breath. "*Lothfalas*," I whispered.

The stone lay quiet in my hand. Drats. I'd know my locus stone when I found it, and this wasn't it.

I tossed the jewel stone aside. It tumbled down the side of the stone heap and dribbled out onto the floor. I stared down at it, shining softly in the late-afternoon light from the cave mouth.

Oh. I was being stupid. The blue stone was a jewel. Just like my first locus magicalicus had been. I looked around the wide, dark cave, at the piles of stones all over the floor. They wouldn't respond to the lothfalas spell because they weren't mine, but all of these stones were locus magicalicii, weren't they? What were they doing here? Had they been collected here? Why?

Not something I could answer now. I got back to my search.

When my voice was hoarse from saying *lothfalas* over and over again, my empty stomach told me it was time for something to eat.

I shuffled through the stones scattered across the floor, picked up my knapsack, and scuffed over to the cave mouth. I looked out. The sun had gone down behind the mountains. Cold air breathed in from outside; I shivered and hunched into my coat. My stomach growled.

I dug through the knapsack, looking for the packet of dried apples. I took a drink of water from the canteen, which was almost empty, and pulled everything out of the knapsack to look again.

The apples were gone.

Just like the biscuit, in the morning. I hadn't miscounted; I'd never miscount biscuits.

The cave must have rats, just like in Rat Hole, where I'd lived in the Twilight. Those rats had nibbled at everything, even soap and books and candles, even the bristles of my toothbrush.

I looked around the cave. A little leftover sunset shone in, but it was almost completely dark except for the glimmer of silver water on the cave walls, way across from me.

"Stay out of my bag, you rats," I said.

No scurry of feet or squeaking.

Oh, well. I broke a biscuit in two and ate one of the halves and put the other half in my coat pocket; then I slung my knapsack onto my back. They were good thieves, these rats, but they couldn't steal my food from under my nose.

I went back to searching until I fell asleep.

CHAPTER 19

In the morning I woke up with the knot of worry in my chest getting tighter. This search was taking too long. It'd take me days to walk all the way back to Wellmet, and I'd be starving by the time I got there.

Arhionvar might be in the city by that time, and I had no way to tell Nevery I was all right and coming home as soon as I could. Sure as sure Rowan would tell him about the dragon, though.

My knapsack was under my head like a pillow. When I checked inside it, another biscuit had gone missing.

"Curse it!" I shouted. I was going to run out of food before I found my locus magicalicus. My pencil and paper were gone, too.

I got out the canteen and the tin cup and, carrying the knapsack, went outside to collect some snow for water.

I stood on the cave doorstep and looked out. The sun was just coming up, and the snowfield and steps before the cave mouth were deep in the shadow of the mountain. I crouched at the edge of the doorstep and scooped up some snow in the tin cup. Thirsty, I ate some mouthfuls of snow, then set the cup down. When the sun came 'round the mountain, the doorstep would get warm and the snow would melt and I'd have water to drink.

As I was standing up, a *swoop-whoosh* shadow passed overhead. I crouched down, covering my head, my heart pounding. Then I got to my feet and looked in the direction the wind had gone.

Clinging to the spire of rock over the cave mouth with all four claw-feet, its tail wrapped around the spire for balance, wings outspread, was the flame dragon, with the sun dazzle-bright behind it.

"Hello, dragon," I said, shading the sun out of my eyes to see it better.

It shook out and folded its wings like a man shaking rain off an umbrella and stared down at me.

"Can you understand what I'm saying?" I asked it.

It kept staring.

Like a guard. It had brought me here. "Dragon," I shouted. "Why'd you bring me here?" Did it want me to find my locus magicalicus? And why should it care if I did? What if it wanted me for something else, and I just didn't know what, yet. Would it let me leave again, once I'd found my locus stone?

It *had* to let me leave.

Testing, keeping an eye on the dragon, I moved slowly to the edge of the doorstep and lay on my stomach, ready to slither down to the first step.

On the spire, the dragon half-opened its wings and clenched its claws, ready to pounce on me.

Right. I eased myself back onto the doorstep. I couldn't leave yet, anyway. Not until I found my locus stone.

I spent the entire day digging through the piles of stones. *Lothfalas, lothfalas.* No light, no luck.

Just before sunset I checked my knapsack for something to eat.

All of the biscuits were gone.

I'd been wearing the knapsack all day; how had the rats gotten into it? Cursed thieves!

Kicking stones out of the way, I went out to the doorstep. The flame dragon was gone from the spire above the cave mouth. I sat down on the edge of the step. The snow in the tin cup had melted down to water, which had a skin of ice on it now that the sun was setting and the air getting colder. The half-biscuit was still in my coat pocket, but I'd save it for later. I ate the last of the cheese and drank the water and stared out at the sky, burning flame-red behind the mountains where the sun was going down.

A bundle of black rags fell out of the sky and landed on the step next to me. No, not rags, a black bird.

"Hello, bird," I said. It hopped onto my knee, cocking its head to look me over with its yellow eye. Its feathers were ruffled; it'd come all the way from Wellmet. A quill was tied to its leg. A note from Nevery written on thin paper.

Boy, when you receive this letter you must return at once to Wellmet. Respond to inform me that you have received this and are coming.

In haste,

—N

Return at once to Wellmet? But I hadn't found my locus magicalicus yet. And the flame dragon wouldn't let me leave.

As I was rereading the letter, another black bird flapped down to land on my knee; the first bird hopped off with a squawk. The second bird had a letter-quill, too.

Conn, if you have sent a letter I have not received it. The situation in Wellmet has changed; you are needed here as soon as possible. You will need at least ten days to travel back down the finding spell, and even that may be too long. Hurry. Wait outside the city, send a bird with message that you have arrived. Write to say you have received this.

—Nevery

Drats. I couldn't go back to Wellmet without my locus magicalicus.

I rummaged inside my knapsack until I found a few biscuit crumbs, all the thieving rats had left.

"Here, birds," I said, giving them the crumbs.

I couldn't write to Nevery to tell him I wasn't coming yet, because the rats had stolen my pencils and paper.

Leaving the black birds to peck at the crumbs, I read Nevery's note again, squinting to see the letters in the gray light. *The situation in Wellmet has changed*, he'd written. What did that mean, exactly? It couldn't mean Arhionvar had arrived in Wellmet, because sure as sure he would've said if it had.

I thought about it while the sky darkened to black and the stars lit up like werelight lanterns. In a while, the moon would come up from behind the mountain.

Out of the darkness came a rustle of wings and a darker shadow. Another bird. It landed on the step and hopped over to me. I untied the quill it carried and pulled out the third note. The paper felt smooth and cool under my fingers.

I sat with the birds perched next to me on the step, waiting for the moon to come up so I could see to read. A breeze blew across the cave mouth, making a hollow, moaning sound, *hooo*, *hoooo*.

Finally the moon peeked up over the edge of the mountain, shining down over my shoulder. I held up the note. The black letters stood out on the bright-white page.

Curse it, boy, where are you? I have received a letter from Lady Rowan, who says you have been taken away by a dragon. Think she must be mistaken, as dragons have been extinct for hundreds of years.

During the past few days, Wellmet has become infested with white predator-cats, like the ones you said accompanied the sorcerer-king everywhere. You know as well as I do the meaning of this: The cats are agents of the dread magic, which means Arhionvar is approaching the city. I have visited the pit where Dusk House once stood; the magic there is behaving erratically. Have tried communicating with it, as you say is possible, but magic does not respond. The duchess's health is failing. The magisters are in disarray. The only defense is the pyrotechnic traps we've been working on. I have contacted the pyrotechnists, Embre and Sparks, and we have made some progress in assembling explosive traps at various points in the city. But you, Conn, are our connection with the magic. You must return at once, with or without your locus magicalicus.

—N.

I dropped Nevery's third letter to the stone doorstep and stood up. Arhionvar was almost in Wellmet. I had to go home.

Grabbing up my knapsack, I headed for the stone steps. Down one, skinning the palm of my hand on the rock; down the next, and the next.

I glanced back over my shoulder. The mountain peak loomed like a black shard across the rising full moon. Clinging to the spire above the cave mouth was a darker shadow and two points of flame—the eyes of the dragon, watching me. I heard the umbrella *whoosh* of its wings opening.

"No!" I shouted. The flaming eyes swooped down toward me. I flung myself down onto the rock, then scurry-climbed down to the next step. It wasn't going to catch me.

Another swoop of wind, and the flame dragon dropped down right onto my step, knocked me over, and grabbed me up in its claw. A great thunderstorm of wings, and we hurtled back toward the cave mouth. The dragon banked and flung me away. I went tumbling into the cave, sliding into a pile; rocks and stones went rattling across the floor.

Ow. Right. I wasn't leaving yet.

CHAPTER 20

"Lothfalas," I said for the thousandth time, my voice hoarse.

Half the night was gone; I hadn't seen even a spark of lothfalas light. The cave darkness pressed around me like when I pulled my black wool sweater over my head. By feel,

shuffling my feet along the floor, I made my way across the cave until I bumped into the next pile of stones. "*Lothfalas*."

I sifted through the pile.

Drats! I didn't have time for this.

The sweater-black cave lightened to gray; the sun was coming up on the other side of the mountain.

"*Lothfalas*!" I shouted.

From the corner of my eye I caught a quick glimpse of light. I whirled around and said the light spell again. From high up on the wall of the cave, another glimmer. The light brightened, dazzle-bright, and the call of my locus magicalicus washed over me.

I jumped from the pile and slithered to the floor, stones rattling down with me, then scuffed a path through the stones to the wall and looked up. Almost at the ceiling, behind a row of spire-spikes, I saw the glow of my locus stone like the sun behind a cloud.

I looked for a way up. Now that I could see them

up close, I realized that the cave walls were strange. They weren't curved like the inside of a bowl the way a cave was supposed to be. They bulged. A rough path was cut into the wall, starting down low, halfway around the cave from me and sloping up toward my locus magicalicus. With one hand on the wall to guide me, I started to follow the wall around to find the place where the path got close enough to the ground so I could climb up.

Now that I was right next to it, with the cave mouth turning pink with the morning, I saw that the wall wasn't wet with dripping water, as I'd thought. It shone in patches, but was covered with moldy black, like tarnish on silver. I stopped and scratched at the tarnish with my fingernail.

Yes, it was shiny underneath. I lay my hand flat on the wall. It felt smooth and warm. Was it vibrating, just a little?

I peered closer at the wall. A long time ago I'd gone snooping in an abandoned workroom in Heartsease, and I'd found a jar full of slowsilver that had gotten so slow that it'd been frozen, like a mirror. This was just like that.

Was the wall made of slowsilver?

I shook my head. *Locus stone.*

I went on until I got to the place where the rut-path came closest to the cave floor. Leaving my knapsack, I climbed up. The black tarnish was thicker here, like the mildew I'd seen in cellar corners in the Twilight.

My locus stone was up there; I could feel its call as a string pulling at my chest. I started climbing. The path grew wider and, as it led upward, rougher, not stairs but a long row of pointed teeth.

Higher and higher I climbed, scrambling over the path-teeth, the call of my locus magicalicus getting stronger. My breath came in short gasps and my hands started to tingle where they touched the path, as if they were being pricked all over with needles. My feet tingled even through my boots.

The path took me to the very top of the cave. I stopped to catch my breath. The air felt thinner up here; it went into my lungs and popped, like bubbles. On either side of the path a line of spire-spikes grew up like a row of tree trunks, each spike twice as tall as I was, brushing against the rock ceiling. The air was dark. From ahead, down the path between the spikes, came a glow.

I gulped down a bubble of excitement and started toward it.

The path grew brighter. There—my locus magicalicus, glowing softly, resting beside one of the spires.

The light went out.

"*Lothfalas*," I said.

The stone started to glow again. I stepped closer. It wasn't like my first locus magicalicus, not a jewel stone, but a chunk of rough, greenish rock the size of a baby's fist.

From out of the darkness behind the spire, something crept out and crouched next to the stone. I stopped and bent down to see better. A little animal. Was it a rat?

No, it had wings, a long tail, a face full of muzzle

and teeth—a dragon. A tiny one, not quite as big as Lady, the cat that'd lived with us in Heartsease. It rested its front claw-paws on top of my glowing locus stone.

"Hello, dragon," I said.

It looked just like the flame dragon but leaf-green, the same color of my first locus magicalicus, shading to gleaming gold on its wings.

I edged a little closer.

The dragon snatched up the stone and hopped backward, twitching its tail.

Oh. "You're the thief!" I said. It hadn't been rats. The dragon had been stealing the biscuits and other things out of my knapsack. Well, it wasn't going to steal my locus stone.

The dragon cocked its head and looked at me with a bright red eye.

I leaned closer and reached for my locus magicalicus.

The dragon opened its mouth like a cat, showing me its needle-sharp teeth.

Oh, no.

It popped my locus magicalicus into its mouth and gulped it down.

"No!" I shouted, and leaped for the dragon. I caught it, grabbing it around the neck. It thrashed its wings and whipped its tail and I held on; it brought its head around and bit me. Ow! I dropped the dragon and it scuttled up the nearest stone spire and jumped from it to the ceiling. It clung there, upside down, like a bat.

Curse it! I stood staring upward; it stared back, twitching its tail like an angry cat. Blood dripped off my hand where it had bit me.

Ah, I knew how to get it down. "*Lothfalas*!" I shouted.

The dragon blinked, gulped, then burped out a gust of light. Its claws let go of the cave ceiling and it tumbled down.

"Got you!" I said. But just over my head, as I leaped up to grab it, the dragon caught itself with its wings and wobble-flapped away, farther down the path. I started after it.

The path shifted and down I fell. Getting back to my feet, I kept my eye on the dragon. It hopped farther away.

The path shook again, harder this time. I landed hard on my knees, then scrambled after the dragon. It led me all the way down the rough path along the cave wall to the cave floor. It hop-flapped across the floor to one of the piles of stones and perched on it, opening and closing its mouth.

I jumped down from the path and started toward it. "Did you think my locus stone was a biscuit?" I said. Reaching the pile, I leaped, grabbing for it, but the dragon hopped away like a grasshopper, landing on another pile.

Drats. I wasn't going to catch it like this.

"*Lothfalas*!" I said.

The dragon coughed out a gob of light. While it shook its head, I crouched down and crept toward the pile of stones it perched on.

"*Lothfalas*," I said again. The word left my mouth and hung in the air.

The cave echoed the spellword back to me.

LOTHFALAS

The spell roared around the cave like a wind, swirling along the walls and the ceiling, and every locus magicalicus, every stone in the piles and scattered across the floor, burst into flame. The light arrowed into my eyes.

I flung myself down on the floor with my arms over my head. The ground trembled, making my bones shiver. I heard stones falling from the piles and settling. Then silence. Slowly, carefully, I opened my eyes, blinking away the brights to see.

I looked up—and up. The cave. The walls were shifting, gleaming patchy silver in the dimming light. Dust sifted down from the ceiling. I felt a low humming in my bones.

A rumbling noise started, like huge stones rubbing against each other. Something shifted in the darkness at the other side of the cave. Looming slowly out of the shadows came a dragon's head as big as the Dawn Palace. Its eye was bigger than the double door leading into the palace. I could've walked through the long, narrow slit in its pupil. It was looking at me.

The cave walls weren't walls at all. They were dragon.

CHAPTER 21

The dragon was so huge, it took up the whole top of the mountain. I'd climbed partway up the dragon's tail to find my locus magicalicus. It'd said the lothfalas spell, and all the locus magicalicus stones had lit up.

Wait. All of *its* locus stones. Dragons kept hoards, didn't they? But why locus stones? What did a dragon have to do with magic?

I crouched beside the glowing pile of stones and gazed up into the dragon's eye. It was like looking into the night sky, deep black and full of stars.

Like a great double-wide door opening and closing, the dragon's eyelid slid across its eye, then back, a giant blink. The floor shook, and with the sound of boulders rolling, the dragon moved its head across the mouth of the cave, a stormcloud moving across the sun. It shifted; the floor shook, knocking me off my feet, and slowly, the dragon rested its head on the ground. Its huge eyes blinked shut. Dust billowed up and locus stones rolled across the floor.

The dust settled. The last stone rattled to a stop. The lothfalas light dimmed and went out.

Trying not to make a sound, I got to my feet. The cave mouth was almost completely blocked by the dragon's head; just a sliver of light shone at its edge.

I stood, staring across the cave at the gap between the dragon and the cave wall. It wasn't very wide. I could squeeze through it if I didn't mind sneaking right under the dragon's nose.

Other thoughts nibbled at the corner of my brain. Had the dragon gathered all the locus stones here? Was there magic here? There must be, for the lothfalas spell to work. Why were the dragon's scales made of slowsilver? It was far too big to fit through the cave mouth, so how had it gotten inside the mountain, and how did it get out? Was the thief dragon the cave dragon's baby? And the question that had bothered me before—why had the flame dragon brought me here?

I shook my head. I could think about those things later. First I needed to get my locus stone out of the thief dragon, and then escape from the cave and from the flame dragon and get back to Wellmet. My stomach gave a hollow growl. And except for half a biscuit, I didn't have any food to help me do it, either. The rock floor trembled. I had a feeling that

I needed to get out of the cave, and soon.

Off to my left, I heard a *tck-tck-tck* sound like little claws on rock. The thief dragon. Probably looking for something else to steal. I crouched down behind a pile of locus stones, then crawled around it.

The light was dim, but I could see a faint golden gleam reflecting from the thief dragon's wings. It crept along the floor until it came to a pile of stones, then started up it, stopping to shake its head and stretch open its mouth. Maybe it had a stomachache. The call of my locus magicalicus came from it, faintly. The dragon could hide from me, but I'd always know where it was.

Still, I wasn't going to catch it by trying to leap on it.

I crawled back behind my pile of locus stones. The only thing the thief dragon hadn't stolen out of my knapsack was the spell-book Nevery'd given me. I took that out, and pulled the half biscuit from my pocket. The dragon liked biscuits, sure as sure.

I sprinkled a few biscuit crumbs on the rock floor,

then put the half biscuit into the knapsack and put it on the floor with the top flap half open. Quietly, trying not to step on any locus stones, I crept 'round the pile and crouched in the shadows, waiting.

After a while I heard a rattle of stones and the *tck-tck-tck* of claws on rock. Slowly, carefully, I crawled out of my hiding place.

The thief dragon crouched next to my knapsack. With one little claw-paw it pulled aside the top flap, then stuck its snout inside. I'd stuffed the half-biscuit deep into a corner. The dragon crawled farther in, its tail twitching.

Now! I burst from my hiding place and dove on the knapsack, pulling the top flap tight and buckling it down. The tiny dragon thrashed around inside, but it was good and caught. "Hah," I breathed, getting the last strap snugged tight.

Now to get out of the cave. I got to my feet, holding the squirming knapsack in my arms. The walls were shifting again, but it wasn't the cave dragon moving. The ground trembled, just enough to make my feet itch. The locus stones scattered around the cave started to glow, faintly.

The tiny dragon kept struggling to get out of the knapsack. "Shhh," I whispered to it.

One thing thieves are good at is creeping without making noise. I started toward the sliver of space between the cave dragon's head and the cave wall.

I glanced over my shoulder. The walls shivered and shone in the lothfalas light. The slowsilver scales were moving, I realized. As I watched, a lump of slowsilver like a giant teardrop flowed down the dragon-wall. Was the dragon melting? The floor stopped trembling and started shaking.

Inside the knapsack, the tiny dragon went very still. A deep hum-thrum rumbled through the cave.

Right. Time to get out, and I didn't need to be quiet about it.

Kicking stones out of the way, I ran across the cave to the sliver of doorway. The dragon lay with its eye closed. A smudge of smoke, like a fire going out, trickled up from its huge nostril. Up close, I could see that its slowsilver skin was tarnished here, too, and crack-wrinkled. The cave dragon, I guessed, was very, very old. Maybe it'd grown old inside this mountaintop, and too huge to squeeze out the cave mouth it'd come in, long ago.

I turned sideways, the knapsack in my arms, and edged into the gap. It was a tight fit, tight enough to scrape buttons off my coat, but I wasn't leaving my locus magicalicus behind. I squeezed past a sharp tooth twice as tall as Nevery, its surface pitted and yellow. A wind tugged at my clothes and hair—the dragon's breath, hot, and with a smell like exploded pyrotechnics. Past another tooth.

And then free, standing on the doorstep, the sun bright in a clear blue sky, the air cold and fresh.

The cave dragon spoke. Its voice rumbled up through the stone step and into me.

TALLENNAR

Inside the knapsack, the tiny dragon squeaked—*Pip!*

A gust of wind burst from the cave mouth, and I

heard the pattering sound of raindrops—slowsilver drops, I guessed, raining down from the dragon. I threw the knapsack over my shoulders and raced for the stone steps. Behind me, the mountain rumbled. Down another step, and another, and five more steps, my breath gasping.

I glanced over my shoulder. Rocks tumbled off the mountain peak, and as I watched, the spire over the cave mouth cracked and tipped over and smashed onto the doorstep, right where I'd been standing. I'd stolen one of its locus stones. The cave dragon was coming after me.

A jagged boulder as big as a horse came leaping down the side of the mountain and bounced down the stone steps toward me. I pressed myself against the stair wall and it crashed past, cracking the stone step where it landed and then flying off into the snowfield. More rocks rained down.

Keeping my head low, I scrambled down another step.

From behind, I heard the whoosh of wings. I looked over my shoulder and flung myself onto the next step. The flame dragon, coming for me. It swooped down in a rush of wind, and without even pausing, snatched me up from the stone step.

I struggled, kicking, pushing at the claws that held me, but it just gripped me tighter. *NO!* It couldn't take me back to the cave, not now.

My stomach lurched as the dragon banked to the side, dodging a hurtling boulder, then it dodged again, its wings pounding, *whump-whump*, lifting us higher.

I braced myself, ready to be tossed back into the cave, but the flame dragon arced away, leaving the rumbling mountaintop behind, gliding over a deep, shadowed valley to another mountain. It circled, then dropped down to a sharp spire of rock and perched there, clinging to the spire with three claws, holding me tightly with the fourth one.

I caught my breath and took off my knapsack to hold it in my arms. The thief dragon kept still. In the tight clutch of the flame dragon I squirmed forward so I could peer around a talon.

Far across the valley, dark gray stormclouds

gathered around the dragon mountain. Silver lightning flashed in the clouds' bellies and crackled around the mountain's sharp peak. A rumbling sound like distant thunder echoed from the other mountains all around.

More rocks tumbled from the dragon mountain; great swaths of snow slid from the snowfields and crashed into the treeline below, sending up clouds of ice crystals.

The noise stopped like a held breath. The mountain shivered, then stilled.

The tiny dragon found a gap in the top of the knapsack and poked out its snout; it gazed toward the mountain.

In a shimmering blaze of light, the entire top of the mountain rose up into the sky and hung there. Stormclouds raged around it; lightning flashed. In a whirl of pyrotechnic flame, the mountaintop burst apart.

The sound of the explosion reached us, a rumbling roar, and then a freezing wind full of grains of rock, and rocks as big as my fist, and rocks the size of the flame dragon, but they all hurtled past us to fall in the snow or shatter on the side of the mountain. The cave dragon. Had it just died?

The tiny dragon made a sad, keening sound.

And then I knew. The hoard of locus stones. The slowsilver. I knew what slowsilver was for; it was for keeping magic in. If the dragon's scales were made of slowsilver, then inside the dragon must be magic.

I stared at the clouds and smoke and the shimmer of slowsilver raining out of the sky.

The cave dragon wasn't dying. A magic was being born.

CHAPTER 22

The flame dragon shot through the fading day. Heading toward Wellmet, I hoped, because that's where the finding spell had come from. I reached up and rested my hand against the flame dragon's claw. Its scales gleamed like liquid flames and felt warm under my fingers. These scales were slowsilver, too, just not silver-colored yet because the dragon was still young.

Outside the flame dragon's claw, the wind shrieked past, cold and thin. Inside the knapsack, the thief dragon was shivering.

I loosened one of the straps and peeked inside.

"Hello, little Pip," I said softly.

It curled in the bottom of the bag and glared at me. The tip of its tail twitched. When a cat twitched its tail it wasn't happy.

Pip was a magical being inside its dragon scales, just as the flame dragon was. Maybe it couldn't understand me unless I spoke its language. From my studying, I knew enough of the spellword language to tell Pip not to be afraid, that I was its friend. But when I reached my hand in to touch it, it snapped at me, then bared its needle-sharp teeth, ready to bite.

Drats. I buckled the bag tight to keep Pip in, then I put the knapsack up under my sweater to keep it warm. I thought I knew why the flame dragon had brought me here. The finding spell had led it to me; it had fetched me because of my locus magicalicus. And, maybe, also so I would find the tiny dragon and take it away before the cave dragon gave up its dragon body and became pure magic.

I curled against the warm claw holding me and thought about the cave dragon. *Tallennar,* it had said after I'd escaped from the cave. I'd learned a lot of words from the spell-language, but I didn't know that one. Maybe I could find the word in a grimoire when I got back to Wellmet.

Dragons. Nevery'd hardly believe it. Or if he did, he'd want me to write it up as a treatise. The dragons were magic, and their slowsilver scales held the magic in. That's what slowsilver did: It confined magic. I'd read that in Jaspers's treatise. The magic itself never really died; it just got too old and too large for the slowsilver to confine it, and it left its old dragon body behind.

The cave dragon. Its slowsilver scales would

seep into the ground, I guessed, holding it there in that place, and the magic would draw people, and a city would grow up there, on the shattered half of a mountain. And all the locus stones the cave dragon had hoarded. Would wizards come and find them, and be the wizards of the city?

If the magic was dragon, it meant Arhionvar had been a dragon once. So had Wellmet. Maybe a long time ago. Knowing that might help us defeat the dread magic. Nevery might know how. "Fly faster," I said to the flame dragon. We needed to get home to Wellmet.

The flame dragon flew all through the night and into the next day until my ears felt battered by the wind rushing past and my stomach was hollow with hunger. I shivered and pulled my coat up over my head and curled around Pip in the knapsack, keeping us both warm.

Then the *whumph-whumph* of the dragon's wings stopped and we went into a glide. I pulled down the coat and peeked out.

Way down below was Wellmet, looking like a city on a map. Dark and smudged on the Twilight side, light and neat on the Sunrise side, with the river winding like a brown snake through the middle of it.

The dragon banked, and we dropped down, and down, circling lower and lower until I could see the black slash that'd been my finding spell cutting across a corner of the Sunrise; and I saw people in the streets looking up at us with their mouths open, screaming maybe, pointing at the flame dragon flying over their heads, and a line of carriages rushing up the hill toward the Dawn Palace, and guards gathering. The dragon circled the palace once, then hovered at roof level, its wings making a sound like thunder.

Nevery wasn't going to like this. It wasn't *circumspect.*

Down below, the guards drew their swords, and I saw Kerrn's long blond braid as she swung around and stared up at the dragon.

With a swoop of wings, the dragon dropped down into a space in the middle of the palace courtyard. I heard screaming and Kerrn shouting orders, and the dragon opened its claw and dropped me onto the gravel drive. The dragon swept up its wings in a swirl of dust and wind, and climbed back into the sky.

I got to my feet and watched it go. The sky was flat and white with clouds, and the dragon shone against it like a flickering candle flame. The dragon glided in a wide circle over the Dawn Palace and the Sunrise, then climbed higher and headed away. Not toward the mountains. Maybe it was going to make its own lair and hoard of locus stones somewhere else. And one day, maybe not for thousands of years, it'd shed its slowsilver scales and become a city's magic.

Still holding my knapsack with Pip in it under my sweater, I turned to face the Dawn Palace. Guards with their swords drawn were lined up before the steps leading to the wide double front door; behind me, a row of carriages rattled into the courtyard.

Somebody broke free of the crowd on the stairs

and, followed by four guards, crunched over the driveway toward me. Rowan.

She stopped a few paces away, catching her breath. She looked pale and had dark circles under her eyes, as if she hadn't slept. The four guards made a circle around us with their swords drawn.

Rowan held up her hand, keeping them off. "Well, Connwaer," she said. "The dragon brought you back, did it?"

I grinned at her.

She glanced at the sky, toward where the dragon had gone, then back at me and looked me up and down. She frowned. "Are you all right?"

"Well, I'm hungry," I said.

"You're always hungry. Is that why—" She pointed at my stomach.

Oh, it looked like I was clutching a lump under my sweater. "It's just Pip." I lifted my sweater and pulled out my knapsack.

Behind Rowan, more guards came across the courtyard, Captain Kerrn in her green uniform striding ahead with her sword drawn. I heard footsteps from behind and looked over my shoulder. Magisters—Brumbee, Trammel, Nimble, and—

"Nevery!" I shouted.

He pushed a guard out of the way and gave me a quick hug.

"Watch out for Pip," I said.

"Hmph," he said, stepping back and pulling on the end of his beard. "Traveling by dragon now, are you, boy?" His bushy eyebrows twitched. Like a cat's tail, that was; it meant he wasn't happy. "Took your time getting home, at any rate."

"Nevery, I—" *found my locus magicalicus*, I wanted to say, and I wanted to tell him that Arhionvar, Wellmet, and Desh had once been dragons, but then Kerrn shouted an order and two palace guards took Nevery's arms and dragged him back, and Kerrn had her sword edge at my throat.

"Do not move," Kerrn said, her eyes colder than ice.

I froze.

"Captain!" Rowan protested.

Ignoring her, Kerrn reached forward and grabbed the knapsack out of my arms.

"What is this?" Kerrn asked. "Some sort of pyrotechnic device?" She nodded at one of her guardsmen, who pointed his sword at me. She lowered her sword and started unbuckling the knapsack straps.

"No, don't—" I started, and felt the guard's drawn sword prick me over the heart when I strained forward.

Too late.

Pip burst from the knapsack in a swirl of lashing tail and needle teeth and golden flapping wings, leaping for the sky.

Kerrn swung her sword up and around, slashing at Pip, but the tiny dragon leaped higher into the air. It wobble-flapped over the courtyard, up higher until it reached one of the flagpoles on the top of the Dawn Palace. It perched there, glaring down at us with its red eyes.

"Get archers," Kerrn snapped.

"No!" I shouted; I pushed the blade away from my chest and started toward the palace, and then two guards grabbed my arms and jerked them behind me. I struggled, and one of them elbowed me in the stomach. I bent over, coughing.

As I looked up, Pip launched itself from the spire, tumbled, then caught itself and flapped away, toward the river.

I heard Nevery shouting angrily, and the worried protests of Magister Brumbee, and Rowan's sharp voice arguing.

But the guards held me tight and dragged me across the courtyard and into the Dawn Palace, Kerrn striding along next to the guards holding me. As we went through the double doors, Kerrn leaned over to speak to me.

"Where did it go?" she asked. Pip, she meant.

I couldn't see Pip, but I knew where it was. I would always know. But sure as sure I wasn't going to tell Kerrn.

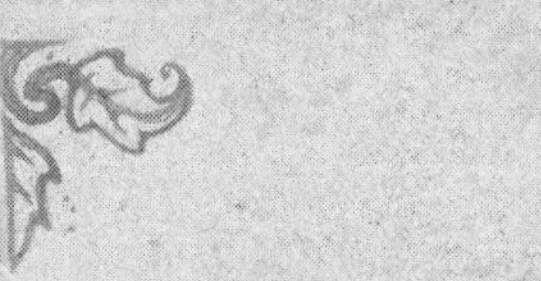

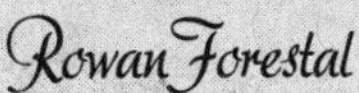

Rowan Forestal

When I got back to Wellmet I thought my mother would punish me for going after Conn, but she was too ill to speak. I am afraid she may be dying. Magister Trammel won't say, but she is as cold and still as stone. I sat by her bed and held her hand, and she didn't seem to know I was there.

If she dies I will have to be the duchess. I will be alone.

I hope she doesn't die.

Captain Kerrn took me to the usual cell. Chair, table, damp walls, not much light.

The guards took my coat, then shoved me in and left; I heard the click of the lock after they slammed the door behind them.

Drats.

I sat down in the chair and

rested my arms on the table, then put my head down on my arms, tired and dizzy from dragon flight and from not eating for too long.

I needed to talk to Nevery, and to the other magisters. To Embre and Sparks, too, because they could help with the pyrotechnics. Most of all I needed to talk to the Wellmet magic. Desh's magic wasn't bad, and neither was the cave dragon. Why was Arhionvar different? Maybe our magic could tell me. It was gathering itself in the Dusk House pit. Maybe that's where its lair had been, when it was a dragon. I had to get out of this cell and find Pip, and then get over to the Twilight.

Arhionvar wasn't in Wellmet yet. The city's magic felt unsettled, but I couldn't sense the dread, cold feeling of Arhionvar, the feeling I'd had in the sorcerer-king's fortress. It must be close, though.

After a while, Kerrn unlocked the door and came into the cell, followed by her bristle-bearded second. Farn, his name was; he was the guard who'd given me phlister the first time Kerrn had caught me.

She stood staring down at me with her ice-chip eyes.

"I'm very hungry," I said.

Kerrn glanced at Farn and gave him a sharp nod; he set the werelight lantern he was carrying on the floor, then left the cell. Going to get me something to eat, I hoped.

"Get up," Kerrn said.

I stood up.

She reached around me, dragged the chair in front of the cell door, and sat down, leaving me standing before her.

Time for questions.

"No phlister?" I asked.

"Be quiet," Kerrn said. "I ask the questions."

"Kerrn, we don't have time for this," I said. "Arhionvar is coming. You know what that means—you were in Desh, and in the sorcerer-king's fortress. I need to talk to Nevery and the other magisters, and to the duchess."

Kerrn shook her head. "*I* ask."

All right. I climbed onto the table and sat with my legs crossed.

Kerrn scowled. "What was that lizard?"

Lizard? Oh, Pip, she meant. "It's a dragon."

"It was thought that no dragons were left in the world."

I shrugged. She'd seen the flame dragon well enough, when it'd landed in the courtyard.

The lantern flickered, reflecting bits of light from the water seeping down one of the cell walls.

"You are a thief," Kerrn said quietly. "And a danger to the city."

Maybe I was a thief. But I felt the city's magic around me, warm, with a tingle of fright in it. "I'm a wizard, too, Kerrn," I said.

Kerrn folded her arms and leaned back against the chair. "If you are a wizard, then where is your locus magicalicus?"

"Pip ate it," I said.

She raised her eyebrows.

"The dragon," I explained. "The dragon is my locus magicalicus."

"A dragon cannot be a locus magicalicus."

"Well, it is," I said. It really was. Unless Pip could cough up the stone, which it would've done before now if it could, and unless I was willing to cut open the dragon to get at my stone, which I wasn't, then Pip really was my locus magicalicus.

"You are not a wizard," Kerrn said.

"I was always a wizard," I said.

She shook her head. "You cannot be a wizard without a locus magicalicus."

I knew what she was thinking. *Gutterboy.* And *thief.* "Kerrn, if you lost your sword, would you still be a guard?"

She didn't answer. But she frowned, like she was thinking about it.

Then Farn came in with the food. Water, bean soup, and a piece of bread without any butter on it. With one last glare, Kerrn turned and walked out with Farn, slamming the door shut.

After eating, I fell asleep at the table with my head on my arms.

A hand on my shoulder woke me up.

"It is time," Kerrn said.

I blinked and rubbed the sleep out of my eyes, stiff from sleeping at the table. Time for what? For breakfast, I hoped. And then Nevery and I would have to convince the duchess and the magisters that Arhionvar was coming. I needed to find Pip, too. The faint call of my locus magicalicus pulled at me from off in the direction of the river.

Kerrn and Farn led me up the stairs and into the hallways of the Dawn Palace. We came to a double door; Kerrn opened it and poked her head in. "Are you ready?" she asked somebody inside.

"Wait a moment," said a voice. It sounded like Nimble.

Kerrn closed the door and stood beside me with her hands clasped behind her back.

"What is this?" I asked.

"Hearing room," Kerrn said, staring at the closed door.

Good. I could tell what I knew, and whoever was in there would hear it. I straightened my black sweater and with my fingers combed the hair out of my eyes. They were more likely to listen if I didn't look too scruffy.

"Is Nevery coming?" I asked.

Kerrn shook her head. "He is not. He was arrested last night and imprisoned. He is likely to be exiled from the city."

Well, once they heard what I'd learned about Arhionvar, they'd know we needed Nevery to stay here. And if I knew Nevery, he wasn't in the cell they'd put him in. I'd taught him how to pick a lock and get himself out.

The hearing room doors opened and we went in.

The room was long and had a polished stone floor that sent the sound of our footsteps echoing off the walls. The ceiling was high, held up by stone pillars carved like tree trunks, for Rowan's family, I guessed, the Forestals.

At the other end was a wide table, where the magisters sat staring as we crossed the room.

Another clump of chairs was set off to the side; some city councilors and rich merchants and other wizards sat there. As we came closer, they shot quick glances at us, whispering. More palace guards stood along the walls. The duchess wasn't there. I didn't see Rowan, either. A little twist of worry tightened in my stomach. Rowan needed to be here.

With a hand on my shoulder, Kerrn stopped me before the magisters' table. The magisters examined me.

Bat-faced Nimble sat in the center chair looking red-nosed and cranky. After giving me a good glare, he glanced down at some papers piled on the table before him. Also at the table was Brumbee, looking worried, and Trammel, sharp and sour as always, and Periwinkle, and the keen Sandera, all the magisters of the city. Except for Nevery.

I glanced over at the clump of chairs. Argent

was there, dressed up in his fanciest clothes. "Hello, Argent," I said, my voice echoey and loud in the silence.

Argent didn't answer, just gave me a wide-eyed look. Not his usual down-the-nose sneer. The last time I'd seen him, he'd tied me to a tree. Maybe he'd thought I was dead. He probably wished I was.

At the table, Nimble cleared his throat. "We shall begin." He nodded at Kerrn. "Captain, we'll need phlister for the prisoner."

The prisoner. That was me. "I don't need any phlister," I said.

"We want the truth," Nimble said. "Get phlister."

"I won't lie," I said.

"If I might interrupt," Brumbee said, from the row of magisters, "I—ah—have never known Conn to lie; he has always been truthful. Rather alarmingly so, I should say."

"Oh, very well," Nimble said, wiping his red nose with a handkerchief. "We can dispense with the phlister." He turned to me again. "Who do you name to speak for you?"

"I can speak for myself," I said. Nobody knew as much about Arhionvar as I did; it didn't make sense to have somebody else speak for me.

At the table, Brumbee whispered something to Periwinkle, who shook her head.

Nimble sniffed. "Very well. We will begin. Do you, Connwaer, admit to collecting pyrotechnic materials, including"— he took a piece of paper from the table and glanced at it—"magnetic rust, atriomated water, and blackpowder?" He handed the list back. "Possession of which is against the law of the city?"

Oh, so they wanted to talk about the pyrotechnics first, and then we'd get to Arhionvar. "Yes," I said.

"So noted," Nimble said with a nod. "You admit to breaking into the academicos in order to use a room there to conduct a pyrotechnic experiment?"

"Yes," I said. No point in denying it; Brumbee had seen me.

"So noted," Nimble said in his dry, high voice.

He was about to say more when the double doors

at the other end of the room burst open and crashed against the walls. I whirled ’round to see. Roaring, Benet bulled into the hearing room. He had a guard hanging on each arm and another leaping on him from behind.

He flung one of the guards off and pulled his truncheon out of his belt and slammed it into another guard’s face; she went down with blood spraying from her nose. Benet caught sight of me and headed across the room.

The magisters at the table jumped up, shouting.

“Guards!” Kerrn ordered.

The guards stationed around the hearing room were already moving, drawing their swords.

“No!” I shouted, starting toward Benet. Farn grabbed my arm and held it tight. “Kerrn, no!”

Kerrn glanced at me.

“No swords!” I said to her.

She gave me a quick nod and, shouting orders at her guards, ran across the room.

Benet gave a roar that echoed off the walls and

swung his truncheon, but two more guards grabbed his arm and another snaked an arm around his neck.

"Benet!" I shouted.

He shook his head like a bear, sending a guard flying, and caught sight of me. "Get out of here, you!" he bellowed.

Then the rest of the guards were on him. They wrestled him to the floor, two to each arm and leg, and he was dragged out, struggling. Other guards helped up the guard with the broken nose and took her out, leaving only a patch of blood on the stone floor.

Kerrn closed the door, shutting out the sound of guards fighting with Benet in the hall.

Farn let me go; my arm hurt where he'd been holding me. My breath came fast. Benet wanted me out of here. He'd come in just to tell me that, and gotten himself into trouble for it. What was going on, exactly?

At the magisters' table, Nimble cleared his throat.

"Well. Thank you for dealing with that disturbance, Captain."

Kerrn, coming to stand beside me again, nodded.

Nimble glanced down at his notes.

My hands were shaking. I wrapped my arms around myself, feeling shivery cold.

"Ah," Nimble said. "We left off here. Did you do the pyrotechnic spell?"

They already knew I'd done it. I nodded.

"Answer aloud," Nimble said.

"Yes." My voice shook. "I did the finding spell."

At the table, Brumbee put his head in his hands; beside him, Trammel looked angry, and Periwinkle gazed down at the table.

"And your master, Magister Nevery Flinglas, assisted you?"

I stared back at Nimble. I wasn't going to answer that question at all.

"You refuse to answer?"

"You're not asking the right questions," I said.

Beside me, Kerrn took a sharp breath. I glanced

aside at her. She was thinking of the time I'd been caught stealing my locus stone from the duchess and she'd given me phlister and asked all the wrong questions.

"Well, he's not," I said to her.

She frowned and shook her head.

I looked back at Nimble, then along the line of magisters at the table. "You should be asking about Arhionvar."

"We have looked into the question of Arhionvar," Nimble said primly. "Arhionvar was a city far to the south in the Fierce Mountains, but it was destroyed many years ago. There is no other Arhionvar than that."

"Yes there is," I said. "Nimble, there was magic in the city of Arhionvar, wasn't there? D'you think it just disappeared when the city did? Arhionvar is a magical being, and it is coming. It'll be here very soon." I looked around at the other magisters, willing them to understand. "Arhionvar isn't like our magic. It won't protect us. We saw what it did to Desh. It'll do the same thing here, if we let it."

"The magic is not some kind of being!" Nimble said loudly.

"We have to figure out what to do once it gets here," I said. "Nevery and I have a plan." They weren't going to like the part of the plan that had pyrotechnics in it. Or the part where the magic had once been a dragon.

"Be silent," Nimble ordered. "Your delusions about magic have no bearing on this trial."

Trial? What did he mean, *trial*?

"It is quite clear," Nimble said. "The accused has readily admitted his crimes. I see no reason not to proceed with the execution."

With the *what*? "Kerrn, what is he talking about?" I asked.

Kerrn glared at me, her gray-blue eyes like ice in her pale face. "You should not have returned to Wellmet."

I stared at her. When I spoke, my lips felt stiff.

"But I had to come back. Kerrn, what execution is he talking about?"

"The sentence for return from exile is death by hanging," she said flatly. "To be carried out immediately."

CHAPTER 24

The guards took me to their commons room. One of them jerked my hands behind my back while the other fetched manacles, then put them on my wrists. Then they shoved me down on a bench to wait.

I sat, my thoughts whirling. This couldn't happen. Rowan had told me about the order of execution, but I hadn't believed they'd actually *do* it. I had to do something. I jumped to my feet, and the guard shoved me down again.

I gulped down a sudden surge of fright. Benet had tried to get me out of the hearing room. Where was Nevery? In a cell, or escaped into the city, hiding?

They were being stupid! If they hanged me, how would Wellmet defend itself against Arhionvar?

The door opened, and Kerrn strode in but didn't look at me.

"You can't do this, Kerrn," I said, getting to my feet.

The guard shoved me down onto the bench.

"They are ready," Kerrn said to the guard.

Rowan. She could help me. "Kerrn, can I talk to the duchess?" Once she heard about the dragons and Arhionvar, and Rowan told her I was telling the truth, she'd have to change her mind about the execution.

"The duchess is too ill to see anyone," Kerrn said, still not looking at me.

Oh. So that's where Rowan was.

"Now," Kerrn ordered.

The guards hauled me to my feet and, pulling on my arms, dragged me out the door, through the hallways of the palace, and out to the wide front steps.

In the middle of the Dawn Palace courtyard a gallows tree had been built out of wood, a high platform with steps leading up and a noose hanging down from a beam.

They must've been working on it all night. The hearing hadn't been a hearing at all; they'd already decided what they were going to do with me.

A crowd had gathered, thousands of people turning to stare as they saw the guards, with me, coming out of the Dawn Palace. More guards surrounded us and I was pulled down the stairs. They pushed through the silent crowd to the steps leading up to the gallows.

Nimble was there. "Has he been searched?" he asked, looking me over.

"Yes, he has," Kerrn said shortly, from behind me.

No I hadn't. I glanced quickly at her as she stepped up beside me, but her face stayed blank, like chiseled stone.

"Very well," Nimble said, adjusting the cuffs of his robe. "Take him up."

The two guards took me by the arms and, with another guard following, marched me up the wooden steps to the platform where the noose was hanging, with a wooden box below it for standing on.

At the top of the stairs I stopped, and the guards dragged me to the box and lifted me onto it. I tried to climb down, and the guards stepped to the side and held my arms so I couldn't move.

As I struggled against their holding hands, the third guard reached up and grabbed the thick-roped noose. "Lift your chin," he said. The two guards kept their grip on my arms.

I put my chin down.

One of the guards grabbed my hair and jerked my head up. I saw the sky, white and blank as a piece of paper, with smudges of cloud ink on it. Then the rope came down over my head, resting heavy around my neck.

I caught my breath and scanned the courtyard. The air was cold. I'd been away so long, winter had settled in over the city. Frost lined the black branches of the trees near the front gates of the Dawn Palace. A cluster of black birds sat in the trees and perched on the iron spikes on the walls around the courtyard, looking cold and bedraggled.

My locus stone called with a low thrumming in my bones; Pip wasn't far away. Maybe the dragon was hiding in a tree with the birds.

I heard footsteps on the wooden stairs, and Kerrn, holding a folded piece of paper, joined us on the platform. "Get on with it," she said gruffly.

The guard snugged the thick-roped noose 'round my neck, turning the knot so it rested just below my ear. The guards let go of my arms and stepped away.

I looked out over the crowd filling the courtyard. The people stood silently, watching. A group of scowling minions stood at the back. Along the front, sitting in a row of comfortable chairs, were the magisters and the duchess's council, but no Rowan, that I could see. At the edge of the crowd I saw a gutterboy waiting for his chance to pick a pocket. If he was smart, he'd wait until the guards pulled away the box I was standing on and people were distracted.

My breath came short. This was happening too fast. They weren't really going to do it, were they? Nevery would be furious if I let them hang me.

Kerrn stepped up to the front of the gallows platform and unfolded the list of my crimes; the crackle of the paper sounded loud in the silence. She started to read the words.

She hadn't searched me for lockpick wires. She had to know I had them on me. Twice before I'd used lockpicks to escape from the jail cells below the Dawn Palace. If I got the manacles off, I might be able to get down from the gallows and escape into the crowd.

It was a chance. Carefully, trying not to jingle the manacles, I felt up my shirt sleeve for the lockpick wire sewn into the seam.

". . . and for willful flaunting of the city's laws proscribing the deployment of pyrotechnic magic . . . ," Kerrn's flat voice said.

I pulled at the lockpick wire, the stitches holding it in place gave way, and it dropped into my hand, a thin strip of metal. The manacles were made with a simple twist plunger lock. With my fingers I bent the wire into the right shape.

". . . and wanton destruction of property both private and public . . . ," Kerrn went on, her voice starting to shake, still reading my list of crimes. But she was reading very slowly, giving me time.

I gripped the lockpick wire.

Quick hands.

Steady hands.

With the wire, I probed the lock. There, the plunger. I slotted the wire into place and gripped it tightly to flick it open.

As I turned the wire, a sudden cold weight settled into me. My fingers slowed, stiffened. The lockpick wire dropped from the lock, falling to the box I was standing on.

I gasped. At the sound, Kerrn whirled around, then glanced down to see the lockpick wire at my feet. She muttered a curse under her breath.

"Kerrn, it's here," I whispered.

She stared at me, her hand on her sword.

"Captain, you must proceed," Nimble called from the row of chairs in front of the gallows.

I looked up at the sky. It was flatter and whiter than before, like the lid of a pot pressing down. The air was completely still. I turned to Kerrn, my heart pounding. "Arhionvar is here," I said, louder this time.

Kerrn stood still as stone, her mouth half open, about to give the order. A guard bent down and took the corners of the box, ready to pull it away. The rope wrapped tight 'round my neck like a snake.

Kerrn raised her hand. The guard paused.

Way off in the distance I heard a faint roaring sound. A wind coming.

Kerrn cocked her head, listening.

The roaring got louder. The banners on the corners of the Dawn Palace started flapping, flowing in the wind like slithering snakes. The tops of the trees outside the gate stirred. In the crowd, people looked up, or off to the east where the roaring sound was coming from. A few hats blew off in the growing wind.

"Hang him, Captain!" Nimble shrieked from the row of chairs.

Kerrn pointed at the guardsman. "Do not touch that box."

"Yes, Captain," the guard said.

In the crowd, somebody screamed. I heard another scream that came from the front of the Dawn Palace; it sounded like Rowan. A prickle of dread ran up my neck like cold fingers.

From where I was standing, I had the best view.

Behind the Dawn Palace, a wall of roiling black clouds, surging, flashing with lightning, boiled up out of the east. The wind rose, whistling through the spires on the Dawn Palace roof.

The whirl of wind and cloud widened along the eastern edge of the city; the air darkened. Nimble, his robe flapping in the wind, stepped up the gallows stairs.

I felt a tug at my hands. I looked over my shoulder.

Kerrn, putting the key into the manacles.

"Hurry," I said.

She gave a quick nod.

The black clouds rose higher, looming over the city, cresting, about to break, to drown us all. Then it did crest, and a black wave of dread crashed down, washing through the courtyard. People screamed and started to flee. At the base of the gallows, the magisters cowered and clung to their locus stones. They didn't know any spells that could stop Arhionvar. The dread gripped me so tightly that I couldn't move.

It was too late. We weren't ready. The city would be lost.

Then the Wellmet magic fought back. From the direction of the Twilight a burst of sparkling starlight and blackest night fountained up from the Dusk House pit, surging across the river, arcing across the white sky in bolts of silver and midnight to crash against the boiling clouds of Arhionvar. The dread magic flinched back. Thunder rolled out, shaking the ground.

The manacles dropped to the floor. I reached up, trying to get the noose off my neck. Too tight. "I can't get the—"

Kerrn pushed my hands out of the way and loosened the knot, then jerked the rope over my head. "Go!" she shouted.

I jumped off the box, my legs shaky.

Nimble reached the top of the stairs. "Captain Kerrn!" he panted, pointing at me.

Kerrn drew her sword. "Go!" she said to me

again, and she swung the sword around until it was pointing at Nimble's chest. "You fool!" she shouted at him. "Do you not see he was right? The dread magic has come. You are a wizard! Do your duty!"

I stumbled, then ducked past Nimble and darted down the stairs. People were still running out of the courtyard. The wind howled. Dread pressed down from overhead. I joined the crowds, fleeing as a blanket of blackest night and dread fell over the city.

Rowan Forestal

I stepped out of my mother's room for a breath of air. Two guards were there, and Argent, who looked frightened. The guards wouldn't let him in, he said. He told me Conn had been put on trial for returning from exile and sentenced to death by hanging, and that the sentence was being carried out right then.

They'd acted too fast—I wasn't ready.

I dashed to my room to get my sword, then ran through the palace to the front doors. When I got there, I saw, over the heads of the crowd, Conn on the gallows, facing away from me. They'd stood him on a box and put a noose around his neck. He was standing very straight and still, and he looked so alone. I screamed at Captain Kerrn to stop—she was too far away to hear—and started pushing my way through the crowd. I had my sword; if a guard had tried to stop me I would have killed him. I feared I would be too late.

Then Arhionvar arrived. I tried to get back into

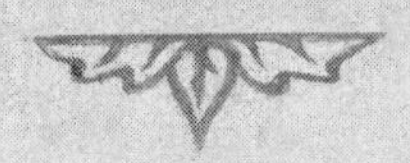

the Dawn Palace to save my mother, but Argent grabbed my arm and pulled me away, and we were caught up in the fleeing crowds. The city's magisters were fleeing with them.

I must find Magister Nevery, and find out whether my mother is still in the Dawn Palace, and I must be sure Conn got down safely from the gallows.

CHAPTER 25

The darkness of Arhionvar's arrival in the city lasted all the rest of the day and into a heavy, black night without stars or moon. The magics battled at the edge of the river, Arhionvar pushing into the Twilight, the Wellmet magic surging up to push it back over the Sunrise,

but not strong enough to push it out of the city altogether.

As night fell, Arhionvar attacked with tendrils of blackest dread that snaked up the Twilight streets, and with fiery rocks that smashed down out of the sky and burned whatever they touched. From outside I heard people screaming, and the howling of wind, and deep rolls of thunder.

I crouched against a wall in a cellar in the Twilight, the cold dread of Arhionvar pressing down on me. The other wizards of the city must feel it, too. No wonder the magisters had run away; they hadn't believed this kind of magic was real. Arhionvar was searching for me. It wanted to use me, as it'd used Jaggus, the sorcerer-king, to finish taking over the city.

During the darkest part of the night, I heard a *tk-tk-tk* on the stone stairs leading down into the cellar. Pip. As the dragon got closer, I felt better, stronger.

"*Lothfalas*," I whispered. My voice sounded hoarse and thin.

At the bottom of the stairs a soft greeny-gold

light glowed—my locus magicalicus inside Pip—and then Pip opened its mouth and breathed out green sparks that spun in a tiny whirlwind up to the low ceiling.

I caught my breath. Near the floor, easing away from Pip's light, hung a snarl of misery eels, twining around each other like ribbons of black smoke. They faded back into a dark corner, not moving. Waiting.

I shivered. If I'd fallen asleep, the misery eels would've had me.

Pip eyed the corner full of eels like a cat eyeing a mouse. Its tail twitched. It crouched, then, breathing out another puff of sparks, it leaped into the middle of the nest of eels. They scattered from Pip, flowing up the walls, oozing into cracks and corners. Pip scrabbled after one of them, crawling straight up the wall, trapping the eel in a corner, where it thrashed. Pip crept closer.

The light was getting dim. "*Lothfalas*," I said again.

Breathing out light, Pip leaped. A spark caught.

Flaming, the misery eel fell from the corner to the floor, twisting and fizzling like a bit of paper flaring up, then burning down to a blackened strip of ash.

Pip hopped down from the corner and stalked along the wall. Looking for more eels, I guessed.

"Thanks, Pip," I said.

It ignored me. After a while it flew up the stairs, away.

I closed my eyes and tried not to feel the heavy dread of Arhionvar or the empty echo of my stomach, and waited for morning.

After a long time, the sound of the wind died, the dread lifted, and gray light seeped into the cellar.

The coming of the light meant that it was time to do something. I uncurled myself from my dark corner. My stomach growled.

I climbed out of the cellar, blinking at the light. I was in an alley off of a street called Needles and Pins in the Deeps, the part of the Twilight not far from the mudflats. Pip was somewhere nearby, tied to me by the string of my locus magicalicus.

I went to the end of the alley and peered out from the shadows. Needles and Pins Street led uphill from the Night Bridge, and it was more crowded than usual, people walking in groups of two and three, leading crying children, carrying sacks and packing cases, and throwing frightened looks over their shoulders.

Overhead, the sky was flat white, as it'd been the day before, and the air was cold. I looked toward the east and saw a line in the sky where a black bank of clouds hung over the Sunrise, ending just at the edge of the river. Arhionvar. Wellmet had fought off the dread magic, but Arhionvar was gathering its strength. It'd go back on the attack as soon as night fell. Then it'd come for me. It needed a wizard, and it wanted me because I had a connection to the Wellmet magic, and it could use me to do even worse things to the city.

I looked toward the north, where the factories lined the river. No clouds of sooty smoke; the factories were closed. Bricks and shards of glass and broken shutters, torn off houses by the wind during the night, were scattered in the street. A pale sun hung behind the clouds, shedding a greenish-gray light. The air was still, no wind, but it tingled like a storm about to break.

Right. I had a locus magicalicus and I knew where the Wellmet magic was, gathering its strength, I hoped. I'd been needing to talk to the magic since the very first time I'd done a pyrotechnic experiment, and now I could. I headed up the hill, toward the Dusk House pit.

I paused in an alley, looking out at Sark Square. Here the crowds were thicker. People were filling the square; they'd fled with everything they could carry on their backs, or stuff into a carriage, or pay a drover with a wagon to carry for them. Sunrise people. Most of them had never been to the Twilight before. The Twilight people stood in doorways or, like me, lurked in alleyways, watching them come.

I wasn't sure what the Twilight people would do. If I'd still been a gutterboy, I might've been working the crowds, picking pockets or stealing things off the back of a wagon to sell to a swagshop. But the city was under attack, and the Sunrise people needed help, not thievery.

I caught a glimpse of something out of the corner of my eye, a flash of white slinking into an alleyway. I followed.

There, hovering in the shadows beside a pile of rags and garbage. A cat, sleek and white, with a flat head and raked-back, sharp ears. Seeing me, it crouched, its tail lashing, and snarled.

Predator-cat. I'd seen a cat like that one before. The sorcerer-king had kept one as a pet. It was a watcher for Arhionvar, just like the black birds were for the Wellmet magic.

With a screech, a black bird plunged out of the sky, landing on the cat. It hissed and swiped a needle-clawed paw at the bird, which fluttered, pecking at the cat's narrow eyes.

I could help; I knew a flame spell from the book Nevery'd given me. Pip—I needed Pip. I glanced wildly around and caught a glimpse of greeny-gold wings, Pip flying up to perch on the edge of a roof.

As I opened my mouth to call Pip, a heavy hand came down on my shoulder and spun me around. The minion Fist.

Drats. I didn't have time for threats and sacks over my head.

"Little blackbird," Fist said. His partner, Hand, loomed up behind him.

"Fist, I have to get to the pit where Dusk House used to be," I said. And get that cat away from the bird.

"You have to get where we're taking you, is what," Fist said, grabbing me by the scruff of my neck.

The black bird and the white cat were still fighting when they dragged me away.

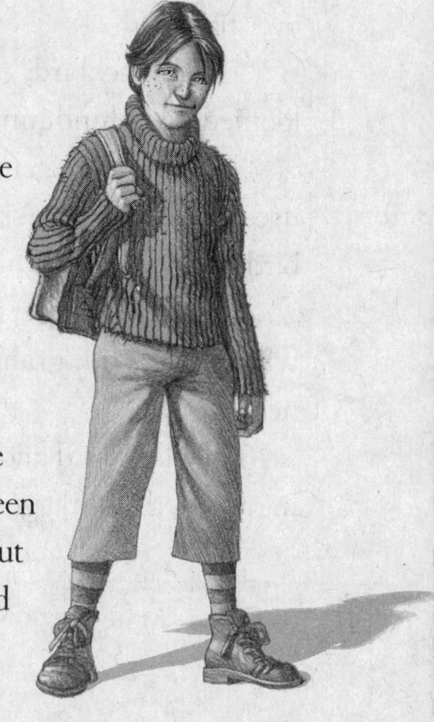

The minions brought me to the old guardhouse on Clink Street, down the narrow stone steps to the cellar with the empty cells and the cobwebs in the corners.

When they'd brought me here before, the room had been empty except for minions, but now a padded armchair stood at the other end next to a desk.

An oil lantern was set on the desk along with an ink-stand and piles of papers.

Sitting in the chair was Embre.

What was *he* doing here?

At the bottom of the stairs, Fist gave me a shove toward the other end of the room; then he and Hand went back up the stairs.

I went across the room and stood before Embre. "Hello," I said.

He looked me up and down, his black eyes sharp. He looked like a bundle of sticks wearing a too-large black suit and waistcoat. He wasn't smudged with soot as he usually was. "You nearly did the rope jig yesterday," Embre said.

The hanging, he meant. I nodded.

From the direction of the stairs came the *tk-tk-tk* of claws on stone. Pip. It crouched at the bottom of the stairs, not coming any closer.

Embre saw Pip and looked at me with his eyebrows raised.

I shrugged.

"I assume this is the arrival of the *bad magic* you

told me about," Embre said.

"Yes, it is," I said. "Arhionvar is here. I have to go talk to the Wellmet magic."

The lanternlight flickered in Embre's dark eyes and made them gleam. Then he spoke quietly. "For a long time I was trying to decide whether to have you killed," he said.

I blinked. Have me killed? By who? And why? "What d'you mean?"

Embre shook his head and gave a half smile. "I thought you wanted to be Underlord. It's what *he* wanted you for."

What Crowe had wanted, he meant.

"Isn't that right?" Embre asked, leaning forward. "Crowe wanted you to be Underlord after him?"

I nodded. But I didn't want to talk about it.

"I couldn't figure you out," Embre went on, sitting back again. "If you were Crowe's, why'd he have a word out on you? Why were you living on the streets like a gutterboy? And then you met up with that wizard and started telling people you were a wizard yourself." He shook his head. "I thought you were lying, especially after Crowe was exiled. I thought you'd try to take over as Underlord then. I was ready to have Fist and Hand knock you on the head and drop you in the river. But instead you came asking me and Sparks for pyrotechnic materials to do magic. It didn't make any sense. Who would want to be a wizard when he could be Underlord?"

I stared at him. He was the one who didn't make any sense. Who'd want to be Underlord when he could be a wizard?

Then I thought about it. "D'*you* want to be Underlord, Embre?" I asked.

His smile sharpened. "I *am* the Underlord, Conn."

Oh. How could I have been so stupid? Of course he was.

"My true name is Embre-wing," he said.

An embre-wing was a kind of black bird with a patch of red and gold feathers like embers on its shoulders. I'd seen embre-wings perched on reeds along the river near the mudflats.

"You're Crowe's?" I whispered. He had to be, with a black bird name. It meant he and Crowe were family.

Embre's face sharpened. "No. Not his." He nodded down at his stick legs. "Crowe did that to me. He broke my legs so I couldn't walk."

I stared at him. My mouth felt dry, full of dust. Embre'd had his legs broken by Crowe. Just as my mother, Black Maggie, had. She'd died of it, and then Crowe had taken me into Dusk House to train me, because my name was a black bird name, too. A *connwaer* was a black bird with a ruffled black crest. But I'd run away, and every time Crowe brought me back and had the minions beat the fluff out of me, I'd run away again until I got better at melting into shadows and he couldn't catch me anymore.

I hadn't known anything about Embre. Embre-wing. I swallowed down some of the dust. "Crowe was my mother's brother," I said.

Embre nodded. "He was my father."

"Why'd he break your legs?" I asked.

"By his calculations, I was too weak to become Underlord after him. He broke my legs to get rid of me." Embre watched me carefully. "To make room for you."

Embre must hate me, then. I shivered and wrapped my arms around myself.

"D'you see why I thought about having you killed?" Embre asked.

I nodded.

"*He* would've done it," Embre said.

He was right; Crowe had hurt people to get them out of his way, or to make other people do what he wanted.

"But I'm not like him," Embre said suddenly.

I hoped he wasn't. "What're you going to do?"

Embre gave me a dry smile. "I'm going to do what the Underlord is supposed to do," he said.

Get minions to beat the fluff out of me, that meant. I hunched into my sweater.

"I'm going to protect the Twilight, Cousin." He gave his half smile again.

Oh. Embre was right. That's what an Underlord did. A good one, anyway. *Cousin*, he'd called me. A sudden bubble of happiness rose up in my chest.

Embre returned my smile. "I am the Twilight's Underlord. And you, as the Twilight's wizard, are going to tell me what the Underlord and his pyrotechnic materials can do to help fight off this Arhionvar magic. Are you ready?" he asked me.

"Yes," I said. "I'm ready."

Before Embre and I made plans, the minion Hand brought another chair and a pot of tea, and a plate of boiled potatoes and carrots with butter, and a roast chicken, and a dish of stewed apples for afters, and while Embre drank tea, I sat at the desk and ate all of the food except for half the chicken, which I took on the plate to the corner where Pip was hiding in the shadows. The dragon skittered away from me, so I put the plate on the floor and went back to Embre.

"He doesn't like you?" Embre asked.

"It's an it, not a he," I said.

"Your locus magicalicus, or so I'm told," Embre said.

I nodded.

He laughed.

But it wasn't funny.

When I'd finished telling Embre what Nevery and I had been doing to prepare the city for Arhionvar's attack, I told him that I had to go to the Dusk House

pit, and he let me go.

The day was getting later. I left Clink Street and ran up Wyrm Street as fast as I could. No people were around.

Over the pit the sky was flat and white with rags of darker smoke drifting across it. The air smelled smoky; fires were burning in the Twilight from the rain of fiery rocks during the night. Embre had minions working with the Twilight people to put them out.

Catching my breath, I crouched behind the shattered stones that had been the gateway leading into Dusk House and peered in. The area around the pit was deserted. The magisters should've been here helping the magic. But they were somewhere else, probably in the cellars below Magisters Hall, cowering and wishing Arhionvar would go away. The air felt thick with the magic, not protecting me as it usually did, not warm, but wound tight with fright. Pip perched at the top of the gate post, drawn by the magic, I guessed.

I got to my feet, crunched across to the edge of the pit, and looked down.

Swirling stars and darkness filled the steep-sided pit. The magic was here. It'd fought off Arhionvar last night, and maybe it was gathering its strength again, but it couldn't hold out for much longer.

Pip flapped over and landed on the ground nearby. That was enough to get the magic's attention. It heaved up from the pit, washing over me, picking me up as it'd done before, and picking up Pip, too.

This time I knew how to talk to it. It could hear me because of my locus stone, in Pip, and ever since I'd become a wizard I'd been reading enough grimoires and spell-books to know what to say.

I shouted spellwords. The magic talked back, spellwords that hum-thrummed in my bones, deeper than my ears could hear. I couldn't understand them all, but I understood enough. The blackness and bright stars whirled around me until I had to close my eyes and listen.

For a moment, behind my closed eyes, I saw the city as the magic saw it. A rolling black plain with a line of glowing slowsilver running through the middle of it where the river was, and patches of warmth and life—that was the city and its people. The magic knew people lived in Wellmet, and it wanted to protect them. It couldn't tell one person from another; they were just points of warmth in the darkness. Only the wizards stood out like twinkling stars in a black sky, noticeable to the magic because of their locus stones. Before I'd found Nevery, I'd been a patch of cold to the magic because I'd been more alone than anybody else in the city. Maybe the magic had found me after my mother'd been killed and Crowe'd had a word out on me, when I'd been trying to sleep in a freezing doorway in the Twilight. Maybe it'd known I was a wizard, and it had saved me, so I could save it.

The magic was alone, too. All the other magics in the world were far away, at other cities. It was sick and weak, too. It'd been weak even before

Underlord Crowe and Pettivox had built their device to imprison it. A city shouldn't be like Wellmet, healthy and whole on one side and rotten and empty on the other. It wasn't balanced. I should've seen it a long time ago.

The magic was barely holding out against Arhionvar. It could fight for another night, maybe two, and then Arhionvar would have it.

The magic told me what I had to do.

I didn't want to do it.

But I would.

My cousin, Embre, had called me the Twilight's wizard. And I was. I would do what the magic needed me to do, but first I had to talk to Nevery. When I saw the city as the magic saw it, I'd seen a cluster of locus stones glowing on the islands that ran through the river.

One of the glowing spots had to be Nevery. He was at Heartsease, busy preparing our defenses. He must've escaped from the Dawn Palace before Arhionvar arrived.

As I left the Dusk House pit, I heard a flutter of wings, and a black bird fell out of the sky and landed at my feet. I crouched down and set it on its feet. It ruffled its feathers.

I took a scrap of paper from a quill tied to its leg. Just one word in Nevery's handwriting.

Heartsease

Yes, Nevery, I knew.

Slinking through alleys, I headed for Fleetside Street and then the Night Bridge.

As I reached the bridge, the heavy, red sun sank behind the dark tenements of the Twilight, making shadows reach out like long, dark arms. The air was icy cold and still. The streets were deserted; people were hiding from the coming of the night.

The bridge was empty, too. All of the Sunrise people had come across during the day, then. The shuttered houses built right on the bridge leaned over me, cutting off the light.

I heard a sound like the distant whine of factory machines. A dusty breeze sprang up and brushed past me, plucking at my sweater.

The darkness at the other end of the bridge was moving.

From behind me, I heard *pip!* and then Pip darted into the narrow crack between two houses.

The factory noise got louder, and from out of the shadows came a whirling column of wind twice the height of a tall man, clogged with dust; it wobbled from one side of the road to the other, bumping up against the houses, ripping off shutters and gutters and chunks of brick, howling toward me.

I scrambled aside into a doorway, crouched down, and put my arms over my head. The shriek of the whirlwind grew louder.

Peering under my arm, I saw the whirlwind spin closer. Then I felt a surge of Wellmet magic rise up like a wall. As it met the wall, the column of wind lifted up like a long finger, and then its winds shredded, flying off like bits of dusty rag. Bricks and nails and shards of glass and splinters of wood spun out and rained down into the road.

Dust swirled in the last eddies of wind. I got to my feet and stepped out of the doorway.

Arhionvar was making an attack on the Twilight. I turned to keep going across the bridge, but the road between the leaning houses had turned white. In the greeny-black light, it seemed to move.

I blinked. The road ahead was flowing with white predator-cats, slinking along close to the ground. They paced closer, their eyes glowing.

Right, I couldn't go this way. I turned and ran.

So many people had rowed across the river from the Sunrise that finding a boat was easy. I wasn't good at rowing, but I could do it well enough. While I rowed I looked over my shoulder, watching the bank of clouds over the Sunrise lower until the Dawn Palace on its hill disappeared in a black fog, and the werelights along the streets winked out one by one.

After a while, the boat bumped against the black rocks along the waterline of the Heartsease island. I set the oars in the bottom of the boat and climbed out onto the rocks.

The new Heartsease was almost finished being built, with windows in place and stairs leading up to an arched front doorway. The builders had stopped their work before finishing the roof.

The ground floor windows glowed with pinkish werelight. Nevery. And Benet, I hoped.

Pip was still in the Twilight, near one of the warehouses along the water. My locus magicalicus pulled at me. I stood waiting for Pip under the big tree in the courtyard, jittering a little, looking out over the dark water.

Pip didn't come. It'd have to come eventually; it couldn't resist the pull from me to my locus stone for too long.

I turned and went across the cobbled courtyard, trying not to make any noise. The werelight was coming from the ground floor, what would be the storeroom and Benet's room when Heartsease was finished. I cat-footed up to one of the arched doorways and crouched beside it in the shadows. I peered in.

Since I'd been here last the floor had been finished, blocks of slate scattered with bricks and bent nails. Somebody had gathered boxes to use as chairs, and planks were set across two barrels for a table. Sitting on the boxes were Brumbee and a few of the duchess's council members, and Argent. The bristle-bearded guard Farn leaned against one of the walls, along with six other Dawn Palace guards. Nevery stood beside the plank table looking down at a piece of paper spread on it; beside him stood Rowan, wearing her sword, pointing at something on the paper; behind Rowan was bat-faced Nimble in his brown magisters robe.

"I wouldn't recommend it," Nevery was saying.

Rowan leaned closer to the paper—a map, I guessed—squinting to see better, and traced her finger along a line. "What about this way, Magister Nevery?"

Nevery frowned. "Hmmm."

Nimble spoke up with his high, whiny voice. "We cannot send the few trained guards we have on a mission that could well be useless. We need them here, protecting us."

Rowan whirled to face him. "Useless?" She opened her mouth to say more, then closed her eyes for a moment and clenched and unclenched her fists. After taking a deep breath, she said, more calmly, "In the absence of my mother, I am the one who must make these decisions."

Across the room, the guard Farn nodded. "Until we find Captain Kerrn, we report to you, Lady Rowan," he said.

Rowan nodded. "Thank you, Farn." She put her hand on her sword. "I will lead the mission myself, with Sir Argent, and the guards will come with us.

We could use a wizard, too."

Nimble gave a shiver. "No wizard with any sense would go to the Sunrise at such a time. And if you are acting for the duchess, Lady Rowan, then you are too valuable to risk on this mission."

Mission? What were they up to? *In the absence of my mother,* Rowan had said. Was the duchess still in the Dawn Palace? I didn't see Benet. He'd been arrested; was he trapped there, too?

I got to my feet.

At the table, Nevery caught sight of me at the edge of the doorway. His eyes widened, then he gave a slight nod.

Come in, that meant.

I stepped into the room.

Nevery said something in a low voice to Rowan; she turned and saw me.

"Conn!" she said. Her face was pale and soot-smudged; her hair was tied back into a tail with a piece of string. She wore a green wormsilk dress with dirty lace cuffs and a torn ruffle along the hem and had her swordbelt buckled around her waist.

"Hello, Ro," I said.

The others in the room turned to stare as I came farther into the room.

"That is the criminal who was to be hanged!" one of the councilors said, getting up from her box-chair, pointing at me.

"He brought that huge dragon here!" said another.

"Guards, arrest him!" Nimble said.

Farn didn't move; Rowan raised her hand and everyone fell silent. She really was in charge.

"Well, Conn?" Rowan asked.

I glanced down at the plank table. The paper was a map of the Sunrise, all the streets drawn in and the Dawn Palace carefully labeled. All under the cloud of Arhionvar.

Rowan saw where I was looking. "Conn, my mother was trapped in the Dawn Palace after Arhionvar arrived, and she's—" She gulped and went on more quietly. "She's been very ill."

I looked across the table at Nevery. "Is Benet there, too?"

"Yes, boy," Nevery said.

They weren't going to like this. But sending guards in didn't make any sense. "I'll go to the Dawn Palace," I said.

After some shrieking and shouting from Nimble and the councilors, Nevery and Rowan took me aside, to give me a talking-to, I figured.

"All right, my lad?" Nevery asked, and put his hand on my shoulder.

I nodded.

"Conn, Nimble overstepped

himself," Rowan said. "I didn't know what he was doing. Argent tried to get in to tell me," she went on. "I was with my mother."

"Ro, what're you talking about?"

"You were nearly hanged!" she said.

"Oh, that," I said.

Nevery gave me a quick, keen-gleam glance.

Rowan shook her head. "You can't go alone on this mission to rescue my mother," she said.

"Kerrn's there, too?" I asked.

Rowan nodded.

I knew Kerrn. While the rest of the guards and wizards had been running away from Arhionvar, she'd done her duty, went to protect the duchess, and got trapped in the Dawn Palace for it.

And Benet, locked in a prison cell.

The magic needed me to do this thing, and I would do it, but I had to get Benet out first. And Kerrn and the duchess.

"Farn will go with you," Rowan said, "and six guards."

I remembered how noisy the guards had been

sneaking into the sorcerer-king's fortress. "Ro, Arhionvar's magic. The guards won't be any help."

Nevery shook his head. "We have no idea what you can expect to find in the Sunrise, boy. I have been reading every grimoire I could get my hands on. I've found nothing to help us."

I knew what to expect. White predator-cats, dusty whirlwinds, and creeping dread.

"I don't like the idea of you going alone, either," Nevery said.

"You should stay here to help Rowan," I said. I didn't want him coming with me. It'd be too dangerous, and I couldn't stand it if something happened to him.

"I know that, curse it," Nevery growled. "This is how you get into trouble, Conn. Inadequate planning." He glanced at Rowan. "Still, if he needs to fight his way out again he'll have Captain Kerrn and Benet to help. Lady Rowan, I think Conn alone might have the best chance of getting to the Dawn Palace." He switched his glare back to me. "As long as he doesn't do anything stupid."

I didn't answer. Going to the Sunrise was exactly what I needed to do—if I was going to do what the Wellmet magic wanted me to. I didn't know if that was stupid or not.

The rest of the magisters and guards and councilors, led by Nimble, went through the tunnels to Magisters Hall to sleep and find supplies.

Nevery and Rowan and Argent, with Farn and another guard, pulled the box-chairs up to the hearth in the shell of Heartsease to wait for morning. One of the guards built a fire to keep the night off. I leaned against the wall beside the hearth, where the guard boiled water for tea. The other guard brought us stale bread and cheese to eat. Lady-the-cat came and climbed into my lap and lay there purring.

I scratched Lady behind the ears and told Nevery and Rowan about the flame dragon and the cave dragon and the slowsilver scales, and the top of the mountain exploding and my ideas about how the dragon gave up its body to become a magical being.

"The magic's original form is dragon, then,"

Nevery said. "Hmmm. Interesting." He was quiet for another moment and said, "Then every city was built on a dragon lair. And pyrotechnics. Clearly dragons have an affinity to smoke and fire, an affinity that must persist even after they have turned into pure magic. Very interesting indeed."

I nodded. Then I told them about how the thief dragon had eaten my locus magicalicus.

"It was not a jewel stone?" Nevery asked.

I shook my head. No, it'd been ordinary.

Nevery looked thoughtful and pulled at the end of his beard. "Hmmm. Anything else, boy?"

Yes, there was something else. "Embre's my cousin," I said. "And he's the new Underlord."

Rowan leaned forward. "You mean Embre the pyrotechnist?" She'd only met Embre once, when we'd gone to him for blackpowder ingredients.

"He's the Underlord, is he?" Nevery said, his eyes gleaming. "While you were gone, Connwaer, I worked with Embre on the pyrotechnic traps."

Right, well, the traps might still be able to help us, but not in the way Nevery expected. He didn't need to know that, though, or he'd get suspicious about what I was up to. "Embre's making preparations to defend the Twilight from Arhionvar," I said.

"Good," Nevery said. But he gave me another one of his keen-gleam glances. He knew that I always told him the truth, but he also knew that I didn't always tell him everything.

"Then Magister Nevery can deal with the pyrotechnic materials," Rowan said. She gave him her sideways look. "I believe he knows a thing or two about pyrotechnics. See what you can prepare to help with the defense of the city. Conn, you take care of your mission to bring my mother out of the palace. Nevery and I will work with this new Underlord."

That'd be a first, the Underlord and the duchess's daughter working together. But it's what the city needed.

After a while, Rowan told me to be careful, and she and Argent left for the Twilight so they could meet with Embre.

Nevery should've gone with Rowan, but he stayed behind to talk to me.

I stared into the fire, my eyes getting heavy with sleep. Lady had gone off to hunt mice. I could sense Pip on the banks of the Twilight side of the river. The pull of my locus magicalicus made my bones itch. Thinking about what the Wellmet magic wanted me to do made my insides feel shivery and scared.

Nevery got up to throw some chunks of wood onto the fire. He sat back down on his box-chair and studied me. "You're up to something."

I was, true. But I didn't answer.

"Don't be stupid, boy," Nevery growled.

"I won't, Nevery," I said.

"Curse it," Nevery muttered. "It's risky for you to go into the Sunrise, boy. After what happened in Desh, the predator magic will be drawn to you."

He was right. When I didn't answer, he glared at me.

"Nevery, it tried to get me in Desh, and I didn't

let it. Now I've got Pip with me. It'll be all right."

"Pip?" Nevery said. "Is that what you're calling your dragon?"

"It's not mine," I said. I remembered something. "Nevery, d'you know what the spellword *tallennar* means?" The word the cave dragon had spoken.

"*Tallennar.* No." His eyebrows bristled. "Pay attention, boy. The dragon is your locus magicalicus, you say." He leaned toward me, lowering his voice. "Can you do magic?"

I shrugged. If Pip got close enough I could.

"I don't like this," Nevery muttered.

Neither did I. But I was the only wizard who knew how to melt into shadows, and under Arhionvar, the Sunrise was nothing but shadows. I could get Benet and Kerrn and the duchess out. They would go back across the river, and I'd stay in the Sunrise to deal with Arhionvar.

After a couple of hours, Nevery left to meet with Embre about the defense of the Twilight, and I went out of Heartsease.

It should've been morning, but the sky was still dark. The air was cold; my breath puffed out in

steamy clouds before my face. Rubbing my arms to stay warm, I went across the cobbled courtyard to stand under the big tree. A few black birds perched there with their heads under their wings.

Pip was there, too; it'd come over during the night. The little dragon glared at me as I went past the tree and out to the tumbled black rocks that lined the shore of Heartsease.

The river was dark and still. I turned my back on the Sunrise and looked across at the Twilight. From here the steep streets seemed empty, desolate. The wind and flame from the first night hadn't come back. Arhionvar was waiting until tonight, I figured, saving its strength so it could finish the Wellmet magic once and for all. I didn't have much time.

I climbed into the rowboat and dropped the oars into the oarlocks. I looked back at Heartsease, a ragged, dark shadow against the black clouds.

Good-bye, Nevery.

The river rippled silver under the gray-black sky.

I rowed myself to one of the docks that led to stone steps that went up to a street along the river.

Black clouds pressed down from overhead; the air was thick with yellow-black fog. Even though it was morning, it was as dark as twilight, but with no stars. The air was cold and still. Even my breaths sounded loud. Prickles of dread picked at me with icy fingers.

I stood on the dock, waiting for Pip, and then felt the pull of my locus stone getting stronger. From Heartsease came a golden blur, skimming over the waves. Pip landed at the end of the dock and perched there, lashing its tail.

Right, time to go. I went up the stone steps and onto the Sunrise street. It led along the riverbank; I turned and headed up a wider street that led uphill, toward the Dawn Palace. As I climbed higher, seeing nobody, hearing nothing, the air grew colder. I was glad for my black sweater.

It was too quiet. The sky grew darker, and the dread pressed down on me; the air grew thick and hard to breathe. The houses on either side of the street were empty, their doors hanging open from people fleeing as fast as they could run from the Arhionvar dread.

I wondered if Arhionvar could see me, a bright point in the darkness, and if it was waiting for me.

I paused and looked back toward the Twilight. Oh, no. Black clouds crept across the sky, crossing the line of the river through the city. As the clouds spread, fingers of whirling wind poked down from them and went skipping across the Twilight side of the river. Wherever they touched, fire leaped up. Nevery was over there somewhere, and Rowan. And the Wellmet magic, readying itself in the Dusk House pit. Arhionvar had made darkness in the daytime; this was its attack. I'd run out of time.

I pushed on through the darkness and dread, seeing nothing and no one, until I reached the Dawn Palace. I paused at the gate, peering in. The gallows tree stood in the middle of the courtyard, the noose hanging down. The air was still, icy cold and stifling at the same time, but overhead the black clouds churned with silent wind.

On cat feet I crept across the courtyard and up the steps to the front doors, and went in. My footsteps echoed as I went through the wide hallway there.

I needed to find Kerrn first. She'd know where Benet was. The duchess's rooms, then. I raced down a dark hallway and up three sets of stairs, then along another carpeted hallway. Pip followed.

There, the duchess's door. It was shut. And locked.

I knocked, the sound faint in the thick air. "Kerrn," I whispered. She'd never hear me. "Captain Kerrn!" I shouted.

The keys jangled in the lock and the door flew open. Kerrn stood there with her sword drawn. Her braid had come unraveled and her face was pale and smudged with soot.

"You all right?" I asked.

She jerked out a nod.

"We need to hurry," I said. "Where's the duchess?"

Kerrn stared at me, her teeth clenched and eyes cold. When she spoke, her accent was very thick. "It is too late."

Oh. Oh, no. Poor Rowan.

Kerrn pointed farther into the room. On the duchess's bed was a long, covered shape—her body.

"She has just died. She has turned to stone," Kerrn said quietly. "We must leave her here. We can go through the streets?"

I nodded. "We have to get Benet first. D'you have keys?"

"I have them, " she said.

We hurried down through the palace to the prison cells underneath it.

They'd put him in the same cell they always put me in. When we opened the door, Benet bulled out, swinging a broken-off chair leg. Kerrn dropped the keys and went for her sword; then Benet saw me and stopped.

"You're not dead," he said.

No, I wasn't. I shook my head.

Benet reached out with a big hand and grabbed me by the scruff of my neck. He bent down and growled into my face, "Next time be more careful, you."

"I will, Benet," I said. My voice sounded squeaky.

"You'd better," he said, and let me go.

Boy is off on mission to lead Duchess, Captain Kerrn, Benet out of Dawn Palace.

Conditions in Twilight worsening. People frightened, growing desperate enough to flee city. All supplies cut off; food already growing short. Winds and fires making organization difficult.

Have met with Lady Rowan and new Underlord, Embre-wing. Can now see family resemblance between Connwaer and his cousin. Embre has set up tents in Sark Square for Sunrise people, organized patrols by minions, set gutterboys and guttergirls hunting down and trapping white predator-cats, spies of Arhionvar. Lady Rowan has sent Twilight and Sunrise people to work in fire teams, with buckets of water in case of sparks.

Went to Dusk House pit. Air there alive with magic.

Have returned to Heartsease. Am preparing pyrotechnic traps. We can set them at various points in the Twilight. Resulting explosions will strengthen our defense, make our weakened magic's spells stronger.

Kerrn and Benet and I headed down the hill from the Dawn Palace toward the bridge. Across the river, fires burned in the Twilight.

"How're we getting across?" Benet asked. Kerrn had been leading us toward the bridge.

"Not that way," I told her. "I've got a boat at a dock off High Street."

"This way, then," Kerrn said, turning right down a narrow alley. She went first, then Benet with his broken-off chair leg, then me.

As we came out onto a wide street, a whirlwind swept out of an alley ahead of us, blocking our way to the bridge. It spun in place in the middle of the street, flinging off shards of glass and splinters; a shard slashed across Benet's face, drawing a line of blood. Then another whirlwind appeared, and as one they turned and roared toward us.

"Get back!" Kerrn shouted. Her sword made a ringing sound as she drew it from its sheath. The whirlwind sent out a tendril of wind like a reaching arm, and Kerrn slashed at it with her sword until it dissolved into dust and stray breezes.

The other whirlwind hurled a chunk of brick, and Benet batted it aside with his chair leg. Benet turned and shoved me back into the alley. "Stay out of the way, you."

Right. I backed away, looking wildly around for Pip. I could help if I did some magic.

There, across the alley, perched on a third-story windowsill, far overhead. Too far for a spell to work very well.

"Pip!" I called.

The dragon cast me a glance and hopped off the windowsill, then flew higher to perch at the very edge of the roof.

At the mouth of the alley the fight with the whirlwinds went on; I heard a *clang* as a sword struck something, and then Benet shouted.

Wait. This was it. Benet and Kerrn were distracted. Time for me to do what I'd come here to do.

I stood in the alleyway, looking up at Pip. I needed it to come down and help me. "Pip, you're being stupid," I called. It didn't need to try so hard to stay away from me. I needed it with me while I dealt with Arhionvar. I wasn't going to hurt it.

Was I?

Oh. No. I was the one being stupid. The little

dragon crouched on the gutter, shivering, curling its tail around itself.

What if I'd been stuffed into an old knapsack and stolen away from my home, and knew that Nevery was gone forever? What if I had to stay with somebody because of a locus stone; what if that person kept using me to do magic? What would I think of the stranger who did that to me?

I'd hate him, was what.

"I'm sorry, Pip," I whispered. The little dragon looked so alone, perched up there.

Alone . . .

The Wellmet magic had chosen me because I'd been alone, because I could understand what that meant.

But I hadn't really understood.

The Wellmet magic had been a dragon. It was the only one of its kind here, but it had a city of people to protect, and we comforted it. Arhionvar didn't have anything. Its city had been destroyed, and all its people had fled. It was a predator because it was a wanderer, trying to steal a new city for itself, so it wouldn't be alone anymore. It was more alone than I'd ever been, even when I'd been a gutterboy sleeping in winter doorways in the Twilight.

"*Arhionvar*," I whispered.

I heard roaring inside my ears. Arhionvar pried at me with fingers made of stony dread. Black spots swam before my eyes. I shook my head and blinked the black away to see.

I just had to tell Kerrn and Benet to go on without me, and then I could deal with Arhionvar.

In the street, Kerrn swung her blade around and sliced the whirlwind in half. Bricks and wooden shards rained to the ground as it fell apart. The other whirlwind spun into an alley and disappeared.

Kerrn sheathed her sword. Benet swung around and spotted me in my alleyway.

"Come on," he said.

I kept my head down. "You go ahead," I said. "I've got something to do here."

I backed away a step, ready to run into the alley to get away, when Benet lunged forward and grabbed me by the shoulder.

"No you don't," he growled. "You said you'd be careful."

"Benet—" I said.

"Master Nevery wouldn't like it," he said. Keeping hold of my arm, he nodded at Kerrn.

I didn't say anything. Benet and Kerrn hurried us away, down the hill to the docks where we'd left the boat. We piled in and Benet set to the oars.

I felt Arhionvar's attention on me the whole way, in the dread pressing down and in the shadows that kept creeping in at the edge of my vision. I crouched in the bottom of the boat, shivering.

When we got to Heartsease, Benet dragged me out of the rowboat and across the cobblestones to find Nevery.

He was there, in the unfinished storage room. Barrels and sacks of blackpowder materials were piled around the room; on the plank table he'd laid out the ingredients for a slowsilver fuse like the one I'd read about in the Jaspers treatise. He sat on a box-chair at the table, measuring out a vial of tourmalifine crystals.

He glanced up, then looked back at the measuring. "Ah, Benet," he said. "Good. Just a moment."

I stared down at the floor. Arhionvar pulled at me, hanging over my head like a cloud of dread. My breath came short.

A clatter of footsteps on the cobblestones outside, and Rowan burst in the door. She spied me and came over.

"I saw Kerrn outside," she panted. "Where is my mother?"

I didn't look up.

"She's dead, Lady Rowan," Benet said.

At the table, I heard a *clink* as Nevery set down the vial, then heard him get to his feet.

Rowan stepped away from me. I stole a quick glance through the gathering darkness; her face was white.

"Conn?" Nevery said.

Arhionvar pulled at me, making it hard to think. "All right," I said. The words felt strange as I spoke them. Arhionvar was here, surrounding me with tendrils of shadow. "Nev—" My mouth felt frozen, like it was turning to stone. "Set—off the—pyrotechnic—traps."

Nevery reached out for me. I saw his lips moving, but couldn't hear him through the gathering dread.

They needed to get away. "Now!" I shouted, and my voice boomed out like a crash of thunder.

At the sound, the unfinished roof of Heartsease blew off, bricks and shards of wood spraying out into the night. Deepest black and silver against the clouds, magic arced down and slammed into me. Another bolt of magic followed, trailing sparks like a shooting star, wrapping me up in a blaze of light.

I threw my head back and looked up, into the blaze of stars and blackest, deepest night that was the magic. It drew me up; my feet left the ground; sparks rained down all around me.

Something pulled at my feet. I looked down through the magic.

Nevery held one leg; Rowan and Benet held the other, anchoring me to the earth.

"*Connwaer!*" Nevery shouted.

He knew my name, like all true names, had power; it smashed through the magic, weakening Arhionvar's hold on me.

I looked down at Nevery and Rowan and Benet. Wind whipped their clothes and they squinted against the bright light surrounding me. They held on to my feet tightly.

If I stayed with them, I couldn't do the thing I needed to do. *I'm sorry, Nevery.*

I kicked my feet free and let the magic pull me out of their hands. I saw a flash of glimmer-gold wings, and Pip shot past me, straight into the heart of the magic. Arhionvar pulled me up, and away.

The magic held me like a dragon holding me in its claw. Black clouds boiled around me; wisps of cloud fluttered in the wind; stars like sparks whirled past and then away. In the middle of the whirlwind, where I floated, it was black and silent and still. Pip hung in the

air near me, its wings stretched wide, its eyes flashing red.

The Wellmet magic had told me what to do next. From the larpenti spell and the embero spell I'd learned the word for *change*; from the finding spell I knew how to ask a question; from the spells in the book Nevery'd sent with me, I pieced together enough words to ask Arhionvar what it wanted. I shouted the spellwords as loud as I could; they went through my locus magicalicus and Pip, and the magic heard them.

It didn't answer in spellwords; it answered by showing me.

Slowly the black clouds opened. Through a gap like a window I saw a shining city in the mountains, surrounded by snow and white clouds and silence. The city of Arhionvar, as it'd once been. The picture shivered, and a crack opened in the middle of the city; I saw people on the streets with their mouths open, screaming, running away, but they didn't make any sound. Then half the mountain slid away, silently crumbling into boulders and clouds of snow, the people going with it, falling down into the darkness.

Dust and snow crystals billowed up, glinting in the sunshine. The slowsilver under the mountain drained away. The surviving people climbed down from the mountain and went to other cities. The Arhionvar magic was left alone, longing for its city full of people, desolate and empty. It wandered for a long, long time, searching, getting emptier and more alone. It wanted what Wellmet had, a city full of people, and to get that it needed a wizard to work its will. Me. It wanted me. Once it had me, it'd devour Wellmet's magic and use me to take over the city.

The cold, dead feeling of stone spread through me. My skin numbed; dread got into my chest and left me gasping for breath.

Then, I felt a prickle. Slowly my head turned. There was Pip, floating beside me, its teeth bared. On my hand, a bleeding bite mark, like drops of blood on white snow.

At the same moment, the warmth of the Wellmet magic flowed into me, pushing back the heavy dread of Arhionvar. Spellwords rattled through my bones, too loud for my ears to hear. Warmth flowed around cold stone. As the magics struggled, like dragons snapping and swirling together, whirlwinds spun down into the city. Fires blazed in the Twilight, sending black smoke-smudges into the sky; buildings crumbled in the Sunrise; the river raged and boiled, washing away the docks along its edges.

The dread stone feeling grew worse. Arhionvar was stronger—far stronger—than weakened Wellmet.

I couldn't let Arhionvar destroy Wellmet.

Then, from the Twilight, far below, I felt the first pyrotechnic trap explode. Nevery'd set it off. Then another, and another—blackpowder explosions that echoed and crashed and roared through the magics. I knew a banishing spell; I knew the spellwords for *exile.* With my help and the pyrotechnics, Wellmet could force Arhionvar out of the city. I opened my mouth to shout the banishing spell; I felt it gather in my throat, loud as thunder.

No.

Arhionvar had been a dragon just like Pip; it was a magic just like the magic of Wellmet. It couldn't be left to wander alone.

With the dread magic flowing through me and the warmth of the Wellmet magic swirling around me and Pip, I looked down at the city, spread out like a map below me. I needed the slowsilver for this spell.

There!

I spoke words and called on the magics, and the river lifted out of its banks, fat and full of fish and trash and mud, hanging above the city like a huge, brown, dripping snake, writhing and flowing in its own wind.

Left behind, in the river's channel through the rock Wellmet was built on, flowing around the wizards' islands, was the city's slowsilver. It was another river, shining like a silver ribbon.

I reached down with the magic and the river of slowsilver flowed from its banks, rippling up into the sky in a glowing arc and into my hands. Both of the magics yearned toward it. I gave one end of it to the Wellmet magic and the other end to Arhionvar, sealing the magics to the city and to each other. Like pyrotechnic materials combining, the magics crashed together and the slowsilver ribbon dissolved into a million shining droplets, hovering in the air, surrounding us.

One breath. Two breaths. Three breaths.

The spell needed one more thing to be completed.

I'd been chosen by both of the magics. I'd given up my first locus magicalicus for the magic, and I'd given up my home, Heartsease. I only had one more thing to give up.

Nevery, I'm sorry.

I gave the magics me.

The spell completed, the slowsilver rained down

and collected in the channel, binding the two magics to the city. The river crashed back down into its place. The whirlwinds spun themselves out and the Twilight fires flickered and died.

The last thing I saw was Pip, diving toward me, a streak of green and glittering gold wings.

And then I was gone.

Tried scrying globe yet again. No sign of boy. Winter nearly over. Grow more certain he will never be found.

City now has two magics, Arhionvar in the Sunrise and the old Wellmet magic in the Twilight, overlapping at the wizards' islands. Thus far, the magics seem at peace. City seems balanced in a way it has not, before.

Still, may leave Wellmet, travel. Duchess needs decent magister while city recovers and adjusts to new magic, and Heartsease nearly rebuilt, but cannot bear to stay here.

I miss him.

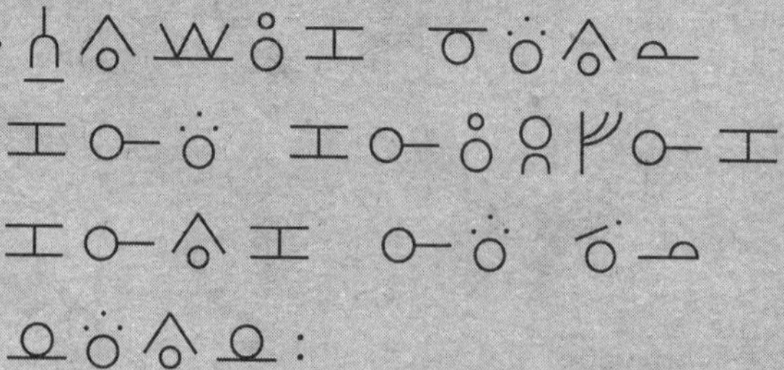

I woke up huddled in a doorway in a Twilight alley, blinking at the early-morning light.

A cold wind blew down the alley, pushing snow fine as dust before it. The sky overhead was gray. I shivered and got to my feet.

I looked down at myself. I had

on a black sweater with too-long sleeves that hung down over my hands. Nobody'd stolen my shoes; I was wearing good stout boots and knitted socks.

I hunched into the sweater and headed down the alley. My stomach was hollow with hunger. Maybe I could find a pocket to pick or I could steal a bit of bread from a Sark Square stall.

I peered out of the alley. The street was busy, full of people walking, a chimney swift and his boy carrying their brushes, a girl selling broadsheets, a woman working to fix a pothole.

The Twilight wasn't usually this busy, was it?

I skiffed back down the alley and headed up the hill toward Sark Square.

The market was busy, too. The air smelled like fish and bread baking. Beside one of the stalls a brazier was set up with magic fire burning in it; a few people stood around it, warming their hands. If I was lucky, one of them might have a pocket I could pick, and then I could buy a sausage in a biscuit for breakfast.

I edged up to the brazier and held up my hands.

The magic fire burned without crackling, giving off a wave of soft warmth like a blanket.

One of the other people at the fire looked up. He was a big man with a wide, ugly face. He nudged the man standing next to him, who was even bigger and uglier, with a lumpy nose and just one eyebrow.

"What, Hand?" the uglier man said.

The man called Hand pointed with his chin toward me.

The uglier man looked, and his eyes widened. "That you, Blackbird?" he asked.

Oh, no. The men were minions, weren't they? I stepped away from the fire.

The two men started around the brazier, coming after me.

As the uglier one reached for me, I ducked under his arm and slipped and fell on the icy cobblestones. I scrambled to my feet and backed away.

"No harm," the man said. "Underlord's been looking for you."

The Underlord? No, I didn't want to see him.

I turned and raced away, heading for an alley to hide in.

"Hoy, Blackbird! Come back!" the man shouted.

Not likely. I ran and hid, and they didn't catch me.

The next morning I woke up shivering in a doorway in Rat Hole, the deepest, darkest part of the Twilight. When I opened my eyes, I saw a little monster like a lizard, greenish-gold, with wings and bright red eyes, sitting in the middle of the alley watching me.

I jerked myself to my feet, ready to run away from it, but the little lizard hopped back, then flapped its golden wings and flew away. It landed on a step leading up to a burned-out tenement house and perched there.

I went to find something to eat. As I headed out of the twisty, dark Rat Hole streets, workers passed me, heading in, carrying ladders and toolboxes, talking loudly. I heard the sound of hammering. Was somebody fixing up the Rat Hole houses?

A good place to find something to eat was a yard behind a chophouse, where the keeper sometimes put out pots and pans with scrapings and crusts of food in them. It was early enough that the chop-house wasn't open yet. I crept into the yard and over to a big kettle half full of soapy water. The back door of the chophouse creaked open.

I looked up, frozen.

The chophouse keeper, a stained apron wrapped around her belly, put her hands on her hips and looked down at me. "Here, now," she said. "Aren't you the wizard's boy?"

I shook my head, *no*.

"Well, you don't need to scrounge for food. You clean those pots for me, and I've got a plate of yes-terday's stew you can have. C'mon in when you're done." She tossed me a rag and bristly brush.

While I worked, a black bird with a patch of white feathers on each wing flew down and perched on the edge of a pot, watching me. Another black-and-white bird flapped down and perched next to the first. *Grawwk,* it said.

After I'd finished rinsing the pots at the pump outside and had gotten wet down my front for my trouble, I went into the dark, low-ceilinged kitchen. The keeper pointed to a stool beside a stove, then handed me a bowl of stew and a spoon.

The keeper went to a table and started chopping up carrots. "What's your name?" she asked, tossing a carrot top into a swill bucket at her feet.

The minions had called me *Blackbird*, but that wasn't right. I took a bite of stew and thought about it. *Boy.* That was my name.

The keeper shrugged when I didn't answer.

I ate the rest of the stew, and left.

The next night was colder, but I found a good sleeping place in a tall house in the deepest part of Rat Hole, an attic where the stairs had rotted away, but there was a ladder leading up to it.

Somebody'd lived here not too long ago; I found ashes in the grate and blankets piled in the corner and rags stuffed into the cracks in the window frame to keep out the cold. And rats scrabbling in the walls. Except for the rats, it was a good place to come back to after picking pockets or stealing a bit of food.

I'd been staying there for a while and was coming back with an empty stomach at the end of a day filled with minions who seemed on the lookout for me on every corner. I climbed the stairs. At the bottom of my attic ladder was a package wrapped in brown paper.

The landing was empty, except for shadows.

I crouched beside the package and opened it. Biscuits. With bacon! Without thinking, I grabbed one and took an enormous bite. Then another. A moment later the biscuit was gone. My stomach gave a happy gurgle. I picked up another biscuit.

From a doorway leading off the landing came a

noise. Getting to my feet, I spun around, and a huge man grabbed me by both arms.

I dropped the biscuit and squirmed, and kicked out at him, but he held me tightly, then gave me a cuff on the head.

"Keep still, you," he said. He had a hard face like a fist full of knuckles; he wore a brown suit with a knitted red waistcoat under it.

Still gripping me by the arms, he brought me through the streets to a tall, stone house down near the bridge. He went inside, past minion-looking guards, up stairs and down cold, stone hallways, to a door. Outside it was the minion who'd almost caught me at the brazier in Sark Square. He nodded at the man holding me. "Benet," he said.

"They waiting?" the man called Benet asked.

The minion nodded and opened the door.

The room inside had a table in the middle of it with a map of the city of Wellmet spread on it, with notes scribbled on the map in red ink. Beside the table, in a comfortable armchair, sat a very thin young man with black hair and a sharp face. At the table, squinting down at the map, stood a tall girl with red hair caught up in a braid that hung down her back. She wore a green velvet dress that had a tree embroidered on the sleeve.

The red-headed girl looked up and nodded when she saw us. "So it worked!" she said. "Well done, Benet. Biscuits?"

The big man nodded and let me go. I headed for the door, but he pushed me away and went to stand in front of it with his burly arms crossed.

The thin young man said something to the girl.

"I don't know, Embre," the girl said sharply.

"We could keep him here," the man named Embre said. "There are cells in the basement."

They wanted to lock me up? I eyed the tall windows. Maybe I could get out one of them.

"Not in the cells," said the big man by the door.

"Benet's right," the girl said. She looked at me and smiled. "I'm very glad to see you, Conn."

"So am I, Cousin," said Embre, adding a sharp smile of his own.

I didn't say anything. I wasn't sure what they were talking about.

The girl who'd called me *Conn* sighed. "Nevery still doesn't know?" she asked.

Embre shook his head. "We weren't sure it was him, or if we could catch him."

"I'll take him, Duchess," said the big man by the door. "Master Nevery's at the academicos."

The girl nodded. "Yes, I suppose that would be best."

"Just don't let him escape," said the boy. "He's hard to catch."

I'd be even harder to catch if they let me get away.

The big man grabbed me by the arm again. "Come on, you," he said.

He took me to the river and put me onto a boat and, after tossing me a blanket to keep warm with, rowed us across the choppy waves to a building on an island. He tied the boat to a dock and climbed out.

Leaving the blanket, I followed.

He kept his hand on the scruff of my neck, leading me into a wide gallery, past people in robes who stared and whispered when they saw me, and up a curved staircase to a door. We went in.

It was a library, full of books and two long tables.

Across the room, at the end of one of the tables, sat a gray-bearded old man, reading a book. He looked tired and stooped; a knob-headed cane rested against the table beside him and a gray robe was thrown over a chair.

The big man gave me a push. "Go talk to him," he whispered.

All right. I walked down the room, my feet quiet on the carpeted floor.

As I got closer, the old man looked up. When he saw me, his eyes widened and his face went very pale. He got to his feet, staring at me, holding on to the edge of the table. "Well, Boy?" he said softly.

Boy, he'd called me. Did he know me?

He pushed aside his chair and took a step toward me. I flinched back. His bushy gray eyebrows lowered, as if he was angry.

I glanced toward the door. The big man was gone.

"Where have you been all this time, my lad?" the old man asked. "I thought I'd lost you."

What did he mean by asking where I'd been? I'd been in the Twilight, hiding from the minions, until the big man had caught me with his biscuit trap.

The old man narrowed his eyes. "What's the matter with you, Boy?" He took another step toward me, and I skiffed toward the door. I could've made a run for it then. Quick-dart out the door and back out into the steep, snow-cold streets of the Twilight. He couldn't stop me. The big man was out in the hallway, though, sure as sure, making sure I didn't get away.

I paused with my hand on the doorknob. "My name is Boy," I said, half asking. My voice sounded rusty, as if I hadn't talked to anybody for a long time.

"It is not," the old man said. He watched me carefully. "You don't remember, do you?"

No.

"Curse it," the old man muttered. He went back to his chair and sat down as if he was very tired. "You don't know who you are," he said.

"I am who I am," I said.

The old man leaned back in his chair and pulled at the end of his gray beard. "Yes, boy, that's true. I suppose you are."

The old man's name was Nevery. He told me about the other me, *Connwaer*, which meant *black bird*. He took me to a tall brick house on an island called Heartsease, where he said I lived with him and Benet. It didn't seem like any place I'd ever been before, not like the Twilight. Nevery said that was because Connwaer had done pyrotechnics and had blown up the other Heartsease and then it'd been rebuilt.

The other me must've gotten into a lot of trouble.

Nevery was a wizard. He said Connwaer had been a wizard, too. "I'm not a wizard," I told him. "I'm a gutterboy."

"You used to be a gutterboy," Nevery said. "But you're not anymore." He fetched a mirror and told me to look at myself.

I looked like I always had. Except I had a patch of white in my black hair. I didn't remember that.

Nevery said I should study books called grimoires, and maybe I would remember. That was all right, because I liked to read. Most of the words in the grimoires were in a magical language that Nevery said had once been spoken by dragons. The words sounded strange and wonderful, but nothing happened when I spoke them.

The little lizard, which Nevery said was a dragon, kept following me around. I'd look up from a book I was reading and it'd be perched outside on the windowsill, shivering in the cold, but when I went over to let it in, it'd fly away.

One day, the wizard took me to see the red-headed girl, whose name was Rowan. She was the duchess and lived in the Dawn Palace. She had an office crowded with a desk piled with papers, and chairs and tables with lace doilies on them, a warm fire in the hearth, and trees in pots. On a cushion set on a chair was a white cat with splotches of black on it, curled up asleep. The cat looked like a predator, with a flat face and sharp ears. It opened one eye, looked me over, and then went back to sleep. The girl wore spectacles with gold rims.

"Hello, Connwaer," she said, getting up from behind the desk and taking off her spectacles.

I didn't answer.

She glanced at Nevery and he shook his head.

"Can I show you something?" she asked me.

I nodded.

She led me through the wide corridors of the palace. She and Nevery walked ahead, talking quietly; I followed, and then came two guards in green uniforms. One of the guards had a long, blond braid down her back and watched me with sharp gray-blue eyes.

I turned and walked backward to see what she was doing. I wondered if she'd known Connwaer.

"I have got my eye on you, thief," she said, but she gave a half smile.

She had, then. I turned back. She was probably watching to see if I got into trouble.

The Duchess Rowan arrived at a double door and waited for me to catch up, then threw it open.

"See?" she said, going in.

I followed her. The room was very fine, a study with a polished wooden table, a patterned red rug on the floor, and lots of shelves stuffed with books. It opened to another room, a bedroom, and a library, and a dressing room.

"These are the rooms of the duchess's magister," Rowan said. She gave me a sharp, sideways glance. "That's you, Conn, once you remember that you can do magic."

Nevery shot her an angry glare, but she just raised her eyebrows and looked duchess-ish.

Nevery took me back to Heartsease.

After dinner, he went to Magisters Hall for a meeting, and I went up to the study to read another grimoire. Benet brought tea and then went away again.

I stared into the fire while the tea got cold in my cup.

It was warm here, and I got plenty to eat, and the books were interesting, but I didn't belong in this place. They all wanted me to be Connwaer, to be a wizard and the duchess's magister, and to eat biscuits. Every time the wizard Nevery looked at me, he was wanting to see Connwaer. It made them all sad that I wasn't him.

Maybe tomorrow I'd go into the Twilight and find a hiding place. I was good at melting into shadows. They wouldn't be able to find me, and after a while they'd stop looking.

I heard a *scrtch-scrtch* at the window.

I went over and opened it, and the tiny dragon, along with a puff of freezing air, hopped in, settling on the windowsill. I closed the window, the latch cold under my fingers.

"Hello, dragon," I said.

It crouched on the sill and wrapped its tail around itself. A line of gray smoke trickled from one of its nostrils.

I went back to the table, to the grimoire I'd been reading. The dragon stayed on the windowsill.

The spell written on the page was a long one. The annotation said it was a spell for protecting a house from burglars.

The dragon language flowed across the page. And then I came across a word that I knew.

Tallennar.

I'd heard it before, hadn't I?

"Tallennar," I said aloud.

On the windowsill, the tiny dragon cocked its head and fixed me with a bright red eye. Then it twitched its tail. With a rustle of its greeny-gold wings, it hop-flew from the window to the table, landing with a scrabble of claws.

It crouched at the edge of the table, watching me.

Slowly, carefully, I reached out, and the dragon closed its eyes, leaned toward me, and let me lay my hand on its back, between its wings. Its scales felt warm and silver-smooth under my fingers.

Pip, the little dragon said.

My hand on its back grew warmer, and then a sudden flash of magic burst from the dragon and flowed over me, wrapping me in sparks and flame flowing with memories like banners in the wind, glimpses of places, people, the sharp smell of pyrotechnic smoke, birds with black feathers, a chophouse in the Twilight, Rowan swinging a sword, the old

Heartsease with the bite out of the middle, Benet, Nevery, everything.

Slowly the sparks faded. I sat back in my chair, blinking the brights from my eyes, and caught my breath. Pip squirmed out from under my hand and crept to the other end of the table.

I remembered where I'd heard the spellword before. I closed my eyes and saw the dazzling blue sky overhead, and breathed in the thin, cold mountain air. I held Pip in the canvas knapsack. I felt the cave doorstep tremble under my feet as the word rumbled up through the rock.

The cave dragon might've been talking to me, Connwaer, when it said the word. I opened my eyes. "But it might've been talking to you, Pip," I said.

The little dragon twitched its tail. It crouched lower on the tabletop. For a moment I thought it was going to fly away. Then it edged closer. I stayed very still, holding my breath. Using its claws, Pip climbed up my arm and perched on my shoulder, clinging tightly to my sweater, and wrapped its tail around my neck like a scarf.

Maybe the cave dragon had been talking to both of us when it'd said the word.

Tallennar.

I knew what it meant. It meant *thief.*

Well, that was all right. Because a thief really was a lot like a wizard.

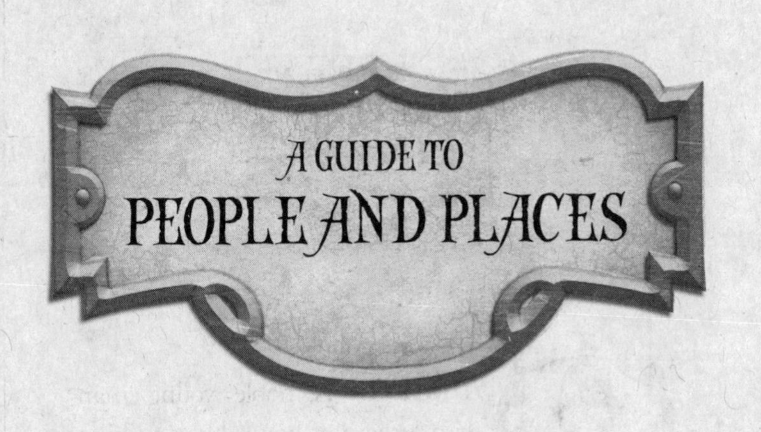
A GUIDE TO
PEOPLE AND PLACES

ARGENT—A noble young man with a sense of honor but no liking for former thieves and gutterboys. He is an expert swordcrafter.

BENET—A rather scary-looking guy but one who loves to knit, bake, and clean. His nose has been broken so many times, it's been flattened. If he were an animal he'd be a big bear. His hair is brown and sticks out on his head like spikes. You wouldn't want to meet him in a dark alley, but you would want to eat his biscuits.

CONNWAER—Has shaggy black hair that hangs down over his bright blue eyes. He's been a gutterboy for most of his life, so he's watchful and a little wary; at the same time, he's completely pragmatic and truthful. He's thin, but he's sturdy and strong, too. He has a quirky smile (hence his quirked tail as a cat). Conn does not know his own age; it could be anywhere from twelve to fourteen. A great friend to have, but be careful that you don't have anything valuable in your pockets in reach of his sticky fingers.

THE DUCHESS—Willa Forestal, the duchess, rules the wealthier part of Wellmet, the Sunrise, from the Dawn Palace. Rowan is her daughter. The duchess doesn't have much of a sense of humor, even less now that she's been attacked and wounded by the Shadows. The wound is still troubling her; it's slowly turning her to stone. Fortunately, she is highly intelligent and foresighted and has trained her daughter well to take over as duchess if necessary.

EMBRE—A young man about eighteen years old. He is very thin and has a sharp face with dark eyes and black hair, and he might have smudges on his hands and face from working with blackpowder. Everything about him is sharp, including his intellect.

KERRN—The captain of the Dawn Palace guards, Kerrn is tall and athletic; she wears her blond hair in a braid that hangs down her back and has sharp, ice-blue eyes. She is an expert swordfighter. She speaks with a strong accent because she comes from Helva, far away from the Peninsular Duchies.

NEVERY FLINGLAS—Is tall with gray hair, a long gray beard, shaggy gray eyebrows, and sharp black eyes. He's impatient and grumpy and often hasty, but beneath that his heart is kind (he would never admit it). Mysterious and possibly dangerous, Nevery is a difficult wizard to read but a good one to know.

NIMBLE—A magister and rather weak wizard, Nimble was a colleague of Pettivox but was cleared of any wrongdoing after the destruction of the Underlord's device. He looks like a bat and is a pen-pushing, officious man. He dislikes Conn very much.

PIP—As Conn says, Pip is an "it," not a "he." Pip is a small dragon, no bigger than a kitten, but it has a very big attitude. Pip does not trust Conn at first—and why should it? Conn stole it from its cave in the mountains, after all. Still, one thief should be friends with another. . . .

ROWAN FORESTAL—A tall, slender girl of around sixteen, with red hair and gray eyes. She is very intelligent with a good, if dry, sense of humor. She is the daughter of the Duchess of Wellmet. She is also very interested in studying swordcraft.

ACADEMICOS—Set on an island in the river that runs between the Twilight and the Sunrise, the academicos is a school for the rich students and potential wizards of Wellmet. Conn enrolls there after becoming Nevery's apprentice.

DAWN PALACE—The home of the duchess and Rowan. The palace itself is a huge, rectangular building—not very architecturally interesting, but with lots of decorations crusted on it to make it fancy.

DRAGON MOUNTAIN—Far away from Wellmet, in the very highest of the Fierce Mountains to the south, is a strange mountain with a huge cave right at its peak. Do dragons live there? Is it a place of magic?

DUSK HOUSE PIT—The place where the Underlord's Dusk House used to stand. It's a pit now because the house was destroyed—blown to bits when Conn freed the magic from the Underlord's evil device. Now the city's magic gathers its strength in this pit, maybe drawn there by the slowsilver left behind when the device exploded.

HEARTSEASE—The old Heartsease, the mansion house with the big hole in the middle, was destroyed in a certain pyrotechnic experiment, so Nevery is building a new Heartsease. When finished, it will have plenty of room for Nevery and Benet and Conn to live there. Conn might even get his own workroom!

MAGISTERS HALL—Seat of power for the wizards who control and guard the magic of Wellmet. It is a big, imposing gray stone building on an island with a wall built all the way around it at the waterline.

WELLMET RUNIC ALPHABET

In Wellmet, some people write using runes to stand for the letters of the alphabet. In fact, you may find some messages written in runes in *The Magic Thief: Found*.

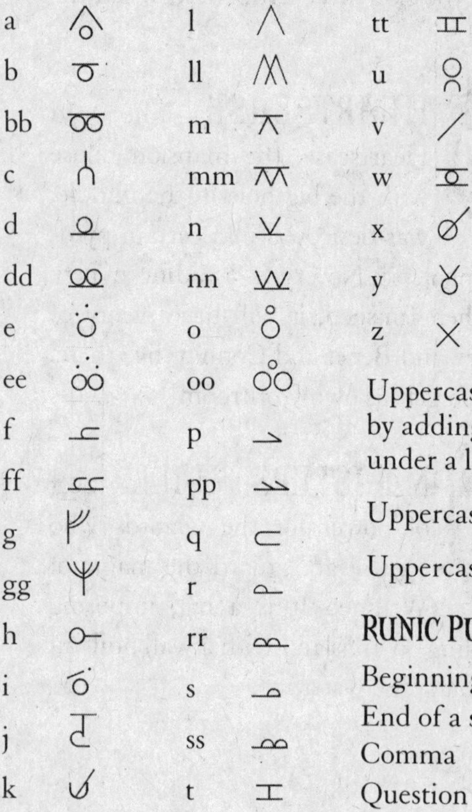

a
b
bb
c
d
dd
e
ee
f
ff
g
gg
h
i
j
k
l
ll
m
mm
n
nn
o
oo
p
pp
q
r
rr
s
ss
t
tt
u
v
w
x
y
z

Uppercase letters are made by adding an extra line under a letter; for instance:

Uppercase A

Uppercase B

RUNIC PUNCTUATION:

Beginning of a sentence ·

End of a sentence (period) :

Comma

Question Mark

BENET'S MAGIC THIEF LOCKPICK SCARF

Benet's scarf has keyholes at both ends and a checkered pattern in the middle.

Materials:

Yarn: 2 skeins nettle green (300m/100gm each) DK weight (Benet used Shilasdair luxury DK in nettle green [color 209])

Needles: 5mm (US 8)

Scissors

Darning needle to weave in ends

Crochet hook for tassels

Gauge: approx 20 sts = 10cm (4 in) in main pattern

Terms

BO = bind off

CO = cast on

K = knit

P = purl

Inc = knit into front and back of stitch

K2tog = knit two together

P2tog = purl two together

Keyhole Panel

CO 32 stitches

Row 1 to 4: knit

Row 5: K3, *K1, P1 repeat from * till last 3 sts, K3

Row 6: K3, *P1, K1 repeat from * to last 3 sts, K3

Row 7: Repeat row 5

Row 8: Repeat row 6

Row 9: K3, *K1, P1 repeat from * five times, BO 6 sts, *K1, P1 repeat five times, K3

You will be working both sides with separate balls of yarn.

Row 10: K3, *P1, K1 repeat from * to end. Attach a new ball of yarn past the bind off and *P1, K1 repeat from * to last 3 sts, K3

Row 11: K3, *K1, P1 repeat from * to end. *K1, P1 repeat from * to last 3 sts, K3

Row 12: K3, *P1, K1 repeat from * to end. *P1, K1 repeat from * to last 3 sts, K3

Row 13 and 14: Repeat rows 11 and 12

Row 15: K3, *K1, P1 repeat from * to last stitch before end, inc1. Inc1, *K1, P1 repeat from * to last 3 sts, K3

Row 16: K3, *P1, K1 repeat from * five times, P1. K1, *P1, K1 repeat from * to last 3 sts, K3

Row 17: K3, *K1, P1 repeat from * five times, K1. P1, *K1, P1 repeat from * to last 3 sts, K3

Row 18 and 19: Repeat rows 16 and 17

Row 20: K3, *P1, K1 repeat from * five times, inc1. Inc1, *K1, P1 repeat from * to last 3 sts, K3

Row 21: K3, *K1, P1 repeat from * six times. *P1, K1 repeat from * to last 3 sts, K3

Row 22: K3, *P1, K1 repeat from * five times, P2tog. K2tog, *P1, K1 repeat from * to last 3 sts, K3

Row 23: K3, *K1, P1 repeat from * four times, K1, P2tog. K2tog, P1, *P1, K1 repeat from * to last 3 sts, K3

Row 24: K3, *P1, K1 repeat from * four times, P2tog. K2tog, *P1, K1 repeat from * to last 3 sts, K3

Row 25: K3, *K1, P1 repeat from * four times, K1. P1, *K1, P1 repeat from * to last 3 sts, K3

Row 26: K3, *P1, K1 repeat from * four times, inc1. Inc1, *K1, P1 repeat from * to last 3 sts, K3

Row 27: K3, *K1, P1 repeat from * five times, inc1. Inc1, *P1, K1 repeat from * to last 3 sts, K3

Row 28: K3, *P1, K1 repeat from * five times, inc1, CO3, join two sides, inc1, *K1, P1 repeat from * to last 3 sts, K3

Row 29: K3, *K1, P1 repeat from * to last 3 sts, K3

Row 30: K3, *P1, K1 repeat from * to last 3 sts, K3

Row 31 and 32: Repeats rows 29 and 30

* If you don't want a keyhole, just repeat rows 5 and 6 for 26 rows

Main checkered pattern

Row 33: K2, K7, P7, K7, P7, K2

Row 34 to 39: Repeat row 33

Row 40 and 41: knit

Row 42: K2, P7, K7, P7, K7, K2

Row 43 to 48: Repeat row 42

Row 49 and 50: knit across

Repeat row 33 to 50 until scarf measures approximately 150cm (60 in)

End panel

For keyhole: repeat rows 5 to 32

For plain end without keyhole: repeat rows 5 and 6 for 26 rows

Knit four rows

BO all sts

Tassels:

1. Cut 60 strands of yarn 30 cm (12 in) long
2. With three strands fold in half
3. Pull loop end through a stitch at end of scarf
4. Pull cut ends through loop
5. Repeat for ten tassels at each scarf end

The scarf can be fastened by looping one end through one of the keyholes.

Use gold or silver yarn to embroider the runes for your name at one end.

Thick pattern at each end of the scarf is perfect for concealing lockpick wires.

A Treatise on Dragons

by

Arista Spyke

Senior Magistress

Torrent City

Peninsular Duchies

After consulting the historical grimoires (found in the great library of Free Ennis), and after translating and transcribing the notes of the wind-mages of the far south, it is possible to draw some conclusions about the creatures known in other parts of the world as

Firedrakes

Wingéd-lizards

Wyrmes

Dragonets (or Dragonettes)

and

Serpentes da magi

And to us as

Dragons.

It is well-known that dragons have been extinct for hundreds of years. According to the crumbling tomes unearthed in forgotten shelves of the library, written a thousand years ago by nameless scribes, dragons were once common in the Peninsula and coexisted peacefully with humans. If these tomes are to be believed, dragons ranged in size from small (the size of a rat or a cat) to quite alarmingly large (the size of a building, or larger). Their colors varied significantly, one dragon displaying scales the deep blue of the ocean, the next as gold as the lost city of Tar-Mentir, the next greener than the finest adamant stone.

One historical source, a scroll faded with age, asserts that dragons' scales were made of some substance impenetrable to conventional weapons (swords, axes, arrows). (If, as another source claims, dragons and humans lived at peace with each other, it is not known how this conclusion could have been reached.)

Dragon lore tells us that dragons were known to be fire-breathers, but no commentary on this ability was found in the sources consulted. One source, a barely legible pamphlet by a writer with the initials L.A.W., notes that "firedrakes" (as she calls them) were often associated with fire, sparks, smoke, and even explosions. It is not noted whether the dragons themselves caused these explosions, or were simply attracted to them.

The dragons' means of reproduction remain unknown. No mention of dragon eggs or offspring has been found. Footnotes in a wind-mage journal mention that dragons were solitary and did not live in family groups.

According to the one drawing of a dragon found—a poor sketch made in the margins of an ancient book—the dragons did fly, yet they were not aerodynamical. If their wings were actually able to lift them into the sky, said wings would require a musculature anchored to a keelbone far larger than that which the sketch indicates. It is possible that dragons fly through the operations of magic, though it is impossible to guess how. It is not possible to conclude that dragons themselves were creatures of magic.

One finding is perplexing. An ancient map of the Peninsula was examined, marked with places called *Dragonlairs*. Strangely, these Dragonlairs correspond exactly to the places where cities exist now.

I can draw no conclusion from this strange finding.

THANKS TO . . .

The usual dear friends, with love: Jenn Reese, Greg van Eekhout, Sandra McDonald.

My steadfast agent, Caitlin Blasdell.

To my editor, Antonia Markiet. Thanks, Toni. You're the best!

The great team at HarperCollins Publishers, including associate editor Alyson Day, copy editor Kathryn Silsand, editorial director Phoebe Yeh, publisher Susan Katz, assistant editor Jayne Carapezzi, associate art director Sasha Illingworth, production supervisor Ray Colon, Tony Hirt, publicist Marisa Wetzel, artist Antonio Javier Caparo.

For their support, friendship, and advice during this crazy publishing ride, Deb Coates, Melanie Donovan, Kristin Cashore, Dori Hillestad Butler, Wendy Henrichs, Ellie Ditzel, Bev Ehresman, Lori Dawson, Jonni Hecker, Britt Deerberg, Katherine House, Lisa Bradley, Laurel Snyder, Dorothy Winsor, Steph Burgis, Tim Pratt, Heather Shaw, and Shawna Elder. And, most particularly, Ingrid Law (three years until our lunch date!).

To the lovely people at Quercus, most especially Roisin Heycock, Nicci Praça, and Parul Bavishi.

Lisa Will for helping me put the sun and moon in their proper places.

Dima Nikolayenko for the explosive chemistry experiment.

Jennifer Adam, who made sure the horses were behaving as horses do.

To the Blue Heaven crew, especially C. C. Finlay.

To Lauren "Deadly Knitshade" for the wonderful "Lockpick Scarf" pattern.

Finally, to all my dear families, especially Theo, Maud, John, Anne and Ward Bing, Pat and Frank Hankins, and that Grrrrrr, Anne Hankins.

Read an interview of Sarah Prineas by her friend and fellow author Greg van Eekhout

Check out cool questions for readers to talk about

Enjoy a secret scene cut from *The Magic Thief,* the first book in the series

INTERVIEW OF SARAH PRINEAS BY HER FRIEND AND FELLOW AUTHOR GREG VAN EEKHOUT

Greg van Eekhout is the author of middle-grade novels *Kid vs. Squid* and *The Boy at the End of the World.* Greg and Sarah have been friends for a long time and always read each other's books before the rest of the world sees them. In *The Magic Thief,* Sarah included Greg's name in one of Conn's magic spells. Greg used Sarah's name in *Kid vs. Squid* for a boat that got shrunk and put in a bottle. They often have conversations about books and writing and silly things. The following is one of those conversations.

Greg: Tell us about a time you got lost.

Sarah: Just yesterday. You know I'm watching this anime series, right? Well, the plot is crazy and twisty, and I'm completely lost with no idea what's going on. Maybe if I go back and watch it again I'll be able to figure out what's happening.

Greg: Are there now, or have there ever been, any places in the real world like Wellmet?

Sarah: The city of Wellmet is a little like the English city of London, the way it was in the nineteenth century. There were nice parts of the city, like the Sunrise, and really dangerous, poor parts, like the Twilight, with a river running through the middle of it. Wellmet is also a little like my hometown, Iowa City, because we have a twisty river running through our city. I live near the bend of the river, where the Twilight is in Wellmet.

Greg: So it's a mix of a sprawling ancient city in England and a college town in the American Midwest. That's wonderfully strange. Have you ever had something stolen from you?

Sarah: Alas, yes. The other day you showed me a picture of your bike from when you were a kid, and it reminded me of this. When I was about Conn's age, I worked a paper route to earn enough money to buy a bike. It was a cherry-red ten-speed, and I loved it. Then some thieves walked right into our garage and stole it (from under my dog's nose, I might add). I didn't get a new bike to replace it, either.

Greg: Bike thieves are the worst! Home is a very important idea to Conn. Describe your dream home.

Sarah: Hm! I think I live in my dream home! It's a little green house with a downstairs that is all one big room so my family can hang out together. It's made even cozier by our two cats and our dog. The backyard is big, with plenty of room to run around, a hammock for lazing in, and a badminton net. We call our house "Primrose Cottage" because our last name, "Prineas," means "Primrose" in Greek. We do eat biscuits here, sometimes, but never bacon because my children are vegetarians.

Greg: That's just heartbreaking. That you never send me biscuits, I mean. What are the best and worst things about living in Iowa?

Sarah: A Californian like you would probably say the worst thing about Iowa is the weather, because we have hot, humid summers, and icy cold winters, and we have tornados in the springtime. But I actually like the changeable weather. So the worst thing, I guess, is that it's so far away from my family, who all live on the east coast. The best thing is that it's so beautiful here. People think Iowa is just flat and field after field of corn, but it's not. As I'm writing this, harvest is going on, and the colors in the countryside are rich brown and golden and burnt orange, and the hills roll out under a brilliant blue sky. So beautiful.

Greg: It does sound very beautiful. I bet the biscuits are beautiful, too. Not that I'd know. If you had to live anywhere but Iowa, where would that be?

Sarah: There are lots of places I'd like to live, many of which have great biscuits, but at the top of my list is New York City. I love visiting New York because it's so full of energy and excitement, and there's so much to do, and so many interesting people. Living there would be *soooo* different from living in Iowa, but I think I'd like it there, too.

Greg: What's your feeling about shoes?

Sarah: I'm really not all that fashionable, but I do have a thing about shoes. I like funky shoes, and Chuck Taylor sneakers, and I love wearing heels to make myself taller. Next time you see me, take a look at my shoes, because they're probably the coolest thing I'm wearing.

Greg: You do wear some pretty cool shoes. Remember that time a bunch of us went shoe shopping in Wisconsin?

Sarah: I do! I think that was the time I got sneakers with gold flowers on them.

Greg: If you could fix one thing about the world, what would you fix?

Sarah: I would make sure every kid in the world had a great education and plenty of books to read, because after a while, as those kids grew up, that would end up fixing everything else.

Greg: You love running. Why? What are you chasing? Is it a bunny? Whatever it is, what will you do when you catch it?

Sarah: How do you know I'm running after something? Maybe something is chasing me!

Greg: I bet you're being chased by a bunny. Have you ever had a job that didn't involve a lot of reading and writing? Did you like it?

Sarah: Well, my paper route was kind of like a job. And I worked as a waitress when I was in high school, and as a gofer on a construction site to earn spending money for college. I liked those jobs pretty well, but the best job I've ever had is the one I have now.

Greg: What noises are you hearing right now?

Sarah: It's early in the morning on a rainy day. I can hear the wind outside and droplets of rain spattering against the windows. I can hear the tick-tick-tick of my dog's toenails as she walks across the wood floor. A cat just came downstairs, so I heard her paw steps. My son is at the table eating his breakfast, while reading a book. He just said, out loud, "Hah! I knew that guy was evil!" Somebody upstairs is walking around; I can hear the floor creaking.

Greg: Look up. What do you see?

Sarah: I see the nubbly white ceiling over the couch where I'm sitting. Pretty boring. What do you see?

Greg: I'm seeing a bookcase spilling over with books, including yours. What are you reading?

Sarah: What I'd really like to be reading now is *The Boy at the End of the World* by this guy named Greg van Eekhout, because I hear it's really good. . . . As you know, I'm reading the Fullmetal Alchemist manga, which a good writer-friend sent to me, and which I'm completely addicted to. I just finished an Amelia Peabody mystery by Elizabeth Peters, and *Scumble* by Ingrid Law, which I loved (Ingrid is also the friend who sent me the manga books). That's about it!

CHECK OUT COOL QUESTIONS FOR READERS TO TALK ABOUT:

If you had a locus magicalicus, what would it look like?

The embero spell turns Conn into a cat, and another time into a blackbird. If the embero spell were done on you, what kind of animal would you turn into?

If you had a pet dragon, what would its name be?

If you had a pet dragon, how big would it be, and what would it look like?

Have you ever been in a place like the Twilight? What would you do if you were in a place like that?

Is Conn a bad person because he's a thief and a lockpick?

Have you ever made up a secret code like the Wellmet alphabet?

If you could make up a magical spell to do with your locus magicalicus, what would it be?

What do you think Conn *wants* most in the world? What does he *need* most?

Who is your favorite character in the Magic Thief books? Would you want to meet this character in real life?

Do you think Benet is *really* a tough guy?

Who (or what) *is* the magic thief??

ENJOY A SECRET SCENE CUT FROM *THE MAGIC THIEF*, THE FIRST BOOK IN THE SERIES!

THE WIZARD'S APPRENTICE

As usual, I was asking too many questions. After growling at me, Nevery fetched three books. "Read chapter five of this one." He *thunked* one book onto the table, raising a little cloud of dust. "And the first three chapters of these." *Thunk, thunk*. He picked up his knob-headed cane and put on his cloak. "Now, I'm going out. While I'm gone, you can mop the kitchen floor, chop a load of firewood, and fill the cauldron in the workroom with water." He pointed at my locus magicalicus. "And *don't* do any magic."

Jamming his wide-brimmed hat onto his head, he swept-stepped out of the study and out of Heartsease.

I looked at the pile of books. How could I read all of that if I had to mop floors, chop wood, and lug water? Anyway, that was work for a servant, not an apprentice!

Hmmm. On the table was Nevery's grimoire—his spell book.

The grimoire made a crackly-cracking sound when I opened it. I turned the pages until I found what I was looking for. *Implement Enchantment: A Directive Spell.*

Nevery'd told me not to do magic. But if I was going to get any reading done, the magic would have to do the chores.

I ran down to the kitchen to find the bucket and the broom. Laying the broom on the floor, I held up my locus magicalicus; then I shouted out the spell from Nevery's grimoire.

In my hand, my locus magicalicus twitched, tingled, and a sizzling ball of green sparks leaped from the stone and fell in a shower over the broom.

I blinked the brights from my eyes. The broom shivered. Then, with a fizzing sound, it lifted from the floor and stood before me. Bending, it bowed.

Right. I bowed back. I pointed at the bucket by the door. "Broom," I ordered. "Fetch water and put it in the cauldron upstairs."

Broom bowed again. The air around it fizzing, it flipped onto its end and hopped over to the bucket and, using the sweeping end like a hand, picked it up and hopped out the door. I followed it out into the courtyard. It bounced up to the well and leaped in, then popped out a moment later with the bucket brimful of water.

Hop, hop, hop, up the stairs it went, up to the fourth floor, where it dumped the bucket of water into the cauldron. Good.

Next, the wood. I crossed the courtyard to a huge pile of logs, more than I could chop in a week. An axe was stuck into one of the logs; I wrenched it out and lay it on the ground and did the thing with the magic spell and my locus magicalicus. Just like the broom, the axe shivered alive and stood before me, waiting for its orders. "Well, Axe," I said. "Go and chop that pile of logs." Axe flew to the first log and whirled around, chop-chop-chopping, sending woodchips flying.

Now the kitchen floor. I went up to the cobwebby kitchen and found the mop. Did the spell. "Mop," I ordered when it stood before me. "Mop the floor."

I'd forgotten about water. Mop swished out the kitchen door and collided with Broom, which was hopping up the stairs with a full bucket of water. Mop leaped on Broom and tried to wrestle the bucket away. The bucket went clattering across the kitchen floor splashing water everywhere. Broom and Mop went after it.

"Stop!" I shouted. They both froze. "Mop," I said, pointing my locus stone at it. "Stop fighting. And you, Broom, go and fetch water for Mop." Broom bowed and picked up the bucket and hopped from the kitchen. Mop flipped its mop-side down and danced across the floor, mopping up the spilled water.

Leaving them to their work, I went back up to Nevery's study to do my reading.

After a while, I leaned back in my chair and stretched, and decided to go check on Axe, Broom, and Mop. Putting my locus magicalicus in my pocket, I went out of the study.

A river was pouring down the stairs, making each step a little waterfall. I turned and saw Broom, hopping down with the bucket. I splashed down the stairs after it.

When I got to the kitchen, I stopped in the doorway. Oh, no. Nevery was going to be furious.

The kitchen was flooded. As I stood in the doorway, Broom pushed past me and flung a bucketful of water onto the floor. Mop twirled through the ankle-deep water, over the floor, up the wall, and across the ceiling, which dripped. Broom hopped past me out to the stairs. "Stop!" I shouted.

I chased it out to the courtyard and saw it disappear into the well. A moment later, it hopped out again with another bucket of water. From across the courtyard came the sound of chop-chop-chopping. I turned and saw Axe, chopping away at the very last log; behind it was a mound of woodchips.

Oh, was I ever going to be in trouble. Taking my locus magicalicus out of my pocket, I held it over my head and shouted, as loud as I could, "STOP!!"

Axe paused in its chopping and whirled over to me. "Come on," I said, and it followed me as I headed into Heartsease and up to the kitchen.

"*Stop*!" I said to Mop, which was sloshing water around in the fireplace. Mop stopped and skated across the wet floor to me.

I heard Broom coming down the stairs. As it passed the kitchen door, I said, "Stop, Broom." It hopped into the room, set down the bucket, and bowed.

"Come on," I said, and led Mop, Broom, and Axe upstairs to the study.

They stood waiting while I looked through Nevery's grimoire. Nothing about how to stop the spell. Drats. I couldn't unmagick them.

All right. I held up my locus magicalicus. "Mop. Broom. Axe," I said. I pointed at the corner. "Go stand in the corner."

Broom bowed and the other two followed it into the corner. Mop bumped into Broom.

"Keep still," I said. They leaned against the wall.

I sat down at the table with the books. I had a lot of pages to read before Nevery got home.

Much later, he came in.

I sat quietly in my chair.

"Well, boy?" Nevery said. "There is a large pile of woodchips in the courtyard. Got a little carried away with the chopping, did you?"

I shrugged. I had, sort of.

"And the kitchen," Nevery said. "It is extremely clean. The ceiling has even been mopped."

I nodded.

"And I expect the cauldron has been filled to the brim with water?"

Yes. Not by me, but yes, it had been filled.

Nevery glanced at the corner, where Mop, Broom, and Axe stood. Broom twitched, shedding a few green sparks onto the floor. He raised his eyebrows. "Have you finished your reading?"

"Almost," I said.

Everything was quiet for a moment. Except for Broom, Mop,

and Axe jostling each other in the corner. I shot them a look, and they stilled.

"Hmmm," Nevery said. "Well, what do you think, boy?"

I shrugged. He was going to tell me I was in trouble, was what.

"Hmmph," Nevery said. "I've got another assignment for you. He pointed toward Mop, Broom, and Axe. "Figure out how to take the enchantment off." He *thunked* down his grimoire before me on the table. "Even if you have to stay up all night to do it."

All right! Now *that* was a job for a wizard's apprentice.